Counterintelligence Theory and Practice

D1606409

Security and Professional Intelligence Education Series (SPIES)

Series Editor: Jan Goldman

In this post–September 11, 2001, era there has been rapid growth in the number of professional intelligence training and educational programs across the United States and abroad. Colleges and universities, as well as high schools, are developing programs and courses in homeland security, intelligence analysis, and law enforcement, in support of national security.

The Security and Professional Intelligence Education Series (SPIES) was first designed for individuals studying for careers in intelligence and to help improve the skills of those already in the profession; however, it was also developed to educate the public in how intelligence work is conducted and should be conducted in this important and vital profession.

1. *Communicating with Intelligence: Writing and Briefing in the Intelligence and National Security Communities*, by James S. Major. 2008.
2. *A Spy's Résumé: Confessions of a Maverick Intelligence Professional and Misadventure Capitalist*, by Marc Anthony Viola. 2008.
3. *An Introduction to Intelligence Research and Analysis*, by Jerome Clauser, revised and edited by Jan Goldman. 2008.
4. *Writing Classified and Unclassified Papers for National Security*, by James S. Major. 2009.
5. *Strategic Intelligence: A Handbook for Practitioners, Managers, and Users*, revised edition by Don McDowell. 2009.
6. *Partly Cloudy: Ethics in War, Espionage, Covert Action, and Interrogation*, by David L. Perry. 2009.
7. *Tokyo Rose / An American Patriot: A Dual Biography*, by Frederick P. Close. 2010.
8. *Ethics of Spying: A Reader for the Intelligence Professional*, edited by Jan Goldman. 2006.
9. *Ethics of Spying: A Reader for the Intelligence Professional*, Volume 2, edited by Jan Goldman. 2010.
10. *A Woman's War: The Professional and Personal Journey of the Navy's First African American Female Intelligence Officer*, by Gail Harris. 2010.
11. *Handbook of Scientific Methods of Inquiry for Intelligence Analysis*, by Hank Prunckun. 2010.
12. *Handbook of Warning Intelligence: Assessing the Threat to National Security*, by Cynthia Grabo. 2010.
13. *Keeping U.S. Intelligence Effective: The Need for a Revolution in Intelligence Affairs*, by William J. Lahneman. 2011.
14. *Words of Intelligence: An Intelligence Professional's Lexicon for Domestic and Foreign Threats, Second Edition*, by Jan Goldman. 2011.
15. *Counterintelligence Theory and Practice*, by Hank Prunckun. 2012.
16. *Balancing Liberty and Security: An Ethical Study of U.S. Foreign Intelligence Surveillance, 2001–2009*, by Michelle Louise Atkin. 2013.
17. *The Art of Intelligence: Simulations, Exercises, and Games*, edited by William J. Lahneman and Rubén Arcos. 2014.
18. *Communicating with Intelligence: Writing and Briefing in National Security*, by James S. Major. 2014.
19. *Scientific Methods of Inquiry for Intelligence Analysis, Second Edition*, by Hank Prunckun. 2015.
20. *Quantitative Intelligence Analysis: Applied Analytic Models, Simulations and Games*, by Edward Waltz. 2014.
21. *The Handbook of Warning Intelligence: Assessing the Threat to National Security–The Complete Declassified Edition*, by Cynthia Grabo, 2015.
22. *Intelligence and Information Policy for National Security: Key Terms and Concepts*, by Jan Goldman and Susan Maret
23. *Handbook of European Intelligence Cultures*, edited by Bob de Graaff and James M. Nyce - With Chelsea Locke
24. *Partly Cloudy: Ethics in War, Espionage, Covert Action, and Interrogation, Second Edition*, by David L. Perry
25. *Humanitarian Intelligence: A Practitioner's Guide to Crisis Analysis and Project Design*, by Andrej Zwitter
26. *Shattered Illusions: KGB Cold War Espionage in Canada*, by Donald G. Mahar
27. *Intelligence Engineering: Operating Beyond the Conventional*, by Adam D. M. Svendsen
28. *Reasoning for Intelligence Analysts: A Multidimensional Approach of Traits, Techniques, and Targets*, by Noel Hendrickson
29. *Counterintelligence Theory and Practice, Second Edition*, by Hank Prunckun
30. *Methods of Inquiry for Intelligence Analysis, Third Edition*, Hank Prunckun

To view the books on our website, please visit https://rowman.com/Action/SERIES/RL/SPIES or scan the QR code below.

Second Edition

Counterintelligence Theory and Practice

Hank Prunckun
Charles Sturt University

ROWMAN & LITTLEFIELD

Lanham • Boulder • New York • London

Executive Editor: Traci Crowell
Assistant Editor: Mary Malley
Senior Marketing Manager: Amy Whitaker
Interior Designer: Ilze Lemesis

Credits and acknowledgments for material borrowed from other sources, and reproduced with permission, appear on the appropriate page within the text.

Published by Rowman & Littlefield
An imprint of The Rowman & Littlefield Publishing Group, Inc.
4501 Forbes Boulevard, Suite 200, Lanham, Maryland 20706
www.rowman.com

6 Tinworth Street, London SE11 5AL, United Kingdom

British Library Cataloguing in Publication Information Available

Library of Congress Cataloging-in-Publication Data

Names: Prunckun, Hank, 1954– author.
Title: Counterintelligence theory and practice / Hank Prunckun.
Description: Second edition. | Lanham, Maryland : Rowman & Littlefield, 2019. |
    Series: Security and professional intelligence education series ; 29 |
    Includes bibliographical references and index.
Identifiers: LCCN 2018044296 (print) | LCCN 2018052200 (ebook) |
    ISBN 9781786606891 (electronic) | ISBN 9781786606877 (cloth : alk. paper) |
    ISBN 9781786606884 (pbk. : alk. paper)
Subjects: LCSH: Intelligence service.
Classification: LCC JF1525.I6 (ebook) | LCC JF1525.I6 P775 2019 (print) |
    DDC 327.1201—dc23
LC record available at https://lccn.loc.gov/2018044296

Printed in the United States of America

During the Second World War, Winston Churchill stated: "In wartime, truth is so precious that she should always be attended by a bodyguard of lies." His epigram suggests that the truth—operational information—is such an important resource that it should never be obtained by the opposition. This book is dedicated to the men and women of the Five Eyes intelligence alliance who have and continue to act as bodyguards for this priceless commodity.

Contents

7 Defensive Counterintelligence: Personnel Security   113

8 Defensive Counterintelligence: Information Security   135

9 Defensive Counterintelligence: Communications Security 157

15 Ethics of Counterintelligence   229

Preface

The English philosopher and scientist Francis Bacon is attributed to saying: "He that will not apply new remedies must expect new evils; for time is the greatest innovator." If intelligence officers and analysts are to avoid "new evils" when it comes to the security of classified information and the secret operations these data underpin, it follows that they must apply new remedies. To do this, a book that addresses the issues of counterintelligence theory and practice is needed.

This book goes some way toward filling the void in the subject literature that has been present for some time. For instance, during my previous twenty-eight years as a practitioner in the fields of security, investigation, intelligence, and research, I have found that there was a dearth of texts available on counterintelligence that discussed in simple, clear terms such as the craft's theory and practice. This is not to say that there are only a few texts on the subject—to the contrary, there are many. However, many of these books tend to be written with disappointingly little practical explanation and no theoretical base. Because of this, many of these texts view counterintelligence simply as "security," which it is not. As such, although there are many texts on library shelves that contain the title *counterintelligence*, they are, in my view, narrow and somewhat limiting in their coverage and do not place counterintelligence in the context in which it needs to sit. For the new counterintelligence recruit, or for the instructor teaching the subject, these texts leave them wanting.

My awareness that such advice was lacking in the counterintelligence field was first realized through my experience as a government investigator, and later as an intelligence analyst and strategic researcher. Then, the revelations of the 9/11 Commission into the U.S. terrorist attacks, as well as other inquiries into the worldwide phenomena of radical Islamic terrorism, underscored the importance for agencies in both the public and private sectors to guard confidential information. The implications of not doing so are discussed in the first chapter. This book was written, therefore, to provide vital, no-nonsense assistance to practicing professionals and students who need "new remedies."

This book, now in its second edition, provides the reader with more than just the basics of counterintelligence; it equips them with an advanced understanding of the underlying theory that supports the art and science of the craft. This book has been updated and new material added. It consists of 15 chapters that take the reader from an examination of the challenges that present for counterintelligence to the practicalities of defensive and offensive counterintelligence.

The book addresses a range of topics in a funnel approach—starting from the general and moving to the specific. The book starts by illustrating some events that encapsulate the key issues for counterintelligence officers as a way of setting the scene. It then moves to explain the fundamentals aspects of what counterintelligence involves, including the practical features of a counterintelligence operation function. Following this scene setting, the book then takes the reader through the theoretical underpinnings of counterintelligence.

The body of the book examines the two main focus of counterintelligence—that is, defensive and offensive counterintelligence. Chapters four through fourteen take the reader through the practice of applying the theory (chapter 3) to real-world situations. The book concludes with an examination of intelligence tradecraft—the techniques used by opposition spies to hide their activities, and a discussion about ethical issues as they apply to the profession (chapter 15). There are also four appendixes that provide examples relating to issues discussed in the text.

As one of the book's purposes is as a text for students and instructors, each chapter concludes with a list of keywords and phrases and several study questions and learning activities. Instructors can use these teaching aids as is or use them as a base from which to develop their own materials for assessment. Students can use these aids to test their understanding independent of whatever assessments their instructors assign, or, if the reader is progressing through the book as some type of "self-paced study" or "self-improvement" undertaking (perhaps as part of their continuing professional development), they can use these learning aids for self-assessment. There are two preliminary pieces of advice for students titled "About the Study Questions" and "Key Concepts to Note" that appear in the front portion of this book.

Acknowledgments

I extend my thanks to the U.S. Department of Defense, the Federal Bureau of Investigation, and other U.S. Government agencies, as well as the various sources cited for the use of the photographs that appears in this book. But, in doing so I point out that their appearance does not imply, or constitute, these providers' endorsement.

Dr. Hank Prunckun
Sydney

About the Study Questions

Here is some advice about the end of chapter study questions and how to approach answering them:

Explain/List/Describe   This type of question asks you to outline the factors associated with the issue under study.

Argue   This type of question asks you to present the factors associated with the issue under investigation, but requires you to select one of the factors so that you can defend it.

Discuss   This type of question asks you to form a view (or judgment) after weighing the "for" and "against" factors, or the factors that influence the issue under study.

Key Concepts to Note

This book addresses counterintelligence from a wide perspective. As a "compass," it uses the definition of "an activity aimed at protecting an agency's intelligence program against an opposition's intelligence service" to facilitate a universal approach to the topic.

So, throughout this book, there are two terms that are used generically; they are the *agency* and the *opposition*. As this book is a treatment of the theory and practice of counterintelligence from the widest perspective, terms that reflect "friend" and "foe," regardless of the "industry" or environment in which counterintelligence is practiced, were needed. The solution was to adopt the generalized terms of *agency* for all friendly forces (whether military, government, business, or private individuals) and *opposition* for all forms of foe (which is consistent with the military concept of an opposing force).

The use of the term *agency* can therefore refer to any organization, or even a nation-state. The term *opposition* can be used to mean any person or group (including a nation-state, etc.) with hostile intent. In this way, such a definition is applied throughout the book to issues that span national security, military, law enforcement, and business/corporate intelligence, or even private affairs. This wide approach makes the treatment of counterintelligence current and applicable across the threat environment.

Chapter 1

Challenges for Counterintelligence

Even though the intersection in Lahore, Pakistan, was crowded, Raymond Davis noticed a motorcycle driver and passenger. When Davis, a Central Intelligence Agency (CIA) contract operative, stopped his car, the motorcycle passed him and stopped in front of his vehicle. In an instant Davis knew he was in danger.

The passenger raised a handgun, leveled it at Davis's head, but before he could fire, Davis shot him five times—Davis's bullets piercing his own car's windshield, then the body of the would-be attacker. Moments after, Davis got out of his car, killed the motorcycle's driver and recorded the two opposition assailants' faces with his camera for intelligence purposes.

Although this was a successful defense, Davis's intelligence mission was now compromised; he could think of only one thing—evasion and escape.[1]

This is a true story and took place on January 27, 2011, in Lahore while Davis's employer was mounting operations against targets openly hostile to the United States and, consequentially, to its allies and their intelligence services—namely, those of Australia, Canada, New Zealand, and the United Kingdom—collectively known as the Five Eyes, as well as other compatriots in the Global War on Terror.

The motives of Davis's attackers were not understood at the time of the attack and were still a mystery at the time of this writing. Nevertheless, someone knew of the role of the American operative and the intelligence agency he worked for, and therefore they knew his movements that day. As such, they disrupted the intelligence operation and, in the process, expose secrets about the operative and the U.S. agency. In the end, Davis was arrested, and an attempt was made by the Pakistani authorities to interrogate him; but his training and personality held and no information, other than some superficial details, were revealed.

The lesson to be drawn from this case is that, at some time during the operation or its planning, details were gathered by forces hostile to the Americans and these data were used to mount a counteroperation to neutralize it. Somewhere along the way counterintelligence failed to protect Davis and his mission's managers. In the end, the counterintelligence practices failed.

Stating these shortcomings is not to try and attribute blame to anyone or any agency—it is acknowledged there are risks in conducting all intelligence operations and all intelligence research projects. But, it is important to understand the consequences of mission failure in addition to understanding how failure occurred. By doing so, an agency can understand how to apply counterintelligence theory to develop better security procedures and practices.

So, was the Davis case in Lahore an atypical event or was it symptomatic of a much wider issue to be considered in the context of counterintelligence? Undoubtedly this was a case of great national security concern that, arguably, crossed over to include aspects of military counterintelligence too. Nevertheless, there are cases much less dramatic than this one that involved law enforcement, private security, and business intelligence that are no less concerning for those involved. Take, for instance, the case involving Heathrow Airport security information. In October 2017, a USB memory stick was found on a London street by a member of the public who turned it over to the *Sunday Mirror*. Upon examination, the device revealed seventy-six folders of unencrypted information, some relating to security of the Queen Elizabeth II when she uses the airport. Other information detailed how to access restricted areas.[2] Then, there was the case involving private investigators hired by Hewlett-Packard who allegedly accessed personal telephone records of some of the company's directors to identify the source of the company's leaks to the media,[3] and, the J. P. Morgan Chase data breach of 2014. Information relating to some eight-three million bank accounts was stolen, including names, e-mail addresses, postal addresses, and telephone numbers. In the past, such data has been used by the perpetrators, or sold to third parties, to facilitate phishing attacks.

Then again, these are not isolated cases—a search of archived media reports will uncover hundreds of security breaches like these. Examples of where counterintelligence was less than adequate can be seen in this list:

- hacktivists stole an approximately 43 GB of data from the Syrian government networks and posted the files—over 274,000—on the Internet;
- a group lobbying for a "free Palestine" hacked the personal e-mail account of CIA's then director, John Brennon;
- a ride-sharing company's cloud server was accessed by unauthorized individuals who downloaded fifty-seven million user records from across the globe that contained their names, e-mail addresses, and cell phone numbers. The unauthorized download also contained the driver's license numbers of some 600,000 of the company's U.S. drivers;
- government-licensed private security guards who had links to outlaw motorcycle gangs;
- security officers who left secret access code-numbers posted in plain view on gates to an airport restricted zone;

- a Pakistani police guard who was assigned to protect dignitaries only later revealed was linked to an insurgent group;
- government legislators who had their computer facilities penetrated by suspected foreign intelligence services;
- a multinational computer company whose corporate database was penetrated by unknown persons who stole thousands of items of personal client information;
- police officers who have sold law enforcement information to private investigators;
- a juror who contacted a defendant during a criminal trial via a social networking website;
- outlaw motorcycle gang members who targeted civil servants in an attempt to bribe them into providing confidential government records, and to modify other records that were maintained by motor vehicle registries and law courts;
- hundreds of government-licensed private security officers who were banned from working in the industry because of drug, alcohol, firearms, and violence offenses; and
- an employee of a U.S. National Security Agency contractor who leaked secret information regarding a highly classified communications intercept program.
- North Korean government was responsible for the 2014 cyberattack on Sony Pictures Entertainment[4] that stole data regarding the personal details of company employees and their family members, the company's executives' salaries, confidential e-mails, and copies of then-unreleased Sony films.

Failure to protect secrets has widespread ramifications, and the perils posed must be addressed. But then again, counterintelligence is more than just keeping secrets. Having said that, too much attention on security can lead to mission failure[5] because analysts and operative cannot access the data they need, or it hampers them in carrying out their jobs. It is a constant challenge between allied agencies and opposition forces. Counterintelligence is one of the most intellectually challenging areas of intelligence work. This is because it is counterintuitive—a "wilderness of mirrors"—where one finds it hard to distinguish between reality and illusion. Yet, practitioners still attempt to use reasoned arguments to establish the truth of puzzling issues via the dialectical method.

Let us examine some selected cases that underscore the depth and breadth of the challenge that counterintelligence must withstand.

Photo 1.1 is a reproduction of Leonardo da Vinci's Room of Mirrors, which demonstrates the inventor's fascination with optical tricks. His room finds metaphor in the craft of counterintelligence as was famously pointed out by the late James Angleton, chief of counterintelligence at CIA (1954–1974) when he was reported to have referred to counterintelligence's challenge in relation to Soviet disinformation and foreign policy as a *wilderness of mirrors*.[6]

PHOTO 1.1 Wilderness of Mirrors. *Source*: Photograph courtesy of the author.

Selected Historical Lessons

Nathan Hale

During the American War of Independence, the colonial forces suffered a serious defeat during the Battle for Long Island (August 27, 1776). This defeat suggested to General George Washington that his forces needed better intelligence to aid battle plans. He is reported to have called for volunteers to go behind the British lines and obtain information on aspects of the British position.

Answering this call was Nathan Hale. As history records, Hale was a patriot of unequaled spirit and one who went undercover without fear to try to penetrate British military operations. But, lacking training in counterintelligence, Hale's intelligence operation was discovered early in the mission. Before he could pass on any useful intelligence, Hale was executed uttering the now famous words: "I only regret that I have but one life to lose for my country."[7]

If only Hale's bravery was matched by skills in the tradecraft of counterintelligence, he may have left the nation with an equally inspiring legacy—other than those loyal words—that is, a successful penetration of a formidable opposition force.

Pentagon Papers

The *Pentagon Papers* was the name given to a study of America's involvement in Vietnam from 1945 to 1967.[8] Its official title was "United States–Vietnam Relations, 1945–1967: A Study Prepared by the Department of Defense." The study was commissioned in 1967 by the then secretary of defense, Robert

S. McNamara. The study was essentially an encyclopedic history of the Vietnam War that comprised "thirty-seven studies and fifteen collections of documents contained in forty-three volumes."[9] These were classified "Top Secret—Sensitive." The study was written by a team of thirty-six analysts—termed the "Vietnam Task Force"—at the Pentagon who used secondary data from official archival sources.[10]

In 1971 the *New York Times* began publishing a series of extracts that were leaked by Dr. Daniel Ellsberg, an analyst who had worked on the secret history. Keeping aside the ethical issues surrounding Ellsberg's motivation for leaking the documents, this case highlights that even, with a document classification system and physical controls over the documents, a person with intent (whether motivated by what they see as a higher principle, just plain greed, the thrill, or the benefit to a foreign intelligence service) was able to photocopy thousands of pages of top secret documents and broadcast their contents.[11] The fact that classified material was released without the sanction of legal authority—one that was repeated in 2010 with the leaking of some 250,000 classified documents (see WikiLeaks Affair below)—is a standout example of the need for a counterintelligence function.

Arguably, the leaking of these classified documents set in motion events that led to several other counterintelligence operations that started off, perhaps, well-intentioned but, in the end, were misguided and, in many aspects, illegal. Known as the Watergate Affair, these events involved the White House Plumbers and an informant with the code name of "Deep Throat."

White House Plumbers

In 1971, and partially in response to the Ellsberg-leaked *Pentagon Papers*, the Nixon White House established a group of counterspies—the Special Investigation Unit (also known as the *Plumbers*—for those who stop leaks). The historical record shows that the individuals who comprised this unit conducted several illegal covert intelligence operations in their attempt to stop government leaks. These included a break-in of Dr. Ellsberg's psychiatrist's office in California, and an aborted attempt to discredit Ellsberg—slipping him the hallucinogenic drug LSD before he was scheduled to speak at a fundraising dinner in Washington, DC.[12]

The low point of these operations came with the break-in of the Democratic National Committee headquarters in the Watergate office complex in Washington, DC, in June 1972. History records the various investigations, hearings, and court trials that followed, with volumes of classified information being revealed because of the operatives' actions. Aside from the ethical and legal issues that this case raised, the lack of understanding of, and/or the lack of proficiency in employing, the principles and practices of counterintelligence was apparent.

In an interesting tangent, in 1988 E. Howard Hunt, one of those convicted of the Watergate break-in, wrote a fictional spy thriller entitled *The Sankov Confession*. In it, Hunt painted a cynical portrayal of counterintelligence through the dialogue of the story's central character, Brent Graves:

Sorting out logistic problems: inventorying boots, uniforms, weapons, radios, field equipment. My heart wasn't in it. Then the program closed down and I came back to another half-assed assignment—counterintelligence. I knew less about it than the average typist.[13]

Hunt's uncomplimentary categorization of counterintelligence and the insinuation that a low-level, office-based clerical staffer might know more about counterintelligence than a field operative is ironic.[14] It could be argued that Hunt's lack of understanding of counterintelligence was instrumental in ending the June 1972 Watergate "black bag" operation he was part of, as well as his and his fellow operatives' subsequent imprisonment for the illegal entry into the headquarters of the Democratic National Committee at the Watergate building in Washington, DC.

Deep Throat

One of the inquiries that was conducted in relation to the Watergate break-in was that of investigative reporters Bob Woodward and Carl Bernstein of the *Washington Post*.[15] Arguably, it was their investigation that exposed the operation and gave rise to the subsequent public events.[16] However, it is acknowledged that their investigation would not have been as successful as it was had it not been for the information provided by an informer—Deep Throat. W. Mark Felt was at the time (1972) the second in charge of the Federal Bureau of Investigation (FBI), but still leaked critical information that guided the two reporters' investigation using this code name.

Deep Throat is an interesting case because it highlights two simultaneous counterintelligence issues—first, the leaking of classified information by a trusted government employee (again, regardless of the motive and ethics) and the inability of the FBI or other security or intelligence agency to identify and prevent leaking; second, the high level of counterintelligence tradecraft practiced by Felt. For instance, until Woodward revealed the identity of Felt in his 2005 book, *The Secret Man*,[17] the identity of Deep Throat was a mystery.[18] Even a team of investigative journalists under the supervision of Pulitzer Prize–winning investigative journalist William C. Gaines could not identify Deep Throat[19] after years of probing.[20]

Woodward's book describes the counterintelligence methods used by Felt when he passed Woodward information. The procedures Woodward described were, by any account, first class and, not surprisingly, the basis on which the secret remained a mystery for over thirty years. Ironically, the lack of counterintelligence controls by government agencies and the high level of controls practiced by Felt are examples of why the counterintelligence profession faces challenges.

Richard Welch Assassination

Richard Welch became the CIA's chief of station in Athens, Greece, in July 1975. His assassination in December 1975 underscores several counterintelligence issues that he should have been aware of and addressed through counterintelligence practice: (1) he stayed in a house that was occupied by a number of his CIA predecessors;[21] (2) his name and address had been published in Greek newspapers (his name and identity as a CIA officer was also published in an East German publication,[22] the left-wing magazine *CounterSpy*[23]); (3) he was able to be followed by four men in a stolen vehicle on his way home; and (4) he was able to be approached without warning or challenge and, hence, killed at a close range after being followed home.[24]

The number of counterintelligence miscalculations that occurred in this case and the magnitude of what took place—his assassination—were surprising given the important position Mr. Welch held in the agency,[25] especially in the hostile political-left atmosphere that existed in Greece at the time.

A counterintelligence officer needs to know what he or she is tasked to protect. The potential number of information items stored by an agency, the sources of this information, and the methods and final products produced through analysis, as well as the operations surrounding all of these considerations, are vast. As counterintelligence resources are limited, the first task is to identify what is secret and what is not. This requires counterintelligence operatives to be skilled in analysis.[26]

Aldrich Ames

Aldrich Ames was a career intelligence officer and analyst employed by the CIA. His area of specialization was Soviet affairs, and at different times in his service he was assigned to recruiting and supervising agents, as well as the behind-the-scenes planning. Reports showed that his performance varied, but one thing bears out: he was successful in providing a large volume of classified information to the Soviet, and later the Russian, intelligence services.[27]

This information led to the execution of several friendly agents. Beginning in 1985 and continuing until his arrest in 1994, Ames was reported to have received US$4.6 million for his espionage activities. Although there were indicators early on, counterintelligence was not able to identify that there was a security issue, and, when it did, it took some ten months to investigate the matter before arresting him on February 21, 1994.[28]

Some of the events that were potential indictors of his espionage activities included alcohol abuse, extramarital relationships with foreign nationals, security violations, and failure to comply with agency administrative regulations.[29] There were purchases made that were far in excess of his annual CIA salary and these occurred over many years—standout items included paying cash for a house and the purchase of a luxury Jaguar motor vehicle.[30] The Select Committee on Intelligence found that the CIA

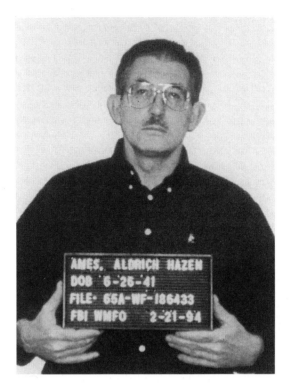

PHOTO 1.2 Aldrich Hazen Ames, a Former CIA Officer, Turned KGB Mole, at the Time of His Arrest in 1994. *Source*: Photograph courtesy of the Federal of Investigation.

failed to aggressively investigate the cases compromised by Ames with adequate resources until mid-1991, six years after the compromises occurred; the CIA had failed to adequately limit Ames's assignments and access to classified information after suspicions concerning him had been raised; and the CIA had failed to advise the oversight committees of the losses caused by Ames despite a statutory requirement to advise of "significant intelligence failures." The FBI had failed to devote sufficient resources to the mole-hunt and delayed for too long in opening a formal investigation of Ames.[31]

The Select Committee found other issues too, like the CIA's failure "to adequately coordinate the operational activities of Ames by allowing him to meet alone with Soviet Embassy officials at a time when he had access to extraordinarily sensitive information pertaining to Soviet nationals working clandestinely with the CIA."[32]

These counterintelligence miscalculations resulted in, as Ames is reported to have declared: the compromise of "virtually all Soviet agents of the CIA and other American and foreign services known to me."[33] This was not the only opposition agent operating with a friendly agency—there were others to come—and collectively these events remind us of the challenges for counterintelligence.

WikiLeaks Affair

WikiLeaks was a web-based organization created in 2007 to bring "important news and information to the public . . . [via] . . . an innovative, secure and anonymous way for sources to leak information."[34] This declaration should be a concern for every counterintelligence officer. Illustrating this point is the alleged leaking in 2010 by Private First-Class Bradley Manning, an intelligence analyst with the U.S. Army stationed in Iraq, of some 250,000 classified documents to the WikiLeaks organization.[35] This event generated a tempest of controversy that resounded in news, academic, and government circles long after the event and was still reverberating at the time this book went to print. Like the Ellsberg leaks regarding the Pentagon Papers almost forty years prior, there were ethical justifications given for the leaking of these documents and the ethical debate was one of the dominant discussions following the wholesale public release of these documents onto the Internet.

The point, though, for counterintelligence is how could a low-level army intelligence analyst in an operational environment (i.e., tactical/operational) been given access to such wide-ranging data, much of which could be considered strategic? How could he have extracted these data from classified computer systems in such volumes and then removed them from a classified area to place them in the hands of an organization that openly admitted it was dedicated to "leaking information"? As U.S. Secretary of Defense at the time, Robert Gates, stated: "The battlefield consequences of the release of these documents are potentially severe and dangerous for our troops, our allies and Afghan partners, and may well damage our relationships and reputation in that key part of the world. Intelligence sources and methods, as well as military tactics, techniques, and procedures, will become known to our adversaries."[36]

This was a mammoth leak, so how could counterintelligence not have noticed and/or acted on the warning signs before Manning handed over these data? For instance, it was reported that Manning was demoted from specialist to private first class for assaulting a fellow soldier,[37] and was sent to a chaplain after officers noticed what was called "odd behaviors."[38] Posts to the social networking website Manning was said to have been using at the time were reported to reflect a psychologically troubled soldier. Even though U.S. Secretary of Defense Gates advised that "we will aggressively investigate and, wherever possible, prosecute such violations,"[39] the ramifications of missing these potentially rich counterintelligence indicators, and promptly acting on them, were reflected in the months of controversy that followed the WikiLeaks affair.[40]

Sony's PlayStation

The ability of the opposition to penetrate national security agencies, as well as the unauthorized release of classified documents by trusted employees, was highlighted in the previous selected cases. But, counterintelligence goes beyond the government and military; it extends to other sectors, including those in the commercial and industrial arenas. The Sony PlayStation case in early 2011 is just one of many examples of how corporate enterprises fail in terms of their counterintelligence responsibilities.

· ·

Sony said that, as a result of the attack, an "unauthorized person" had obtained personal information about account holders, including their names, addresses, e-mail addresses, and PlayStation user names and passwords. Sony warned that other confidential information, including credit card numbers, could have been compromised, warning customers through a statement to "remain vigilant" by monitoring identity theft or other financial loss.[41]

· ·

It could be said that, if a person's house is burgled, the owner knows it—the TV may be gone, jewelry stolen, and cash missing—but, when data is stolen, the "original" is still there. This makes "information burglary" more difficult to detect. When it comes to computer systems, the only clue that data has been "taken" may come in the form of an entry in an access log (i.e., if the person penetrating the system has not deleted his trail or altered it to throw counterintelligence investigators off track).

In the case of the Sony PlayStation penetration, the impact was troubling in several ways: "Sony has estimated that the hacker attacks will cost it at least 14 billion yen (about $175 million) in damages, including spending on information technology, legal costs, lower sales and free offers to lure back customers."[42] There were a number of counterintelligence issues raised by this case, including the identification of data that needed classifying (and hence protection), storage, access, and compartmentalizing.

John Deutch

It is not just staff of agencies—officers, operatives, and agents—who are the subject of counterintelligence mistakes. When John Mark Deutch left the post of director of central intelligence there was an allegation that he had mishandled classified information. It was alleged that he stored sensitive data on his unclassified home computer and that this information was susceptible to being compromised when he visited Internet websites.[43] The CIA's Office of Inspector General investigated the matter and found that

Deutch was aware of prohibitions relating to the use of unclassified computers for processing classified information. He was further aware of specific vulnerabilities related to the use of unclassified computers that were connected to the Internet. Despite this knowledge, Deutch processed a large volume of highly classified information on these unclassified computers, taking no steps to restrict unauthorized access to the information, and thereby placing national security information at risk.[44]

Chief of MI6

Normally, the chief of Britain's secret intelligence service would keep a low profile, as would any serving intelligence officer. This is because the potential for exploitation by opposition forces by publishing personal information about these persons carries serious consequences, as was pointed out in the case of CIA Chief of Station Richard Welch, who was assassinated in Greece in 1975.

However, in July 2009, the world's media carried the story that Sir (Robert) John Sawers—the soon-to-be chief of Britain's secret intelligence service (MI6)—had his personal details along with a number of photographs publicly displayed on his wife's social networking profile on Facebook.[45] As innocent as this may seem, a skilled intelligence analyst could use these details to complement existing data holdings on Sir John to develop, say, a psychoanalytic profile[46] of him as a leader, his decision-making aptitude for intelligence matters, and so on.

. . . .

Criminals search social networking sites for people to exploit. The process is known as *whaling* because crime groups are looking for "big fish." Their targets are usually prominent people in the business world but can include politicians. They are looking for personal information that will allow them to use a pretext to con the target into paying a fake invoice or other fabricated debt. Politicians are targeted because their personal information can lead them to their government related computer systems.

. . . .

From a counterintelligence point of view this was a security risk that showed naïveté. Although the James Bond-esque image of the British secret intelligence service no longer completely cloaked in secrecy, experience has shown that there is a reason why personnel security forms an important part of counterintelligence practices and procedures. In this case, it may be impossible to assess what long-term harm may have occurred by MI6 because of such a pause in security.

News of the World and Alleged Telephone Hacking

In mid-2011 the world's news media published articles alleging that a wide range of people's personal cell phone messages and records were illegally accessed, and details purchased by the now-defunct British newspaper *News of the World* to be used as part of the stories they were reporting. Several of the newspaper's executives who were alleged to be involved in the scheme were arrested. It also caused the head of the Metropolitan Police to resign because he employed a former *News of the World* executive as a media adviser, unaware of his past involvement in the scandal.

The hacking allegations centered on the unauthorized access of the telephone accounts of various celebrities, politicians, and members of the British royal family. There were also allegations that the voicemail of a young murdered schoolgirl, relatives of deceased British soldiers, and victims of the 7/7 London bombings were also accessed. The allegations "that may have included identity theft and bribery of police officers"[47] outraged the British public and as a result, the newspaper's advertisers withdrew their support. The lack of advertising revenue was reported to have contributed to the *News of the World*'s closure on July 10, 2011 (after 168 years of publication). In January 2012 over thirty civil settlements, which included financial compensation for damages as well as legal costs to some of the alleged victims, were announced.[48]

. . . .

Ashley Madison is a website that promised confidentially for people wanting to have extramarital affairs. However, in July 2015 it was hacked. Tens of gigabytes of data from the dating website were stolen and those claiming responsibility held it for ransom, demanding that the company close the website. The perpetrators, calling themselves The Impact Team, claimed to have user information that it would release into the public domain if their terms were not met. These data included user names, their email and home addresses, their sexual fantasies, their credit card information, and many gigabytes of Ashely Madison company emails. The data also included information of users who paid an additional fee to have their information deleted. Between 18 and 21 August 2017 The Impact Team released the data.[49]

. . . .

Abdul Qadeer Khan

A. Q. Khan was a Pakistani nuclear scientist who was instrumental in developing Pakistan's atomic bomb project. He was also instrumental in establishing a black market for the sale of nuclear information, production designs, and methods to third parties. Investigations revealed that he sold designs of Pakistan's P1 centrifuge to Iran. He sold the design of the improved P2 centrifuges to several other countries. And, he sold drawings for a uranium processing plant to Libya.[50]

In September 2003, the director of Central Intelligence, George Tenet, confronted the then president of Pakistan, Pervez Musharraf, with blueprints of the secrets A. Q. Khan sold. Although Khan confessed, he was never arrested or tried in a court of law. His subsequent house arrest was challenged in the Islamabad High Court and he was freed. As disappointing as this result is, Khan is no longer profiting from the proliferation of nuclear secrets. This can be attributed to the counterintelligence work that was done by the small CIA team that pursued Khan for almost a decade. They need to be acknowledged for their sterling work in closing down Khan's network.[51] But, how long will it be before another Khan emerges, and rather than selling nuclear secrets to nations, they sell them to terrorist groups?

Mossack Fonseca and the *Panama Papers*

In April 2016, the obscure Panamanian law firm of Mossack Fonseca & Co. became the center of world-wide media attention when it realized that it had suffered a massive data leak. The leak was dubbed the *Panama Papers*. At that time, the legal company was reported to be the fourth largest offshore financial services provider, representing over 200,000 companies, and some of the most politically and financially influential people in the world. The term *massive* is not an exaggeration—it was reported that the data hemorrhaged by the law firm's inadequate computer security was around 11.5 million documents. These were documents with detailed financial and attorney-client confidential information. Some of the data dated back to the 1970s, the time the firm was created. Presidents, kings, former prime ministers, heads of state, and family members of these people were identified in the leaked documents. The data also revealed corrupt activities of politicians, dictators, drugs and arms dealers, and some not-for-profit organizations.[52]

Appleby and the *Paradise Papers*

Like the Panama Papers leak, the so-called Paradise Papers was a cyberattack that, in late 2017, made public some 13.4 million confidential electronic documents. These documents from the Bermuda-based law firm, Appleby, related to over 120,000 people and companies, including Queen Elizabeth II. The e-files are reported to include confidential e-mails, court documents, bank statements, and detailed client information. The timeframe these documents covered was extensive—from 1950 to 2016. Data security experts estimated the size of the leak was in the order of 1.4 terabytes (1000^4 bytes). Beside the loss of client trust the leak caused, these data could potentially be sold to third parties to be used in criminal activity.

- -

A secret is something you haven't told yet.—Anonymous

- -

Global Surveillance Disclosures

In 2013, Edward Joseph Snowden, a former computer security technician, who was once employed by the CIA, stole tens of thousands of classified documents from the U.S. government.[53] He then leaked the classified material he took from the National Security Agency, where, at the time, he was a contractor for Booz Allen Hamilton. The documents he made publicly available revealed various global surveillance operations that were being run by the NSA, as well as the Five Eyes intelligence alliance.[54] Soon after his leak, U.S. Federal prosecutors filed criminal charges against Snowden, alleging theft of government property, and under the *Espionage Act, 1917*, "unauthorized communication of national defense information" and "willful communication of classified communications intelligence information to an unauthorized person."

It is estimated that Snowden stole 1.7 million secret documents. It is understood that he has leaked some 200,000 documents to journalists when he traveled to Hong Kong. It is not publicly known how many documents he still has, so implications of this are disturbing for national security, because from 2014 to the time of this writing, Snowden has lived under the patronage of the Russia security intelligence services in Moscow. In this regard, Russian exhibits perverse logic when it comes to handling defectors, because in March 2018, Russian state television broadcast a threat to Russian defectors: "I don't wish death on anyone, but, purely for educational purposes, I have a warning for anyone who dreams of such a career [i.e., spying for a foreign government]. The profession of a traitor is one of the most dangerous in the world."[55] Days earlier, the Russian state was linked to an assassination attempt on defector Sergei Skripal and his daughter, Yulia, in Salisbury, Wiltshire, England.

· ·

The increase in classified information within the entire government has diminished respect for it and encouraged carelessness in handling it. Steps to correct the situation will be difficult, but they must be taken.[56]
—Admiral Stansfield Turner, Director of Central Intelligence, 1977–1981

· ·

CIA Secrets "Vault"

In March 2017 WikiLeaks posted some 9,000 classified CIA documents to the Internet. These documents discussed the CIA's cyber weapons program, revealing methods and software programs that could, for instance, convert computers, Internet routers, iPhones, Android equipment, web-enabled televisions, and other electronic devices into instruments that are able to collect data covertly. The leak of these documents was reported to have been provided by a former American government contractor. A month later, CIA director Mike Pompeo stated, "It is time to call out WikiLeaks for what it really is, a non-state hostile intelligence service often abetted by state actors like Russia."[57]

Some Concluding Thoughts

It would be a naïve person who would argue that an opponent has not thought thoroughly about how to use information to develop intelligence, and how to use this insight to attack—whether that attack is to undermine national security, to defeat a military in whatever battle-space it might be fighting, or to dominate business enterprises throughout the world.

Carl von Clausewitz once wrote: "So long as I have not overthrown my opponent I am bound to fear he may overthrow me. Thus, I am not in control: he dictates to me as much as I dictate to him."[58] These are words of caution that should be heeded, as dominance in one area of the intelligence rubric does not mean dominance in all. There are without doubt some determined opponents in the world, and, until we find a way to wreck not only their ability to attack, but their *will* to attack, counterintelligence practitioners must stand vigilant against their persistent probing of information defenses. But, an over emphasis on counterintelligence can lead to a degradation of the agency's core business because security measures can paradoxically hamper "doing the job." Moreover, as ruthless as these opponents might be, they are smart enough to evolve their methods and practices in response to each innovation that counterintelligence theory and practice brings.

There is a Latin proverb that states that a wise man learns from the mistakes of others, whereas a fool learns from his own.[59] Although said in a different era, and no doubt in a different context, this saying seems to have application for the challenges of counterintelligence today and certainly provides food for thought as we consider the fundamentals of counterintelligence.

Review of Key Words and Phrases

The key words and phrases associated with this chapter are listed below. Demonstrate your understanding of each by writing a short definition or explanation in one or two sentences.

Five Eyes   WikiLeaks affair
MI6   wilderness of mirrors

Study Questions

1. Describe three challenges that counterintelligence professionals face in protecting classified information.
2. It could be argued that one of the weakest links in securing information is the human element. Taking this position, explain why this might be the case.
3. Using archived media reports, compile a list of five counterintelligence events that have taken place within the state or province in which you work or live (the time frame is not relevant). Distinguish whether the events were related to a national security, military, law enforcement, or private security/investigation event.
4. Describe the types of information that might be of interest to the opposition who might be (a) a foreign political state or (b) a business competitor.

Learning Activity

An article appeared in *The Times* (London) by Defence Editor Michael Evans that stated, "All members of the [British] Armed Forces are warned about Facebook and other social networking websites. Although they are not banned from the website, they have been told not to include details that could compromise their security. The same warning has been issued at MI5, MI6, and GCHQ, the Government's eavesdropping center in Cheltenham."[60] As a learning exercise to demonstrate how such information could be complied by the opposition, use the Internet to assemble a dossier on *yourself*. Use only Internet-based information from the results of search engine queries—for example, media archives, social networking websites, other websites, and so forth.

Notes

1 Raymond Davis with Storms Reback, *The Contractor: How I Landed in a Pakistani Prison and Ignited a Diplomatic Crisis* (Dallas, TX: Benbella Books, 2017). Compare this event with the successful intelligence operation that culminated with the assassination of an Iranian nuclear scientist in January 2012 by unknown covert operatives. See Rick Gladstone, "Iran Tightens Its Security for Scientists after Killing," *New York Times*, January 18, 2012, A6, New York edition.

2 Associated Press, "Heathrow Airport Security Information Found on USB stick on London Street," http://www.abc.net.au/news/2017-10-30/heathrow-security-information-found-in-usb -on-london-street/9097792 (accessed November 1, 2017).

3 Matt Richtel, "Hewlett-Packard Settles Spy Case," *New York Times*, February 14, 2008.

4 U.S. Federal Bureau of Investigation, *Update on Sony Investigation*, Media Release (Washington, DC: FBI National Press Office, December 19, 2014).

5 As an example of "over planning," see Prunckun's discussion regarding "good idea fairies." Henry Prunckun, *How to Undertake Surveillance and Reconnaissance: From a Civilian and Military Perspective* (South Yorkshire: Pen & Sword Military, 2015), 92–93.

6 The saying is attributed to a passage in T. S. Eliot's 1920 poem "Gerontion" (T. S. Eliot, *Selected Poems* [New York: Brace and World, 1964]). It was subsequently the title of David C. Martin's book on CIA counterintelligence during the Cold War (David C. Martin, *Wilderness of Mirrors* [New York: Harper and Row, 1980]).

7 M. William Phelps, *Nathan Hale: The Life and Death of America's First Spy* (New York: Thomas Dunne, 2008).

8 Neil Sheehan, Hedrick Smith, E. W. Kenworthy, and Fox Butterfield, *The Pentagon Papers as Published by the New York Times* (New York: Quadrangle, 1971).

9 Although the covering memo to the secretary of defense (through Mr. Paul C. Warnke and Dr. Morton H. Halperin), written by Dr. Leslie H. Gelb, chairman of the Office of the Secretary of Defense Task Force, stated that there were forty-three volumes, the notation on the index shows that there were forty-six volumes, plus the index volume, thus making the study a forty-seven-volume set. In June 2011 the entire study was declassified and made public except for eleven words, which remain classified.

10 In my book on intelligence analysis (Hank Prunckun, *Scientific Method of Inquiry for Intelligence Analysis,* 2nd ed. [Lanham, MD: Rowman & Littlefield, 2015]), I point out the value of archival data in relation to intelligence research. This secret history of the Vietnam War is a case in point, as no primary data in the form of interviews, surveys, or focus groups were sought, yet the goal of the classified research project was accomplished.

11 Daniel Ellsberg, *Secrets: A Memoir of Vietnam and the Pentagon Papers* (New York: Viking, 2002).

12 G. Gordon Liddy, *Will: The Autobiography of G. Gordon Liddy* (London: Severn House Publishers, 1980), 170.

13 E. Howard Hunt wrote *The Sankov Confession*, as well as several other spy novels under the pseudonym of P. S. Donoghue. P. S. Donoghue, *The Sankov Confession* (New York: Donald I. Fine, 1988), 117.

14 This view was prevalent at the time. Take, for instance, John Prados's (U.S. National Security Archives) comments, "Counterintelligence officers tended to have low rank (an average grade of GS-9), they had little experience (five years or less on average), and only one in four had advanced or even basic training in counterintelligence operations." John Prados, "The Long View," in

Bruce Hoffman and Christian Ostermann (eds.) *Moles, Defectors, and Deceptions: James Angleton and His Influence in U.S. Counterintelligence* (Washington, DC: Wilson Center), 88.

15 Carl Bernstein and Bob Woodward, *All the President's Men* (New York: Simon and Schuster, 1974).

16 For instance, see Gerald Gold, ed., *The White House Transcripts* (New York: Viking, 1974).

17 Bob Woodward, *The Secret Man: The Story of Watergate's Deep Throat* (New York: Simon & Schuster, 2005).

18 Leonard Garment, *In Search of Deep Throat: The Greatest Political Mystery of Our Time* (New York: Basic, 2000).

19 Which is a curious phenomenon—that is, a group of investigative journalists trying to expose the confidential source of another investigative journalist.

20 John W. Dean, *Unmasking Deep Throat: History's Most Elusive News Source* (San Francisco: salon.com, 2002).

21 Bob Woodward, *Veil: The Secret Wars of the CIA, 1981–1987* (New York: Simon & Schuster, 1987), 264–65.

22 Julius Mader, *Who's Who in CIA: A Biographical Reference Work on 3,000 Officers of the Civil and Military Branches of Secret Services of the USA in 120 Countries* (Berlin, East Germany: Julius Mader, 1968).

23 Philip Agee, *On the Run* (Secaucus, NJ: Lyle Stuart, 1987), 130–34.

24 Woodward, *Veil*, 264–65.

25 Richard Helms, *A Look Over My Shoulder: A Life in the Central Intelligence Agency* (New York: Random House, 2003), 433–34.

26 Dr. Petrus "Beer" Duvenage (State Security Agency, South Africa), personal communication, January 23, 2012.

27 Pete Earley, *Confessions of a Spy: The Real Story of Aldrich Ames* (New York: Putnam, 1997).

28 David Wise, *Nightmover* (New York: HarperCollins, 1995).

29 David Wise, *Nightmover*. But, see also, Tim Weiner, David Johnston, and Neil A. Lewis, *Betrayal: The Story of Aldrich Ames, An American Spy* (New York: Random House, 1995); and Peter Maas, *Killer Spy: The Inside Story of the FBI's Pursuit and Capture of Aldrich Ames, America's Deadliest Spy* (New York: Warner, 1995).

30 David Wise, *Nightmover*.

31 Select Committee on Intelligence, *Special Report, Committee Activities of the Select Committee on Intelligence, United States Senate, January 4, 1993, to December 1, 1994* (Washington, DC: U.S. Government Printer, 1995), 16.

32 Select Committee on Intelligence, *Special Report, Committee Activities of the Select Committee on Intelligence, United States Senate, January 4, 1993, to December 1, 1994*, 16.

33 Aldridge Ames reported in *New York Times*, April 29, 1994, A16: 1.

34 WikiLeaks, "About," wikileaks.org/About.html (accessed July 5, 2011).

35 Andrew Fowler, *The Most Dangerous Man in the World: How One Hacker Ended Corporate and Government Secrecy Forever* (New York: Skyhorse Publishing, 2011).

36 Department of Defense, *DoD News Briefing with Secretary Gates and Admiral Mullen from the Pentagon* (Washington, DC: Office of the Assistant Secretary of Defense [Public Affairs], July 29, 2010). In support of this assertion, *Newsweek Magazine* published a story on August 1, 2010, alleging that some of the WikiLeaks documents contained names and villages of Afghans who were secretly cooperating with the American military. The news story said that "just four days after the documents were published, death threats began arriving at the homes of key tribal elders in southern Afghanistan. And over the weekend one tribal elder, Khalifa Abdullah, who the Taliban believed had been in close contact with the Americans, was taken from his home in Monar village, in Kandahar province's embattled Arghandab district, and executed by insurgent gunmen [i.e., Taliban insurgents]." See Ron Moreau and Sami Yousafzai, "Taliban Seeks Vengeance in Wake of WikiLeaks," *Newsweek Magazine*, August 1, 2010. This story was preceded by others, such as the one that stated: "The Taliban yesterday threatened to decapitate informers revealed in uncensored intelligence documents published on the internet. In their first response since WikiLeaks placed thousands of secret documents online detailing names and locations of anti-Taliban informers, Afghan militants said, 'we know how to punish them'—a reference to beheading, the usual Taliban punishment

reserved for 'Traitors.'" David William, "Taliban Threatens to Behead Informers," *The Advertiser*, Adelaide, Australia, July 31, 2010, 67.

37 Fowler, *The Most Dangerous Man in the World.*

38 Fowler, *The Most Dangerous Man in the World.*

39 Department of Defense, *DoD News Briefing with Secretary Gates and Admiral Mullen from the Pentagon.*

40 For example, as highlighted in Patrick F. Walsh, *Intelligence and Intelligence Analysis* (New York: Rutledge, 2011), 210–18.

41 An excerpt from a newspaper report of the data theft incident. Nick Bilton and Brian Stelter, "Sony Says PlayStation Hacker Got Personal Data," *New York Times*, April 26, 2011, B1, New York edition.

42 David Jolly and Raphael Minder, "3 Detained in Spain in PlayStation Attack," *New York Times*, June 11, 2011, B1, New York edition.

43 Valerie Plame Wilson, *Fair Game: My Life as a Spy, My Betrayal by the White House* (New York: Simon & Schuster, 2007), 347.

44 Central Intelligence Agency, *Inspector General, Report of Investigation: Improper Handling of Classified Information by John M. Deutch* (Washington, DC: CIA, February 18, 2000).

45 Sarah Lyall, "On Facebook, a Spy Revealed," *New York Times*, July 6, 2009, A1, New York edition. One could argue that because Sawers was not an SIS officer at the time of his appointment as Chief (most his career, which spanned 1984–2009) was as a senior diplomat, it is not surprising that his details were in the public domain. However, contrast this event with the news report that President Barack Obama, who used social media during his 2008 election campaign, refused to allow his two daughters to join his Facebook page, stating, "Why would we want to have a whole bunch of people who we don't know knowing our business?" See David Jackson, "Obama: No Facebook for Malia, Sasha," *USA Today*, December 14, 2011.

46 See, for example, a description of this technique in Hank Prunckun, *Scientific Methods of Inquiry for Intelligence Analysis,* 65.

47 John F. Burns, "Victim's Family Appears amid Rage at Tabloids," *New York Times*, July 13, 2011, A14, New York edition.

48 Sarah Lyall and Don Van Natta, Jr., "An Arrest and Scotland Yard Resignation Roil Britain," *New York Times*, July 17, 2011, New York edition, A1; and Sarah Lyall and Ravi Somaiya, "Murdoch Company Settles with Dozens of Hacking Victims," *New York Times*, January 20, 2012, New York edition, A4, as well as "Phone-Hacking Damages Claims Settled," *Weekend Australian*, January 21, 2012: 10.

49 Steve Mansfield-Devine, "The Ashley Madison Affair," *Network Security* 2015, no. 9: 8–16.

50 George Tenet with Bill Harlow, *At the Center of the Storm: My Years at the CIA* (New York: HarperCollins), 285.

51 Tenet, *At the Center of the Storm,* 287.

52 Bastian Obermayer and Frederik Obermaier, *The Panama Papers: Breaking the Story of How the Rich and Powerful Hide their Money* (London: Oneworld Publications, 2017).

53 Glenn Greenwald, *No Place to Hide: Edward Snowden, the NSA, and the U.S. Surveillance State* (New York: Henry Holt and Company, 2014).

54 Edward Jay Epstein, *How America Lost Its Secrets: Edward Snowden, the Man and the Theft* (New York: Alfred A. Knoff, 2017).

55 Russian state television news broadcaster, Kirill Kleimenov, cited in Andrew Higgins, "To Putin, Spy Case Bolsters Image," *The New York Times*, International Edition, March 16, 2018: 4.

56 Stansfield Turner, *Secrecy and Democracy: The CIA in Transition* (Boston: Houghton Mifflin Company, 1985), 276.

57 Warren Strobel and Mark Hosenball (Reuters), "CIA Chief Calls WikiLeaks a Hostile Intelligence Service," https://www.reuters.com/article/us-cia-wikileaks/cia-chief-calls-wikileaks-a-hostile-intelligence-service-idUSKBN17F2L8 (accessed November 5, 2017).

58 Carl von Clausewitz, *On War*, trans. Michael Howard and Peter Paret (Oxford, England: Oxford University Press, 1976), 16.

59 A saying that seems to have its origin in an ancient Latin proverb and has been quoted in different forms, but with the same intent.

60 Michael Evans, "Wife of Sir John Sawers, the Future Head of MI6, in Facebook Security Alert," *Times* (London), July 6, 2009.

Chapter 2

Fundamentals of Counterintelligence

Individuals, corporations, the military, and entire nations owe their safety and well-being to counterintelligence. Without it the intelligence function in all its manifestations could not be as effective as it is. If espionage were a sport, those who practice the craft of counterintelligence would be considered the game's goal keepers. Without these practitioners, the opposition would have carte blanche to raid the unprotected goal and score never-ending points. In chapter 1 we saw examples of how poor counterintelligence practices manifest themselves.

Intelligence Quadrangle

To understand counterintelligence, one needs first to understand the interdependence between the various intelligence fields and how these fields of practice are interrelated. The term *intelligence* has several meanings, so it is important to offer a definition for each of the contexts in which the term is used. *Intelligence* can be defined in the following four contexts:

1. Actions or processes that are used to produce knowledge;
2. The body of knowledge produced because of processing;
3. Organizations that deal in knowledge (e.g., an intelligence agency); and
4. The reports and briefings that are the result of the process or are produced by such an organization.

Sometimes raw data are referred to as *intelligence*, but this is not correct. It can only be considered intelligence after it has been analyzed and meaning given to the question being asked of the data. Nevertheless, the common theme in these definitions is *knowledge*. In intelligence work, knowledge equates to *insight*. Or, stated another way, it is the ability to *reduce uncertainty*. Intelligence is important, as insight and certainty offer decision makers the ability to formulate policy, propose options, and take actions to better control "the unknown."

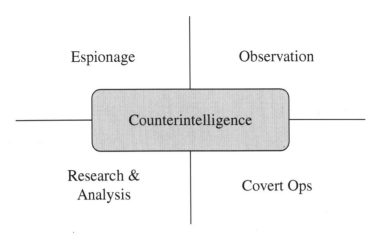

FIGURE 2.1 Intelligence Quadrangle Linked by the Keystone of Counterintelligence.

Intelligence can be categorized into four broad functions—espionage, observation, research and analysis, and covert operations. Two of the quadrilateral's sectors—espionage and observation—support a third sector, which is research and analysis. In turn, the combination of these three quarters supports a fourth—covert ops. Counterintelligence, therefore, is the keystone that locks these pieces of intelligence mosaic to one another—it is common to all other functions (Figure 2.1).

Espionage

Espionage is the archetypal method for gathering information. It dates back centuries with biblical references to it. For instance, in the fourth book of the *Old Testament* (Numbers), it states in chapter 13: "The Lord said to Moses, 'Choose one of the leaders from each of the twelve tribes and send them as spies to explore the land of Canaan.'"[1] "When Moses sent his spies out, he instructed them: 'Find out what kind of country it is, how many people live there, and how strong they are. Find out whether the land is good or bad and whether the people live in open towns or fortified cities. Find out whether the soil is fertile and whether the land is wooded. And be sure to bring back some of the fruit that grows there.'"[2]

This example demonstrates how agents were tasked to collect data about the issue under consideration so that this information could guide action. The word *espionage* is derived from the Old French, meaning *spy*; so, it is understandable that it is sometimes simplified to *spying*. This biblical reference points out that espionage utilizes agents to go undercover to gather information. This is distinct from *observation*. So, the way the term "observation" is used here should not be confused with reconnaissance. Reconnaissance is scouting; although it is allied to observation, it has a different purpose. Observation in the context of this book is information gathering in the broadest sense.

An agent is someone who acts on behalf of another person or an agency (e.g., a private investigator, or a private inquiry *agent*). An agent is someone who an intelligence officer recruits to obtain secrets on behalf of the officer's agency. In such situations, the recruiting officer is termed a *case officer*[3] (or, in some instances, a recruiter or a *handler*[4]). Those who perform operational duties are termed *operations officers* or *field officers* (field officers may even have specific role designations, such as *counterintelligence investigators* and the like). There are times when *dummy agents* are created for the purposes of deception. These dummy agents then perform invented activities, such as sending dummy messages or performing invented acts of espionage or sabotage, which form part of the deception plan. These activities give currency to the dummy agent's "existence," ultimately promoting carefully crafted disinformation to the opposition.

The role of agents is to place themselves in a position that allows them to obtain information—by viewing, overhearing, participating in discussions, or by other means so that the desired information can be obtained. In the biblical example, the tribal leaders that Moses is reported to have sent to Canaan were tasked with collecting certain data items. However, with vast technological improvements, *observation* by technical surveillance and unobtrusive methods is a favored source over the use of human agents (though human sources should never be discounted).

- -

The techniques of secret operations are as old as the human race; they are by no means diabolical inventions . . . or symptoms of a human decline.[5]

- -

Operatives are of two forms—those with some form of official cover and those without.[6] *Cover* is best described as a plausible story about all facets of the operative's life. If the operative is operating under official cover they can assume the role of a minor diplomat or other person in an embassy or consulate, thus giving them an excuse for being in certain places or undertaking certain activities. Those operating under nonofficial cover (NOC, pronounced *knock*), sometimes referred to as *commercial cover*, may work for a phantom company created and maintained by an intelligence agency. These operatives have no connection with their government. As has been pointed out by those in the trade, "the best way to protect your cover as a spy is to inhabit your cover identity as much as possible."[7]

NOC operatives have been described as the truest practitioners of espionage as they operate on their own, always. They are afforded no protection from their government while overseas. If they are caught abroad, they may be tortured during interrogation and risk execution. If this happens, it is most unlikely that a media conference will be held and, therefore, no one will hear about the event. NOC operatives operate alone and die alone.

It could be said that espionage worked reasonably well during the Cold War years (1945–1991) when intelligence agencies faced actors that were states, as electronic and other technical means of data gathering were possible. But, since the al-Qaeda terrorist attacks of September 11, 2001, intelligence agencies have recognized the importance of having undercover officers and agents in place to gather information. This is because such groups are ill defined—there are no geographic borders to monitor, no specific land-based targets to reconnoiter, and no organized communities (whether military or social) to assess. Today's targets are bound by ideology and can live within the agency's country or one of its allies.

During the Cold War, one reason for shifting to technically gathered data was the comparatively high cost of "running" human agents as well as improving the reliability of the data collected. For example, aerial and satellite photographs are not susceptible to an exaggeration of the truth as an agent might be. Technical data simply show what is there and what is not. Furthermore, technological advances have now made much of these data available in real time. As a case in point, take the May 2011 joint CIA and U.S. Navy SEAL operation that targeted Osama bin Laden at his safe house in Abbottabad, Pakistan. This secret operation was transmitted live into the White House Situation Room. However, the events of September 11 and the subsequent terrorist attacks in Madrid, London, and Bali, as well as the others that followed this initial wave, showed that, despite the advantages of technically gathered data, these data may be of little value when faced with terrorist cells operating in a vastly different fashion to that of, say, a foreign government's military.

. . . .

One of the rules of thumb of espionage is to never give away a piece of information. Instead, it should be sold or traded for information that is of equal or greater value.

. . . .

Loosely structured groups related by an ideological bond and other nontraditional challenges to a state-centric paradigm have changed the nature of confrontations. Nations now face threats from weak and corrupt governments, rogue states, substate and transstate actors, as well as international organized criminal groups, radical ethnic and religious groups, and right- and left-wing political groups. These threats pose special data collection problems that defy a purely technical collection approach.

Observation

Observation refers to those methods for gathering information that center on *viewing*. It employs methods other than placing an agent in a position to obtain confidential information. Observation includes collecting data via technical means such as audio surveillance devices, radio frequency devices, and special photographic equipment, including space-based reconnaissance satellites. It is a catch-all category for a variety of methods other than espionage (as pointed out in the section on espionage above).

The use of technical means of observation through, say, remotely controlled drone aircraft can yield results no other method can. Examples of this can be seen in accounts of how U.S. unmanned aerial vehicles (UAV) were used to hunt down Taliban insurgents in Afghanistan throughout the first decade of the 2000s and continued up until this book went to press.[8] However, it is at the peril of an intelligence agency that it neglects data collection by human sources.

Moreover, observation is also concerned with collecting data that is in the public domain through what is termed *open-source* data collection. In some cases, the collection of information from open sources can provide an intelligence analyst with an exponential gain in both the quantity and, under the right circumstances, the quality of the information gathered.[9]

Research and Analysis

Research is sometimes seen as probing esoteric issues and obtaining findings, the applicability of which to real-world situations may at times be difficult to see. In academic disciplines this is termed *basic research* or *theoretical research*. Such research is concerned with discovery for its own sake—that is, when undertaken, it has no practical application. It is knowledge for the sake of knowing. The findings of this type of research can be used later in an applied setting, but, at the time of conducting the research, the goal is not to apply the knowledge to solve particular problems.

By contrast, *applied research* has a practical purpose—to offer a basis for making a decision (i.e., to provide *insight*). Intelligence is, in this sense, applied research: it is the outcome of processing raw information that has been collected from a variety of sources—open sources, semi-open sources, official sources, clandestine sources, and/or covert sources. This function is sometimes termed *positive intelligence* or *positive collection* depending on the context. Once such information is made available to an intelligence analyst, it is evaluated, and any irrelevant information discarded. The pieces of information pertinent to the matter under investigation are then analyzed, interpreted, and formed into a finished "product."

This product can take the form of an oral briefing, a written briefing, a target profile, a tactical assessment, a strategic estimate, or any number of different types of reports. These products are then disseminated to the end users. In intelligence parlance, end users are called *customers*.[10] The intelligence process can be summarized as analysis that leads to the production of deep, thorough, or meaningful understanding about an issue.

Covert Operations

Covert operations lay in a somewhat gray area of intelligence work. Sometimes referred to as *covert action*,[11] *special activities*,[12] and in Britain, *special political action*,[13] these operations use various methods of information gathering, including those of research and analysis, but incorporates advice and counsel, financial and material support, and technical assistance to individuals, groups, or businesses that are opposed to, or working in competition with, a target or adversary.

Covert ops and *black ops* are shorthand names for a function by which the perpetrator uses the information it collects through espionage, observation, and analysis to strengthen its allies and to weaken or destroy its opponents.[14] Covert action is "the practice of trying to influence events, decisions, and opinions covertly in other states with a measure of plausible deniability."[15]

The effectiveness of covert operations is contingent upon the perpetrator's involvement remaining hidden, or deniable. At this point it needs to be stressed that despite the portrayal of covert action in cinema and spy thrillers, it is highly improbable that an agency with legislative oversight can initiate and maintain a covert operation without some form of approval (see offensive counterintelligence tenets 1, 2, and 3). The notion of a rouge intelligence unit, or an entire agency carrying out covert ops as it sees fit, is how it is depicted in novels—pure fiction.[16]

On one hand, if a plausible denial[17] can be maintained, then the rewards of such ventures can be enormous. On the other hand, if the perpetrator's involvement is discovered, the consequences of this activity can be catastrophic. For example, in 1985 the French government was concerned about protests by Greenpeace regarding nuclear testing on the Pacific atoll of Mururoa. So, on July 10, 1985, French intelligence operatives from the *Direction Générale de la Sécurité Extérieure* (or, in English, the Directorate-General for External Security) mined Greenpeace's *Rainbow Warrior* in Auckland Harbour, New Zealand, with two explosive charges. The second charge was intended to sink the vessel, and as a result, one person on board drown.

New Zealand police mounted an investigation into the incident and two French operatives were arrested, tried, and found guilty. They were then sent to prison. The other French operatives involved in the black op managed to evade capture and escaped. The incident was not only an embarrassment to the French government but carried political ramifications that affected the French government for many years.

Had the operation been carried out successfully—that is, had the operatives managed to escape undetected—then the results of the op would have been different. As the former director of Central Intelligence, the late Richard Helms, advised "Covert action should be used like a well-honed scalpel, infrequently, and with discretion lest the blade lose its edge."[18]

Role of Security in Intelligence

If one was to speculate about the origins of mankind's need for security, it is possible that it began with primitive man who required a sanctuary, haven, or retreat from the threats of nature and the wilds. As man developed his security apparatus for the preservation of his life, it may further have developed to protect lands and chattels under his control, which, in turn, allowed him to project power and influence over others.

This early security is likely to have been defensive—employing tactics such as simple barriers, hiding places, natural camouflage, subterfuge, and evasion, along with others. It is likely that, once man started to organize into social groups, security took on more of an offensive role. For instance, feudal states (and their forerunners) formed armies to defend the clan's land from threats by neighbors. The strategy of striking at an external threat to prevent it from attacking (i.e., a preemptive attack) can be viewed as the precursor to offensive security.

Applying this theory to intelligence, one can see that to protect information that is vital to decision-making, some form of security is required. This is the role of counterintelligence.

Anatomy of Counterintelligence

Just as the human anatomy comprises different parts, counterintelligence also comprises different components. But, unlike intelligence—which comprises espionage, observation, research and analysis, and covert operations—counterintelligence is made up of two fields of endeavor: counterintelligence and counterespionage. These fields are related and interdependent. To understand how and why these fields of practice are codependent, we will discuss each in turn.

Counterintelligence

"Secrets range in importance, from what someone might have bought you for your birthday, to the nuclear launch codes. Personal secrets are kept avoiding embarrassment and to avoid judgment; but business secrets, law enforcement secrets, and secrets relating to national security are kept to protect people's lives, as well as to safeguard society. . . . To protect secrets, a branch of intelligence work has developed and is known as *counterintelligence*."[19] Counterintelligence is concerned with deterrence and detection. It is a security-focused function, but it is not security. However, security is used defensively within counterintelligence. That is, the thrust of counterintelligence is to protect an agency (or its client) from infiltration by an adversary, to protect against inadvertent leakage of confidential information, and to make secure its installations and material against espionage, subversion, sabotage, terrorism, and other forms of politically motivated violence, and the transfer of key technologies and/or equipment. It is an active model that calls on defensive, as well as offensive, methods of security and uses research and analysis that is core to the intelligence function.

Even though there is a clear distinction between intelligence and counterintelligence, this demarcation line can be thin. That is, information discovered via the counterintelligence function concerning an adversary's attempts to penetrate one's own or partner agency can feed the intelligence side, revealing an opponent's information voids as well as highlighting their capabilities and possible intentions. So, counterintelligence is both an activity that is carried out and a product that is produced to inform decision makers.

Counterespionage

Counterespionage is concerned with detection, deception, and neutralizing the effectiveness of an adversary's intelligence activities. On the surface, counterespionage presents as a form of spying—collecting classified information through, say, a network of agents. And it is, but the difference is that it is the acquisition of data not from another nation's government or military, but from the opposition's intelligence service. It is in some ways related to counterintelligence but differs in others. Counterintelligence can be seen as the defensive side of the craft, whereas counterespionage is the offensive side. An agency cannot have the latter without the former, so the two work in tandem.

Counterespionage is a precise function that is, arguably, the most subtle and sophisticated of all intelligence functions. It calls for the engineering of complex strategies that deliberately put one's agent(s) in contact with an opposition's intelligence personnel. This is done so that classified information can be obtained, or the adversary can be fed disinformation, which should lead to confusion, thus disrupting the adversary's operations, thus allowing the perpetrator to prosper. False information can also be planted, so, like a "barium meal," the route that this information travels within the opposition's intelligence apparatus can be traced to confirm penetration by a mole, or perhaps, expose other security leaks. It could be argued that counterespionage could not carry out its mission without the support of the methods and practices of counterintelligence.

• •

If counterespionage were a religion, then case officers would be its high priests.[20]

• •

Security, Law Enforcement, or Intelligence

If viewed with a superficial eye, counterintelligence could easily be confused with the humble role of security. After all, it oversees many of the methods for securing facilities, materiel, and personnel. It also includes investigations where breaches of security are suspected or have taken place; so, does this make it a law enforcement role? Counterintelligence also involves research and analysis; so, does that make it an intelligence function?

It is all of these—a fusion of security, law enforcement, and intelligence into a form uniquely termed *counterintelligence*. Because it is a composite of the three, no one function can be separated from the whole without leaving it incapacitated. In practice, this means that counterintelligence officers will liaise with their counterparts in the fields of security and police (including regulators and compliance), as well as intelligence. But, unlike their counterparts, counterintelligence officers will have responsibilities that span all three fields.

Taxonomy of Counterintelligence

Although intelligence can be classified into three categories—operational, tactical, and strategic—counterintelligence's taxonomic categories are those of *defense* and *offense*. Although these categories have been articulated in other ways by others in the intelligence community, viewing counterintelligence this way enables a more refined picture to emerge. For instance, the U.S. Marine Corps presents a taxonomy of counterintelligence along the lines of "[1] operations; [2] investigations; [3] collection and reporting; and [4] analysis, production, and dissemination."[21]

Nevertheless, by viewing counterintelligence according to the two categories advocated here—defense and offense—we see that defensive counterintelligence gathers together those activities that contribute to deterrence and detection, whereas offensive counterintelligence is comprised of those activities that contribute to detection, deception, and neutralization. The reason detection has been included in both categories is because its role can be to provide a means that secures information and the facilities that hold that information, as well as "hunting" those who have breached those controls.

Figures 2.2 and 2.3 show the relationship between the two taxonomic models—Figure 2.2 is the U.S. Marine Corps model and Figure 2.3 is the preferred model. The reason the defensive/offensive model is preferred to the U.S. Marine Corps model is that each of the four functions described in the Marine Corps model can be part of both defensive and offensive, and hence the model makes no real distinction. As such, viewing it the way the Marine Corps has done raises the question as to how these functions are employed, as opposed to the clarity provided in the defensive/offensive model (Figure 2.3). Under the defensive/offensive model, these four functions simply become *methods* of achieving the mission's objective—that is, to defend or go on the offensive.

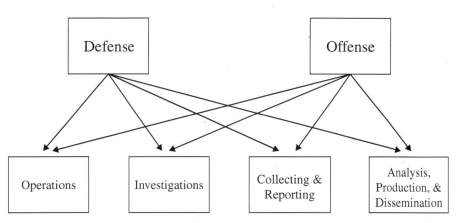

FIGURE 2.2 U.S. Marine Corps Model with Overlapping Relationships that Makes No Real Distinction. *Source*: Courtesy of the author.

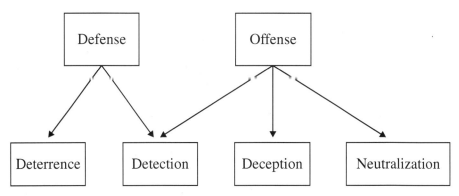

FIGURE 2.3 The Preferred Defensive Offensive Model for Counterintelligence. *Source*: Courtesy of the author.

Arguably, this model is equally applicable to the five types of counterintelligence that are about to be discussed—national security, military, law enforcement, business, and private.

Typology of Counterintelligence

One way to understand counterintelligence is by examining its typology. Counterintelligence types are based largely on the environment in which the agency operates. As such, there are five major counterintelligence types: national security, military, law enforcement, business, and private. However, having defined these types it is important to note there can be substantial overlap—for example, an investigation into the leaking of information regarding a troop deployment to a foreign country would be of interest to military intelligence units as well as agencies involved in national security, and perhaps some private security firms operating in the country. In addition to the typological overlap, the same functions—defensive and offensive—are used by each intelligence type.

Take for example the U.S. intelligence community. At the time of writing, the intelligence community was structured in an alliance that comprised sixteen agencies, all of which came under the control of the executive branch of government and lead by the director of National Intelligence.[22] Although these agencies worked on cases individually, they may work collaboratively in sharing resources, expertise, and information depending on the issue under investigation. While these agencies are intelligence focused, many have dedicated units devoted to counterintelligence or, at least, counterintelligence functions that are performed within the agency. These agencies are the following:

1. United States Air Force, Twenty-Fifth Air Force;
2. United States Army, Intelligence and Security Command;
3. Central Intelligence Agency;
4. United Sates Coast Guard, Coast Guard Intelligence;
5. Defense Intelligence Agency;
6. Department of Energy, Office of Intelligence and Counterintelligence;
7. Department of Homeland Security, Office of Intelligence and Analysis;
8. Department of State, Bureau of Intelligence and Research;
9. Department of the Treasury, Office of Terrorism and Financial Intelligence;
10. Drug Enforcement Administration, Office of National Security Intelligence;
11. Federal Bureau of Investigation, Intelligence Branch;
12. United States Marine Corps, Intelligence Department;
13. National Geospatial-Intelligence Agency;
14. National Reconnaissance Office;
15. National Security Agency/Central Security Service; and
16. United States Navy, Office of Navy Intelligence.

Opposing Forces

If counterintelligence is generally concerned with identifying areas of weakness within an agency that could be exploited by those hostile to the agency (or its client), it warrants discussion as to who these persons or entities might be.

A term commonly used in counterintelligence circles is *foreign intelligence service* or FIS for short. Although the word *foreign* is used, it is synonymous for an *opposing force* (OPFOR) or the *opposition*, whoever or whatever that may be.

The opposition may be a country when discussed in relation to national security intelligence, or another nation's military in relation to military intelligence, and so on as it applies to other types of intelligence. The opposition may be a traitor who works within the agency or a transnational group, such as a terrorist cell or a criminal enterprise. Opposition may also include an insurgent group that opposes government authority through criminal, paramilitary, or guerrilla methods.

. . . .

Security Intelligence—Intelligence on the identity, capabilities and intentions of hostile organizations or individuals who are or may be engaged in espionage, sabotage, subversion or terrorism.[23]

. . . .

So, in this book the terms *foreign intelligence service*, *opposition*, and *perpetrator* will be used interchangeably, depending on the point being made, to denote the forces that are in conflict with the agency, or its client. As pointed out in the section at the beginning of the book on the use of the "Key Concepts to Note," the term *agency* will be used to represent the organization that is trying to keep its secrets safe.

National Security Counterintelligence

National security counterintelligence can be conducted by various branches of a nation's armed forces, as well as its foreign diplomatic services. It can also be conducted by a law enforcement agency. Table 2.1 displays the national security agencies for the Five Eyes intelligence alliance.

TABLE 2.1 **The Five Eyes—National Security Counterintelligence Agencies**

Country	Selected Agency Examples
Australia	Australian Security Intelligence Organization (ASIO)
Britain	Security Service (MI5)
Canada	Canadian Security Intelligence Service (CSIS)
New Zealand	New Zealand Security Intelligence Service (NZSIS)
United States of America	Federal Bureau of Investigation (FBI), National Security Branch Department of Energy, Department of Intelligence and Counterintelligence Department of State, Intelligence and Research

TABLE 2.2 Selected U.S. Military Counterintelligence Agencies

Military Agency	Exemplar Counterintelligence Units
U.S. Department of the Army	Office of the Deputy Chief of Staff for Intelligence (ODCSINT) Army Intelligence and Security Command (INSCOM) Army Tactical Counterintelligence Elements (e.g., at battalion level)
U.S. Department of the Navy	Naval Criminal Investigative Service (NCIS) Director of Intelligence, U.S. Marine Corps (DIRINT)

Military Counterintelligence

Aside from the overlay between national security and military counterintelligence that was highlighted in the introduction to this section, by and large, military counterintelligence falls to units of the military itself. By way of example, Table 2.2 shows two U.S. military agencies to demonstrate the types of units that have responsibility for counterintelligence. These are not exhaustive, but indicative examples, as there are numerous units that may have direct and indirect responsibility, or coordination/oversight of counterintelligence.

Law Enforcement Counterintelligence

Intelligence units involved in law enforcement intelligence are usually clear as their aims are typically well articulated—for instance, to increase the accuracy of decisions of operational commanders. By contrast, law enforcement counterintelligence units can be spread across several disjointed areas and not defined well at all, yet they still perform the function. For instance, a police force may use its detective bureau to conduct counterintelligence investigations on a case-by-case basis. That is, the matter is assigned to a detective for investigation like other alleged criminal offenses. Or, the matter may fall to investigators assigned in the police force's internal investigations branch, or an external oversight body set up to make inquiries into alleged police and political corruption. So, the form and role of counterintelligence may not be clearly defined, and this situation exists in the security role counterintelligence performs.

The role of securing facilities and information could be spread thin and wide in the law enforcement context. Take, for example, data security. A police force may share its computer network with other government agencies (especially at local government and state government levels). As such, data security may be the province of a data security manager who is an employee in the information technology department of government, not the police force. Building security may be the responsibility of a facilities manager who comes under the direction of not a police officer, but a supervisor in the resources branch (i.e., building management) of government. Vetting of personnel could be the role of a private sector firm contracted to carry out security and background checks, or they could be done by another law enforcement agency.

The exact configuration of a counterintelligence function within law enforcement is hard to describe as its role at the lower levels of government is commensurate with the risks posed, along with the resources management is willing and able to devote to maintaining security. However, at national levels of government, whole divisions or branches can be established—as is the case with the Federal Bureau of Investigation (FBI)—and these units are specifically labeled "counterintelligence."

Business Counterintelligence

Business intelligence is concerned with the acquisition of trade-related information and commercial information that is held confidential from competing firms. It is also termed *competitor intelligence* (or *competitive intelligence*) and *corporate intelligence*.[24] Therefore, business counterintelligence concerns itself with protecting trade information. Although the media has portrayed the unethical behavior of some business intelligence practitioners as "spying," it is safe to say most information that is gathered in business intelligence is through open- and semi-open sources. So, by and large, the focus of intelligence activities is on monitoring what competitors are doing in the marketplace, whether that is local, regional, national, or international.

Therefore, business counterintelligence can involve units within commerce and industry that deal with issues as disparate as security, on one hand, and marketing, on the other. It can also include private investigation firms that specialize in protecting information or investigating breaches of trademarks, copyright, or trade secrets. Government intelligence agencies, both domestic and foreign, have units that monitor the transfer of information and technology. For example, the U.S. Department of Commerce's Office of Export Enforcement, and its Office of Enforcement Analysis (OEA), enforces export business regulations relating to prohibited dual-use items, such as computer hardware technology, software,[25] chemicals, and nuclear material. It does this to prevent weapons proliferators and terrorist being able to buy these sensitive items. For instance, between 2013 and March 2018 "nearly 3,000 people have been swept-up by Homeland Security investigations alone for trying to smuggle weapons and sensitive technologies—including circuits or other products that can be used in ballistic missiles, drones or explosives devices. . . . Russia, China, North Korea and Iran are some of the countries most active in trying to acquire American military technology."[26]

. . . .

At what level ought company policy be decided[?]   At the topmost level, in other words, by the Chairman and the Board of Directors.[27]

. . . .

Private Counterintelligence

Private counterintelligence can take a variety of forms, but, for the purposes of this book, it will be limited to those firms and private agents who offer their services for fee or reward. Although the term *private* implies an individual, there is some overlap in what constitutes private counterintelligence and what may be business counterintelligence, or even national security counterintelligence. The final determinant is who is contracting the security agent.[28]

Private counterintelligence practitioners offer a range of specialist services that go beyond the bounds of what the average private investigator can provide. Although private investigators do feature largely,[29] often, however, the private counterintelligence practitioner comes from a background in law enforcement (including compliance or regulatory work), security, risk management, military intelligence, military police, national security intelligence, or a country's diplomatic corps.

Their specialties may be in fraud or background investigations, or counter-surveillance and physical or information security. *Information security* should not be confused with *computer security*. Information security is used here in its widest context—that is, documents and papers, electronic data, software, knowledge, and artifacts. Practitioners may have extensive training in the use of state-of-the-art electronic audio surveillance equipment, so they are able to offer advice on *de-bugging* (i.e., electronic/audio countermeasure "sweeps," or *technical surveillance countermeasures—TSCM*).[30]

They may also specialize in providing close personal protection (i.e., bodyguards) for important public figures or wealthy private persons. When the late Richard Nixon was president, the White House hired former New York City detective Tony Ulasewicz as a private investigator. Ulasewicz, who was a former operative in the New York Police Department's Bureau of Special Service and Investigation (BOSSI), wrote in detail about the operations he conducted on behalf of the presidency in a private capacity. This is an amazing arrangement given that the presidential office had vast government investigation and intelligence resources at its disposal. Nonetheless, the president still relied on a private investigator who could be called on to conduct discreet inquires, free of the fear of leaks.[31]

The consulting group Control Risks is one of several companies that could be considered a private counterintelligence agency:

> We are a specialist global risk consultancy that helps organisations succeed in a volatile world. Through insight, intelligence and technology, we help you seize opportunities while remaining secure, compliant and resilient. When crises and complex issues arise, we help you recover.[32]

Private counterintelligence agencies could, arguably, include businesses that simply sell and install closed-circuit television (CCTV) equipment and other security hardware, but this may be too wide an interpretation. In the same vein, it could include businesses that sell or install alarms or access controls or provide audit or similar services to track and account for pieces of information. Again, this would be too liberal an interpretation. However, private counterintelligence could include practitioners who design integrated protection systems that incorporate several security functions.

Overall, private counterintelligence practitioners are viewed by some of their government counterparts as an important way to augment situations where resources are constrained by shrinking budgets. Such augmentation is done through outsourcing or contracts.

PHOTO 2.1 An Example of Private Counterintelligence (Physical Security)—Devices that Appear in Circles are CCTV Cameras, Those in squares are floodlights, and those in diamonds are warning signs. Note also high wall and double-glazed windows with reflective foil treatment. *Source*: Photograph courtesy of the author.

Review of Key Words and Phrases

The key words and phrases associated with this chapter are listed below. Demonstrate your understanding of each by writing a short definition or explanation in one or two sentences.

agent
applied research
basic research
black ops
business counterintelligence
case officer
counterespionage
counterintelligence
cover
covert operations
customers
de-bugging
defensive counterintelligence
dummy agents
espionage
field officer

handler
intelligence
law enforcement counterintelligence
military counterintelligence
national security counterintelligence
observation
offensive counterintelligence
open sources
operations officer
positive intelligence/positive collection
private counterintelligence
research and analysis
spying
sweeps
technical surveillance countermeasures

Study Questions

1. Explain the role security plays in intelligence work and how it provides protection to the four intelligence types—espionage, observation, research and analysis, and covert operations.

2. Describe the difference between counterintelligence and counterespionage and explain how each element performs its mission separately, as well as how it supports the other.

3. Explain the differences between defensive counterintelligence and offensive counterintelligence. Give an example of each.

4. List the four types of counterintelligence, and then explain similarities and differences among them (perhaps use a table to facilitate this).

Learning Activity

Research the intelligence community at one of these levels in the jurisdiction where you live or work: local, state/province, or national. First, list the agencies and describe whether the entire agencies, or units within them, have responsibility for counterintelligence. Then, discuss whether these agencies work individually on cases or work collaboratively to share resources, expertise, and information. Finally, assess whether this structure could be improved by advancing a hypothetical structure, with explanations as to why this might provide improvements, and in what ways.

Notes

[1] United Bible Societies, *Good News Bible: Today's English Version* (London: The British Foreign and Bible Society, 1978), 142–43.

[2] United Bible Societies, *Good News Bible*, 143.

[3] Case officers are also known as *operations officers*.

[4] Though the role and skills of a recruiter and a handler can be quite different. See, Melissa Boyle Mahle, *Denial and Deception: An Insider's View of the CIA from Iran-Contra to 9/11* (New York: Nation Books, 2004), 134–35.

[5] Christopher Felix, *A Short Course in the Secret War* (New York: Dutton, 1963), 9.

[6] Generally, the role of a nonofficial cover officer is to identify people who can potentially provide information to the agency. In doing so, the assessment would include determining whether they are willing to do so. Once these details are established, the actual recruitment is handed over to an officer with official cover. The reasoning for this is that, by definition, NOC officers have no connection to their government. If they were to make such an approach they would "break cover" and expose their true affiliation. See Laura Rozen, "Becoming a NOC," in the Afterword to Wilson, *Fair Game*.

[7] Rozen, "Becoming a NOC," 327.

[8] For instance, in June 2011 it was reported that the CIA planned to deploy armed drones in Yemen to hunt down and kill al-Qaeda militants as part of its strategy to combat the threat posed by this organization (Siobhan Gorman and Adam Entous, "CIA Palms Yemen Drone Strikes," *Wall Street Journal*, June 14, 2011. Also see, Joby Warwick, *The Triple Agent* (New York: Doubleday, 2011) for a more detailed discussion of the uses and the targets of intelligence-driven drone attacks. Accounts of how certain environmental activists have used

drones as part of their intelligence-gathering activities have been reported in the world's press. See, for instance, "Donated Drone in Hunt for Whalers," *The Advertiser*, Adelaide, Australia, December 26, 2011: 34.

9   For instance, CIA analysts employed in the CIA's Open Source Center (formerly the Foreign Broadcast Information Service) are reported to monitor an estimated five million social media postings a day to gain an understanding of public sentiment in places like the Middle East, North Africa, and various parts of Asia, as well as other intelligence requirements. See Kimberly Dozier, "CIA Following Twitter, Facebook," November 4, 2011, retrieved from: http://news.yahoo.com/ap-exclusive-cia-following-twitter-facebook-081055316. html, December 24, 2011.

10   For example, if the president or the prime minster of a country were the audience for an intelligence report, they would be referred to as the *first customer*.

11   Not to be confused with "executive action," or more crudely put, "assassination." Richard Helms with Hood, *A Look Over My Shoulder*, 170. And, William Colby with Peter Forbath, *Honorable Men: My Life in the CIA* (London: Hutchinson & Co., 1978), 266–69, regarding the Phoenix Program in Vietnam.

12   William J. Daugherty, *Executive Secrets: Covert Action and the Presidency* (Lexington: University of Kentucky Press, 2004), 13–15, and note seven at 228.

13   Roy Godson, *Dirty Tricks or Trump Cards: U.S. Covert Action and Counterintelligence* (Washington, DC: Brassey's, 1995), 2.

14   See, for instance, Dennis Fiery, *Out of Business: Force a Company, Business or Store to Close its Doors... For Good* (Port Townsend, WA: Loompanics Unlimited, 1999).

15   Roy Godson, *Dirty Tricks or Trump Cards*, 19.

16   William Colby with Peter Forbath, *Honorable Men*, 462.

17   U.S. Senate Committee to Study Governmental Operations with Respect to Intelligence Activities, *Alleged Assassination Plots Involving Foreign Leaders* (Washington, DC: U.S. Government Printer), 17–17. See also, Richard A. Best, Jr. and Andrew Feicket, *CRS Report for Congress: Special Operations Forces (SOF) and CIA Paramilitary Operations: Issues for Congress* (Washington, DC: Congressional Research Service, Library of Congress, December 6, 2006), 5.

18   Richard Helms with William Hood, *A Look Over My Shoulder*, 184.

19   Frank J. Stech and Kristin E. Heckman, "Human Nature and Cyber Weaponry: Use of Denial and Deception in Cyber Counterintelligence," in Henry Prunckun (ed.), *Cyber Weaponry: Issues and Implications for Digital Arms* (Switzerland: Springer International Publishing, 2018), 13.

20   Adapted by the author from a passage about Mossad that appeared in David Ignatius, *Agents of Innocence* (London: W. H. Allan, 1988), 337.

21   U.S. Marine Corps, *MCWP 2–14, Counterintelligence* (Washington, DC: Department of the Navy, September 2000), 2–1.

22   Office of the Director of National Intelligence, *About the Intelligence Community*, www.intelligence.gov/about-the-intelligence-community/ (accessed November 16, 2011).

23   U.S. Marine Corps, *MCWP 2–14, Counterintelligence*, G–20.

24   Leonard M. Fuld, *Competitor Intelligence: How to Get It—How to Use It* (New York: Wiley, 1985); and Richard Eells and Peter Nehemkis, *Corporate Intelligence and Espionage: A Blue Print of Corporate Decision Making* (New York: Macmillan, 1984), 78.

25   For a discussion of how certain commercial software programs and various pieces of standard computing hardware can be used as cyber weapons, see Hank Prunckun, "Bogies in the Wire: Is There a Need for Legislative Control of Cyber Weapons," *Global Crime 9*, no. 3 (2008): 262–72.

26   Ron Nixon, "Smuggling of U.S. Technology Rises Sharply," *The New York Times*, International Edition, March 19, 2008: 4.

27   Peter Heims, *Countering Industrial Espionage* (Leatherhead, UK: 20th Century Security Education Ltd, 1982), 133.

28   In the private sector there are private intelligence agencies, so it follows that there are private agencies and persons that perform counterintelligence functions. See, for example, Eells and Nehemkis, *Corporate Intelligence and Espionage*, 57–60.

[29] For instance, the British Broadcasting Corporation (BBC) was reported to have spent £310,000 hiring private investigators on more than 200 occasions during a six-year period starting around 2006. See *The Times* (London), "BBC spent $459,000 on Private Detectives," *Australian*, January 25, 2012: 10.

[30] The term "countermeasure" refers to control, and control in the context of counterintelligence is the ability to implement plans or actions that will mitigate risk. *Risk*, of course, is likelihood and consequence.

[31] Tony Ulasewicz with Stuart A. McKeever, *The President's Private Eye: The Journey of Detective Tony U. from N.Y.P.D. to the White House* (Westport, CT: MACSAM Publishing Company, 1990).

[32] Control Risks, www.control-risks.com (accessed November 15, 2017).

Chapter 3

Counterintelligence Theory

In the realm of financial investment, the concept of *risk* is used as a means of understanding *yield*. That is, if an investment has low risk, its return on investment is likely to be low as well. This prospect does not stop investors from longing to eliminate risk yet achieve high yields. If this metaphor is applied to intelligence work, one can see how operatives and analysts might yearn for a low-risk operation to, say, obtain information, yet still be able to yield high-grade intelligence.

Unfortunately, real-world experience suggests that the factors of low risk and high yield are not destined to meet in either financial investment or secret intelligence. Nevertheless, risk can be mitigated, and in intelligence work, this falls to the role of counterintelligence—to keep safe methods and operations while engaging in the activities that will ultimately produce a focused intelligence product.

To reduce the risks that are characteristic of intelligence work there needs to be a theoretical base on which the practice of counterintelligence can rest. Without a theoretical foundation an efficient and effective counterintelligence program is less likely to be achieved. It follows that, if this cannot be accomplished, risk management is also not likely to be realized. So, this chapter puts forward a theory of counterintelligence.[1]

. . . .

No intelligence service can for very long be any better than its counterintelligence component.—An anonymous source cited by the former CIA Director, the late-Richard Helms[2]

. . . .

Background

Entities, whether they are individuals, corporations, the military, or even entire nations, have their safety and well-being enhanced by the protection afforded by counterintelligence. This is because counterintelligence supports the intelligence function in all its manifestations, and, in turn, intelligence supports the development of sound, rational policy.[3] If espionage were a game, those who practice the craft of counterintelligence could be considered the game's "goal keepers." Without these practitioners the opposition would have carte blanche to raid the unprotected goal and score endless points. Without counterintelligence, the intelligence goal would be wide open to such raiders.

Given this analogy, it is not difficult to see why the role of counterintelligence is commonly thought of as *security*. In fact, Johnson pointed this out well over twenty years ago when stating, "People like to confuse counterintelligence with security."[4] The role of counterintelligence likely has been misunderstood because there is little if any formally articulated theory of counterintelligence to guide practice.[5] Practitioners are therefore left to formulate what they do and how they do it based on need and not on an understanding of its theoretical principles. Though there is nothing inherently wrong with a necessity-based experience approach, it does however make for a less efficient and, hence, less effective practice.

What makes intelligence work different from the research and analytic functions found in industry and commerce (which includes collecting information) is, arguably, the fact that some aspect of the endeavor is secret.[6] Secrecy is therefore a primary objective of counterintelligence. Johnson put it bluntly when he stated: "[counterintelligence] is aimed against intelligence, against active, hostile intelligence, against enemy spies."[7]

There is some confusion between *security* and *counterintelligence*, so it is understandable that this confusion extends to the relationship between counterintelligence and other intelligence functions, such as counterespionage. Duvenage said:

> Counterintelligence is often sensationalized and misrepresented in the popular media—it is certainly distorted in fiction. Counterintelligence is portrayed as spies outgunning spies. This is, of course, not the case. [Counterintelligence sometimes] has the more mundane connotations of being principally about computer passwords, restrictions on the use of computing equipment, security guards, access control, guard dogs, and the like. This is also a skewed view.[8]

Duvenage's argument is perhaps why counterintelligence practitioners may have gotten lost in their own *wilderness of mirrors* as James Angleton famously quoted the T. S. Eliot poem, "Gerontion."[9] The confusion between security and counterintelligence—and between counterintelligence and other intelligence functions, such as counterespionage—is understandable.

Despite recognizing this confusion, James Angleton—once iconic head of CIA's counterintelligence staff—never advanced a theory on which counterintelligence could be based.[10] Whether by design or because of the genuine absence of such a theory, when Angleton was questioned before the *Select Committee to Study Governmental Operations with respect to Intelligence Activities* (i.e., the Church Committee), he let slip an opportunity to provide a matchless description. As a result, at best, we have been left with many cobbled-together definitions that, over time, have appeared in various academic journals, professional manuals, and military field manuals, as well as in media accounts about counterintelligence.

Rationale for Developing a Theory

Varouhakis argued that there was a theoretical vacuum in the literature relating to intelligence. He pointed out that "the large theoretical structure of the field of intelligence does not extend into counterintelligence."[11] In pointing out this theoretical vacuum, he drew on the subject literature that underscored the fact that there were only two studies published in the last few decades that attempted to specifically address the issue of counterintelligence theory. This is important because without a theoretical foundation an efficient and effective counterintelligence service is less likely to be achieved. Such inefficiencies have long held counterintelligence to ridicule.

> Within the CIA, counterintelligence officers are sometimes held in disdain by operations officers. The CI-nicks are seen as information misers gloating over their stashed jewels but never doing anything with them.[12]

Four attempts to formulate a theory of counterintelligence are those by John Ehrman,[13] Miron Varouhaskis,[14] Loch K. Johnson,[15] and Vincent H. Bridgeman.[16] Ehrman's treatment resulted in not so much a theory but an essay on the importance of developing a theory, and this was acknowledged by that author: "As a foundation for theoretical work it remains incomplete."[17] The Varouhaskis treatment was an attempt "to provide a framework by which counterintelligence officers will be able to ultimately understand, explain, and predict the intelligence-gathering behaviors of intelligence agencies domestically and abroad, as well as the employee behavior at those agencies"[18]—or, in other words, it was an examination of organizational behavior with counterintelligence as its focus.

Johnson's contribution was a section in a large theory he developed on *strategic intelligence*. This section put forward two theoretical propositions: (1) the affluence of the entity conducting intelligence work will affect its ability to protect its secrets; and (2) a feedback loop must be incorporated into counterintelligence operations to ensure that if there is a failure, the causes can be addressed.[19]

Bridgeman's treatment however did try to structure a theory around what he described as three advantage areas or modes—denial, insight, and manipulation.[20] Nevertheless, even this could be argued was less than a comprehensive theory.

Having drawn attention to the limitations of these studies does not detract from their importance; on the contrary, these are studies of importance and their contribution to the literature needs to be acknowledged. In fact, the work of these scholars underscores the need to develop a theory: "I hope others will contribute to the development of counterintelligence theory and help further develop what this article attempts to begin."[21]

Good theory should have an explanatory power, parsimony, and the attribute of falsifiability.[22]

One could argue that there is already a considerable base of evidence within the subject literature that explains such aspects as why and how intelligence practitioners collect data, and how these data are used to support intelligence products, and so on. There is no doubt that there has evolved a rich stockpile of information on intelligence and intelligence analysis.[23] Likewise, there is ample information on counterintelligence practice and the need for improvement.[24] This is not in dispute. What observers like Ehrman pointed out, however, was the lack of a systemic presentation of these practices via a theory that explains why they are performed and how each principle relates to the other.

Although there have been scholarly attempts that have achieved some levels of success in advancing work toward a theory, unfortunately these have not achieved what could be considered full success.[25] Ehrman underscored this issue when he wrote: "Almost from the start, scholars have called for a theory of intelligence. None has been advanced. Although some authors entitle sections of their work 'theories of intelligence,' to my knowledge no one has proposed concepts that can be tested."[26,27] Although he wrote of intelligence in general, it applies equally to counterintelligence, and to the five types of counterintelligence discussed in chapter 2—national security, military, law enforcement, business, and private.

There are likely to be tens of thousands of personnel practicing the craft of counterintelligence within the Five Eyes countries. It is reasonable to assume that these practitioners know what to do instinctively—through practice—because there is no theoretical basis reflected in the subject literature. The absence of an articulated theory, therefore, forms the rationale for this chapter in exploring the question: What is the theoretical base that underscores counterintelligence?

Context

There are many definitions of counterintelligence and Ehrman[28] lists a number of these in his study. Without debating the finer points of these and no doubt other definitions, it is reasonable to view counterintelligence definitions as being context specific. For instance, the definitions cited by Ehrman appear to treat counterintelligence as if it only applies to foreign policy intelligence or national security issues. However, experience has shown that, when a nation deals with, for example, a non-state actor or a transnational criminal organization, there is little demarcation between what might constitute a national security issue and, say, a law enforcement problem. Perpetrators, or targets of interest, that fall into these types of categories as "threat-agents" traverse the "radar screens" of a number of functional agencies.

William R. Johnson's definition of counterintelligence as an activity that is "aimed against intelligence, against active, hostile intelligence, against enemy spies"[29] is probably as close to the mark as one could get. However, if his definition is truncated to *an activity aimed at protecting an agency's intelligence program against an opposition's intelligence service*, it might be closer to being what could be considered a universal definition. This is because the term *agency* could be used to mean any organization or even a nation-state. The term *opposition* could be used to mean any person or group (including a nation-state) with hostile intent. Such a definition could then be applied equally to issues that affect national security, the military, law enforcement, or even corporate and private affairs. This wide approach to defining counterintelligence is the approach taken in this book.

Theory Construction

Although David C. Bell stated that "creating theory is an art,"[30] it does require structured thinking. It is through structure that transparency and replicability of the methods used to conduct the research can be established. Transparency and replicability are at the core of the scientific method of inquiry,[31] thus making it not only an art but a science.

The research method that is widely used for developing theory is that of *grounded theory*.[32] Grounded theory usually finds its home with qualitative researchers, as it is a method for theorizing by *grounding* the theory being developed in observation or, in other words, practice.[33] Grounded theory method is simple, but it is an iterative process. The iterative process requires the identification of themes, followed using inductive logic to assign meaning to those themes.[34] The process is equally applicable to primary or secondary data.

Because there was no shortage of secondary information that either explains or discusses the counterintelligence practice, secondary data were deemed an appropriate source in developing this theory. These data offered both depth and breadth of information, and a practical way to obtain the required information (i.e., through library research as opposed to the unrealistic approach of trying to arrange personal interviews or focus groups). Even more appealing was that these data included practitioners who wrote about their experiences, as well as academics who have studied the craft of counterintelligence. In brief, the subject literature ranged from accounts by private investigators and security operatives through to those at the highest levels of national security. The tactical issues covered in these texts ranged from the commonplace (e.g., losing a surveillance tail) to the most complex operational issues to face counterintelligence (e.g., running a double agent, or "walking back the cat" after a leak or penetration by a hostile intelligence service).

Data were therefore collected from secondary sources that were in the public domain; these included scholarly journal articles and textbooks of various descriptions, but mainly pertaining to counterintelligence, intelligence, investigation, and security. Military field manuals and training texts that had been used by in-service practitioners were also reviewed, as were government reports and publications and memoirs of former intelligence operatives and agency chiefs.

The research process began with the posing of the question: What constitutes the principles of counterintelligence, and then moved to collecting qualitative data from the sources just described. From these data items, key themes (or concepts) relating to counterintelligence principles were separated, like light passing through a prism. Then, connections between the themes were hypothesized, thus yielding a set of counterintelligence assumptions and propositions—or, in other words, the construction of a theory of counterintelligence.

The thematic counterintelligence concepts were collated and connected using the technique known as *mind mapping*.[35] The themes were then organized into a logical structure, or model, that then formed the theory presented in the findings section below. In short, a simple stepwise process was used that was based on the original grounded theory method espoused by Barney Glaser and Anselm Strauss,[36] which involved

1. observation—by collecting data through empirical means;
2. theme notation—through content analysis, then identifying and recording key themes; and
3. meaning formulation—based on inductive reasoning, assigning meaning to the observed themes.

Theory of Counterintelligence

From a theoretical perspective, counterintelligence rests on seven assumptions.[37] These assumptions are based on the concepts of deterrence, detection, deception, and neutralization[38] of the opposition's efforts to collect information, regardless of why the opposition is collecting these data—whether for intelligence, subversion, sabotage, terrorism, weapons proliferation, or competitive advantage.

Intelligence can include planning for any number of purposes—criminal, national security, military, business, and private. Subversion can include such acts as rebellion, treason, and insurrection. Sabotage is damage, disruption, and incapacitation of services and process of a variety of descriptions. Terrorism can include the violent acts themselves and how politically or ideologically motivated groups express their violent messages. There may be others, but for illustrative purposes this list is sufficiently wide.

Because this study is a "universal" theory of counterintelligence, the four concepts of deterrence, detection, deception, and neutralization have been used because they apply across various contexts; that is, military, national security, law enforcement, and business.

These four concepts can be categorized as being passive defense and offensive defense; or stated another way, defensive counterintelligence and offensive counterintelligence. This categorization is shown in Figure 3.1. The two categories are sometime referred to in the subject literature as *denial* and *deception*.[39] Defensive counterintelligence (i.e., denial) comprises the concepts of deterrence and detection, and offensive counterintelligence (i.e., deception) encompasses the concepts of deception and neutralization. Offensive counterintelligence to some degree shares detection (hence the line between the two concepts in the diagram).

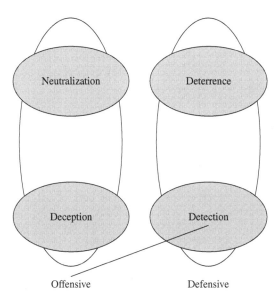

FIGURE 3.1 Categorization of Counterintelligence Concepts. *Source*: Courtesy of the author.

The theory contains seven *propositions*[40] that contain statements of condition. The propositions are deemed to be axiomatic.[41]

Proposition 1—Operational Surprise

The purpose of counterintelligence is to support other intelligence functions, so these functions can achieve operational surprise.[42] It does this by establishing and maintaining secrecy. Surprise may take many forms; in the military sense it might be an attack, or in a national security sense the ability to call the bluff of a foreign leader regarding a geopolitical issue. Law enforcement officers may translate surprise into a scenario where they are able to provide the community with safety by being able to execute search warrants against gangs for illegal firearms. Businesses may be able to use surprise in developing and launching a new range of services or products ahead of their competitors.[43]

Proposition 2—Data Collection

The second proposition is that an opposition force will use various means to collect data on an agency's operations. An opposition that does not intend to collect data on the agency, by this fact itself, does not warrant a counterintelligence program. This proposition also considers that the means employed by an opposition will include *all* available avenues to collect data—ethical and unethical; legal and illegal.[44] By grounding this axiom in this most dangerous possible attack vector, the theory therefore provides counterintelligence practitioners with the ability to formulate several possible solutions.

By assuming the worst case, such strategies allow analysts to identify the resources they need to deal with a range of possibilities, from the most minor situation up to and including the catastrophic.[45] If reasoning such as this did not form part of this proposition, the possibilities would be limited, thus providing inadequate countermeasures for all risks. By incorporating a worst-case premise, it allows analysts to formulate a few contingency plans. Should the countermeasures be circumvented by the opposition, it also allows for analysts to estimate what resources will be needed to mitigate the effects of a successful attack and recover from that attack.

Proposition 3—Targeting

An opposition will direct its data collection efforts toward obtaining information that will lay bare an agency and how it operates (as well as the entities the agency serves to protect). That is, the target of a hostile information collection operation will focus on data that will expose an agency's structure (legal and constitutional, as well as its chain of command and its personnel), its sphere of operations and influence (e.g., geographic, economic, and political/social), its current capabilities (in all regards), and its future intentions. Moreover, it will target the factors that limit the agency's operations and its administrative, managerial, and functional vulnerabilities.

The reason why these areas are targeted is that it allows an opposition to concentrate its efforts on vectors that will offer surprise, allows it to inflict the most damage (however defined), or allows it to leverage the most advantage to neutralize the agency's operations, and to protect itself and its clients (if any).

⬩ ⬩

As the shield is a practical response to the spear, so counterintelligence is to intelligence.[46]

⬩ ⬩

Proposition 4—Resources

Counterintelligence cannot be performed without staff and recourses that allow them to carry out defensive operations. Physical security equipment is expensive and the better the equipment, the more it cost to purchase and maintain. The same is true of information security devices and communications equipment. The cost of conducting personnel vetting is expensive if it is to be done thoroughly by competent staff. Each of these aspects of defensive counterintelligence comes with a cost: "The more affluent the [organization], the less porous its counterintelligence defenses are apt to be."[47]

Physical, personnel, information, and communications security are important parts of the funding issue. Well-crafted counterintelligence architectures are only as effective as the staff an agency can recruit and retain. And, this is often contingent on offering generous remuneration packages *and* supportive working environment.

Proposition 5—Paradox of Fiction

Defensive measures provide the essential framework to the central challenge of counterintelligence; that is, the battle of wits played out between an intelligence service and its opposition service. This contest requires an offensive approach that is termed *counterespionage*. These types of operations must be performed by agency staff who are able to perform illusions by exploiting the *paradox of fiction*. The paradox of fiction is condition everyone experiences when fictional performances, such as in literature and cinematic presentations take place. The paradox relies on altering a person's perception so that they experience emotions that lead them to believe are real when they do not exist. It is an illusion or a distortion of the senses that the brain interprets as factual. The strategy comes from

> the literary theory known as the *paradox of fiction*. The theory states that for a story (fiction) to achieve believed, it must convince the reader that it is true. Although the reader knows the story is fiction, the writer can, to a large degree, convince (i.e., deceive) the reader into believing the story though the use of various literary tropes, techniques, and imagery. This is evident when a reader says, "the book was a page turner," "I couldn't put it down," "the writing made my heart race," and so on.[48]

Intelligence agencies leverage the paradox of fiction to project illusions in a form of real-live stage production by creating situations that the opposition will view real, and act on accordingly, but what they perceive as real is merely a deception. Take for instance the case of "The Man Who Never Was" that is discussed in detail in chapter 14. Illusions can be optical (e.g., camouflage), auditory (produce sounds that replicate some real occurrence—like the laugh track on television situation comedies), tactile (e.g., production of false documents), temporal, taste, or combinations of various senses.

Proposition 6—Operational Failures

It is fair to say that risk is inherent to all enterprises, and this applies to counterintelligence operations as well. Where there is risk, there is the change of failure. Although intelligence failures have been dramatized in the press and entertainment media, counterintelligence failures are no different to failures in any other type of endeavor—take the Financial Crises of 2007–2008 as just one example.

When counterintelligence failures occur—and there will—these events should not paralyze an agency. Agencies need to respond to these events with renewed vigor to lean for the failure and review the adequacy of defensive measures, but need to be mindful that any new, measures do not inhibit smooth operations. Balance needs to be maintained between defensive pasture and being able to operate operation well. Remedial measure should never impede intelligence staffers from carrying out their duties.

Wherever, possible, any intelligence failure needs to be avenged by launching an offensive operation(s). Strategic thinkers are of the view that a purely

PHOTO 3.1 Intelligence Analysis. *Source*: Courtesy of the Federal Bureau of Investigation.

defensive posture cannot provide adequate safeguards—if the stakes are high, then offensive operations must be undertaken.

Proposition 7—Analysis

Counterintelligence is more than a security function. It has at its core analysis. The craft of counterintelligence could not function efficiently or effectively without producing policy options and operational plans that are based on fact and reason. Reasoned argument is analysis. So, counterintelligence practice needs to be based on analytic output. This may in turn join with the research function of positive intelligence, and perhaps it should as a matter of course, as the two could work hand in glove to achieve the same overall objective.

As for the practice aspects that counterintelligence analytics informs, these too are more than traditional security. Defensive measures constitute only half of the practice—deterrence and detection. These aspects of counterintelligence are more than simply "blunting the opposition's ability to...," as the saying goes. These defensive functions need to dovetail with the offensive side of the craft—to deceive and to neutralize, which is arguably at the heart of counterintelligence. Deception and neutralization could be described as "the real contest."

Defensive Counterintelligence

Deterrence: Deterrence is the ability to prevent an opposition from gaining access to information. Deterrence in this context can be the ability to both discourage an opposition from attempting to conduct a penetration operation and deny an opposition's data collection operation once a penetration operation has been launched and is underway.

Underlying deterrence are three premises that must be met or else it will fail. The first premise is that of *unacceptable damage*. An organization must be able to deliver some form of harm upon its opposition for that opponent to be deterred. Deterrence in the counterintelligence sense is different from that used in the context of, say, international foreign relations, where it is used to, for instance, contain the aggressive behavior of an opponent state through the threat of retaliation. In a counterintelligence context, deterrence is simply an agency's ability to persuade its opposing force (OPFOR) that the costs or the risks of mounting an information collection operation outweigh the benefits (in a sense, this could be construed as a form of "retaliation").

The second premise is that the threat must be *perceived* by an opposition. If an agency wants an opposition to cease unethical or illegal data collection, then the opposition must realize that such a threat has in fact been made; it is of no value if the threat is not communicated.

The third premise is that of *credibility*—the threat must be credible to succeed. Credibility, in turn, comprises two elements, the first that the organization making the threat is *capable* of delivering the "unacceptable harm" and second that it has the *will* to do so.

Deterrence forms the bulk of what comprises defensive counterintelligence, and it mainly takes the form of physical security, information security,[49] personnel security, and communications security. Security is the bedrock on which deterrence relies. Although security does not act as an absolute deterrent, it is the keystone.

Detection: Detection is the act of noticing that an event has taken place and that the event is somehow associated with a breach or potential breach of confidential information. The following are five premises that underwrite detection:

1. Identifying an event of concern;
2. Identifying the persons who were involved in the event;
3. Identifying the organizational association of the person(s) of interest;
4. Identifying the current location of the person(s) of interest; and
5. Gathering the facts that indicate that the person(s) committed the event.

An *event of concern* is used here as a generic term that could be anything that could be at the center of a hostile information collection operation. For instance, it could be the temporary removal of documents from an office for copying. It could be the passing of information from an employee to an opposition organization. Or, it could be the unauthorized observation of classified information. The examples are endless but suffice to say that the event of concern is, in law enforcement terms, the "alleged breach." Regarding counterintelligence, it is the event that has given cause for concern.

To be able to identify such events, counterintelligence officers need to have in place systems that will bring these events to their attention. Systems might include the observations of a person in the office who has been trained to report issues of this nature; or they might be technical systems, like alarms or digital image recordings of people's activities within the office. Regardless, without systems in place detection is diminished—the event may go unnoticed, which is after all what the hostile information collection operation is anticipating.

If an event is detected, then the perpetrator needs to also be identified. Without this, the ability of assessing the damage caused by the breach is lessened. For example, a counterintelligence officer could not conclude with confidence who was interested in the data, how it was to be used, and what ramification this "lost" information could result in for the agency. Counterintelligence officers could nonetheless estimate the damage and the intended purpose, but this would not be as valuable as knowing the identity of the person and the details surrounding the breach.

Closely associated with detecting the person involved is identifying the person's association with any organization (opposition or otherwise). It would be hard to envisage an individual acting solely on their own without any association with anyone else or with any other organization. Spies collect data and, in the normal course of their employ, pass it onto intelligence analysts in a headquarters setting who then analyze and synthesize this information and produce intelligence reports. Even in the case of small operations in, say, the business community, where a competitor is seeking insight into a competitor's service or product, the data is handed from the information collector to someone who will (formally or informally) process this information and use it for planning.

Unless the case involves a private individual, who has unilaterally embarked on a personal mission to, for instance, "expose" some dealings of the agency (or its client), then it is hard to conceive of a situation where no one else is involved. But, even in a situation of such a "man-on-a-mission" case, they would presumably hand over the information they collect to some legal authority or the news media as a way of exposing the disagreeable behavior at the core of their mental disquiet.[50]

Regardless, it is important that the person's association with others is identified for two reasons. It allows the counterintelligence officer to understand what needs to be done in terms of damage control, and it also helps detection and evidence gathering—given that motivation is key to many a successful counterintelligence investigation. Knowing whom one is looking for, by name and other identifying traits, increases the likelihood that the person will be located.

Finally, the ability to gather facts that directly or indirectly indicate a person's complicity in an event of concern concludes the principle of detection. With the facts of the events in hand, the counterintelligence officer has the full picture of the event—who, what, where, when, why, and how (the five Ws and H of information gathering). Generally termed *criminalistics* or *forensics*, this includes the use of science and scientifically based techniques to locate, collect, and preserve evidence of the event. However, unlike a pure criminal investigation, the end purpose of collecting evidence in a counterintelligence investigation may not be prosecution in a court of law, but instead to mount a counteroperation (see offensive counterintelligence below) to obscure, confuse, or deceive the opposition.

So, with any event of concern, the ability to detect and identify the perpetrators would cause an opposition to be less inclined to attempt a hostile operation to target an agency's information. If it does not, and the opposition is still inclined, it forces them to become far more sophisticated, which may place them beyond their technical capability, or it places them at such risk that the consequences outweigh the benefits. If the opposition does carry out a more sophisticated operation, then it makes the counterintelligence officer's job harder, but, paradoxically, the counterintelligence officer can deduce the likely identity of the perpetrator, and by doing so contribute to the first principle of counterintelligence theory—deterrence.

Offensive Counterintelligence

Deception: Deception involves misleading an opposition's decision makers about some aspect of the agency's operations, capabilities, or intentions (or those of its client), or concealing *who* is perpetrating an operation. The end state is to have the opposition form a view that makes them act (or not act) so that these actions prove futile. Or, deception operations may be aimed at causing confusion, thus delaying an opposition's ability to react effectively, or projecting a false understanding that sends the opposition down a path that wastes its time and resources, thus placing the agency in a far stronger position than before.[51] Double agent operations are classic in regards to the latter,[52] and so is the use of dummy agents, who form a part of campaigns to sow disinformation or to project false pictures of what is truly occurring.

Legendary examples of counterintelligence deception are the various operations carried out in the lead up to the Allied invasion of Nazi-occupied Europe during the Second World War. One was Operation Bodyguard. This operation was designed to convince German leadership and decision makers that the Allies' invasion would be timed later than it was, and that the invasion would be at locations other than the true objective of Normandy. For instance, Allied forces understood the Nazis were collecting information on the preparations they were making for invasion with the view to determine the landing sites.[53] With such intelligence, the Nazis could have mounted a formidable defense that repelled the attack, as they did in 1940 when British, French, and Belgian troops were forced to evacuate Europe from a beachhead at Dunkirk, France (i.e., Operation Dynamo).[54]

Other examples of deception are discussed in chapter 13 (Offensive Counterintelligence: Deception) and include decoys, camouflage, and pretexts and ruses.

Neutralization: The blocking of an opposition's intelligence collection operation can be done though the method of *neutralization*. This principle is based on the concept of "defeat"—that is, collapse, failure, rout, or ruin.

The ability of an opposition to be successful with its intelligence collection operation is predicated upon the premise that it will be successful. This suggests that hostile operations can be thwarted by either destruction or paralysis. It can also be achieved by causing a loss of interest or enthusiasm in carrying out the operation (or continuing to carry out an operation), or by inflicting a loss of confidence in an opposition that in turn will be unable to achieve its objective (in whole or part).

Destruction in the military sense is easy to visualize—say, the destruction of forward observation posts, whether they are manned or electronic, or the killing of reconnaissance forces sent forward to reconnoiter. However, in other intelligence operations it might be the arrest of a spy cell or the transfer of a suspected spy to a remote office or location where they have no access to classified data (e.g., where not all the elements of *detection* have been established).

Although neutralization by paralysis is not as dramatic as destruction, it can be as effective. With paralysis an agency must be able to cause an opposition to halt any actions that might lead it to gain access to classified or sensitive information (or further access if already underway). Unlike destruction, where "demolition" of the operation is the goal, paralysis is concerned only with inflicting a temporary disruption of, say, a key process or a temporary disruption to communications so that direction, leadership, coordination, or command is lost, thus dooming the operation to failure. The intent is to cause the abandonment of the operation and the dismantling of, perhaps, a spy ring, by the opposition to avoid detection. Paralysis can be actions that are initiated by an agency as a preemptive measure to flush out an opposition operative or as part of a counterintelligence investigation.

It could be argued that destruction and paralysis are defensive counterintelligence strategies, whereas loss of interest and loss of confidence could be classified as offensive. For instance, loss of interest is predicated on the notion that, if an agency can project the belief that the financial, political, or other costs of collecting the information are greater than the benefits of collecting the information by legal or ethical means, it will cause an opposition to lose interest in the operation. Another approach to causing a loss of interest is if the agency can project the belief that the value of the information is so low that it is not worth collecting, or by presenting a more tempting alternative, which might also form part of a deception strategy.

Causing a loss of confidence is a more esoteric method. It involves an organization being able to inflict upon an opposition's operative—an event or set of events that cause that operative (or his master controller) to become dysfunctional to the point that he is either detected or is paralyzed to the point that he is ineffective. Take, for example, two business competitors aggressively vying for the same market. If an agency can erode the opposition's faith in their operative's ability to succeed, defeat will occur.

Methods for neutralization are numerous but the standout is the one made classic in the fictional spy genre of counterespionage. Counterespionage "calls for the engineering of complex strategies that deliberately put one's agent(s) in contact with an adversary's intelligence personnel. This is done so that an adversary can be fed with disinformation which should lead to confusion, thus disrupting the adversary and allowing the perpetrator to prosper."[55] Accordingly, "counterespionage is like putting a virus into the bloodstream of the enemy."[56]

Conclusions

If we return to the analogy of financial investment, one could argue that anyone promoting the notion of a low-risk, but high-yield investment is akin to the alchemist peddling the idea he can turn lead into gold. Extending the financial analogy to intelligence work, one would be hard pressed to argue that running an intelligence operation, or conducting a secret research project, could be performed without the need to mitigate risk.

To provide utility to the support of sound counterintelligence practices, this study sought to formulate a theory of counterintelligence that was grounded in empirical observation. The study used secondary data from the subject literature as the basis for its observations.

What can be concluded from these findings? With regard to offensive counterintelligence, the theory highlights the active role it plays in misleading an opposition's decision makers through deception and in destroying or paralyzing the opposition's ability to continue with its intelligence operation. Neither of these functions can be effectively performed without considering the defensive functions interaction. Without such a theoretical understanding, a successful agency counterintelligence program would be hamstrung.

Nevertheless, by viewing counterintelligence in the context of these two categories—defense and offense—we see that defensive counterintelligence gathers together those activities that contribute to deterrence and detection, whereas offensive counterintelligence is comprised of those activities that contribute to deception and neutralization. But, having said that, detection may also be included as part of offensive counterintelligence. The reason detection can be included in both categories is because its role can be to provide a means that secures information and the facilities that holds these data, as well as "hunting" those who have breached those controls.

In sum, this theory of counterintelligence is not one that could be described as conceptually dense; nonetheless it is one that clearly articulates the seven propositions that explain why counterintelligence practice is performed as it is or, arguably, as it should be. It also presents the four assumptions that lay the conditions on which these propositions rely. Therefore, an understanding of the relationship between theory and practice can be used not only to improve a counterintelligence program's performance but to help avoid catastrophic security failures (e.g., penetrations).

Theory can do this by providing scholars with the ability to formulate hypotheses that can be tested: for example, *a purely defensive approach to protecting information is less effective than one that incorporates offensive measures.* Because this is a universal theory of counterintelligence, it allows the context to be varied so it too can be tested: for instance, *a purely defensive approach to protecting national security information is less effective than one that incorporates offensive measures, but, in a business context, incorporating an offensive role will be counterproductive.* Using such hypotheses, scholars can then define variables and operationalize them. Take the first hypothesis above as an example: *offensive measures* could be operationalized into, say, double agents, agents provocateurs, "sleepers," walk-ins, or any number of other manifestations of the concept.

Finally, having a basis to explain why and how counterintelligence practitioners carry out their craft in a testable form also gives rise to the possibility of exploring metrics that could be used to measure counterintelligence processes, outputs, and outcomes.

"Intelligence is . . . not a form of clairvoyance used to predict the future, but an exact science based on sound quantitative and qualitative research methods. Intelligence enables analysts to present solutions or options to decision makers based on defensible conclusions."[57] The same is true for counterintelligence. With what is advanced here the profession may continue to refine the theoretical base that underpins the craft. All being well, one would anticipate that, in the fullness of time, this and other yet to be articulated counterintelligence theories will spawn better policy options. These policy options will therefore be based on defensible conclusions that are grounded in empirical research.

Review of Key Words and Phrases

The key words and phrases associated with this chapter are listed below. Demonstrate your understanding of each by writing a short definition or explanation in one or two sentences.

deception	event of concern
detection	neutralization
deterrence	

Study Questions

1. List the three underlying assumptions that support counterintelligence theory.
2. List the four categories that comprise the theory of counterintelligence.
3. List the three premises that comprise the theory of deterrence.
4. List the five premises that underwrite the theory of detection.

Learning Activity

Consider the concept of an *event of concern*. Using either your current workplace or a notional one, brainstorm at least five situations that could be considered as events of concern. List the event and next to it the reasoning for it being of concern. Rank them in terms of risk (i.e., likelihood and consequence) from highest at the top to lowest at the bottom. Select the highest ranking event and a system that will bring this type of event to the attention of a counterintelligence officer. If there is already such a system in place for this, evaluate it in terms of whether it could be improved from the point of view of effectiveness and/or efficiency.

Notes

1 This chapter presents the results of a study conducted by the author that was originally published in *American Intelligence Journal* 29, no. 2 (2011): 6–15 and subsequently circulated in

revised form as a chapter of the first edition of this book, *Counterintelligence Theory and Practice* (Rowman & Littlefield, 2012). Stemming from this research, the author developed a paper based on these two publications for presentation at a classified forum of intelligence scholars at the University of Adelaide in 2014. The paper was subsequently cleared for publication as, "Extending the Theoretical Structure of Intelligence to Counterintelligence," *Salus Journal 2,* no. 2 (2014): 31–49. This chapter is therefore a consolidation of the author's thinking on a counterintelligence theory.

2 Richard Helms with Hood, *A Look Over My Shoulder,* 154.
3 Godson, *Dirty Tricks or Trump Cards.*
4 William R. Johnson, *Thwarting Enemies at Home and Abroad: How to be a Counterintelligence Officer* (Bethesda, MD: Stone Trail Press, 1987), 1; and William R. Johnson, *Thwarting Enemies at Home and Abroad: How to be a Counterintelligence Officer* (Washington, DC: Georgetown University Press, 2009), 1.
5 John Ehrman, "Toward a Theory of Counterintelligence: What Are We Talking About When We Talk About Counterintelligence?" *Studies in Intelligence* 53, no. 2 (2009): 18.
6 Patrick F. Walsh, *Intelligence and Intelligence Analysis.*
7 Johnson, *Thwarting Enemies at Home and Abroad* (1987), 2; and Johnson, *Thwarting Enemies at Home and Abroad* (2009), 2.
8 Petrus C. Duvenage, "Counterintelligence," in Hank Prunckun (ed.), *Intelligence and Private Investigation: Developing Sophisticated Methods for Conducting Inquiries* (Springfield, IL: Charles C. Thomas, 2013), 130.
9 Michael Holzman, *James Jesus Angleton, the CIA, and the Craft of Counterintelligence* (Amherst: University of Massachusetts Press, 2008), 3.
10 Holzman, *James Jesus Angleton, the CIA, and the Craft of Counterintelligence,* 3.
11 Miron Varouhakis, "An Institutional-Level Theoretical Approach for Counterintelligence," *International Journal of Intelligence and Counterintelligence* 24, no. 3 (2011): 495.
12 David Atlee Philips, *The Night Watch* (New York: Antheneum, 1977), 52.
13 Ehrman, "Toward a Theory of Counterintelligence."
14 Varouhakis, "An Institutional-Level Theoretical Approach for Counterintelligence."
15 Lock K. Johnston, "A Theory of Strategic Intelligence," in Peter Gill, Stephen Marrin, and Mark Phythian (eds.), *Intelligence Theory: Key Questions and Debates* (London: Routledge, 2009), 49–50.
16 Vincent H. Bridgeman, "Defense Counterintelligence, Reconceptualization," in Jennifer E. Sims and Burton Gerber (eds.), *Vaults, Mirrors and Masks: Rediscovering U.S. Counterintelligence* (Washington, DC: Georgetown University Press, 2009).
17 Ehrman, "Toward a Theory of Counterintelligence," 18.
18 Varouhakis, "An Institutional-Level Theoretical Approach for Counterintelligence," 498.
19 Lock K. Johnston, "A Theory of Strategic Intelligence," 50.
20 Bridgeman, "Defense Counterintelligence, Reconceptualization," 128.
21 Ehrman, "Toward a Theory of Counterintelligence," 18.
22 Lock K. Johnston, "A Theory of Strategic Intelligence," 33.
23 As examples, see: Robert M. Clark, *Intelligence Analysis: A Target Centric Approach* (Washington, DC: CQ Press, 2007); Richards J. Heuer, Jr. and Randolph H. Pherson, *Structured Analytic Techniques for Intelligence Analysis* (Washington, DC: CQ Press, 2011); Mark M. Lowenthal, *Intelligence: From Secrets to Policy, Fourth Edition* (Washington, DC: CQ Press, 2009); Prunckun, *Scientific Methods of Inquiry for Intelligence Analysis*; Jerome Clauser, *An Introduction to Intelligence Research and Analysis* (Lanham, MD: Scarecrow Press, 2008); and Walsh, *Intelligence and Intelligence Analysis.*
24 Frederick L. Wettering, "Counterintelligence: The Broken Triad," *International Journal of Intelligence and Counterintelligence* 13, no. 3 (2000).
25 See, for instance, Michelle K. Van Cleave, *Counterintelligence and National Security* (Washington, DC: National Defense University Press, 2007). Nevertheless, this is a praiseworthy piece of research.
26 Ehrman, "Toward a Theory of Counterintelligence."
27 See, for instance, the critical appraisal of some existing models of intelligence and whether these accommodate a clear understanding of counterintelligence, by Petrus "Beer" Duvenage

and Michael Hough, "The Conceptual Structuring of the Intelligence and the Counterintelligence Processes: Enduring Holy Grails or Crumbling Axioms–Quo Vadis?" *Strategic Review for Southern Africa* 33, no. 1 (May 2011): 29–77.

[28] David Kahn, "An Historical Theory of Intelligence," *Intelligence and National Security* 16, no. 3 (2001): 79.

[29] Johnson, *Thwarting Enemies at Home and Abroad* (1987), 2; and Johnson, *Thwarting Enemies at Home and Abroad* (2009), 2.

[30] David C. Bell, *Constructing Social Theory* (Lanham, MD: Rowman & Littlefield, 2009), 61.

[31] Hank Prunckun, *Scientific Methods of Inquiry for Intelligence Analysis.*

[32] Anselm Strauss and Juliet Corbin, *Basics of Qualitative Research: Grounded Theory Procedures and Techniques* (Newbury Park, CA: Sage, 1990).

[33] Earl Babbie, *The Practice of Social Research*, 9th ed. (Belmont, CA: Wadsworth, 2001).

[34] Bell, *Constructing Social Theory.*

[35] Tony Buzan, *How to Mind Map* (London: Thorsons, 2002).

[36] Barney Glaser and Anselm Strauss, *The Discovery of Grounded Theory* (Chicago: Aldine, 1967).

[37] In the first edition of this book, these *assumptions* were referred to as *principles.*

[38] There may be synonyms for these concepts that apply to specific contexts; for instance, the concept of *detection* might be equated to *identification*, and so on.

[39] See, for instance, Abram Shulsky, "Elements of Strategic Denial and Deception," *Trends in Organized Crime* 6, no. 1 (Fall, 2000): 17.

[40] In the first edition of this book, *propositions* were referred to as *axioms.*

[41] John Hospers, *An Introduction to Philosophical Analysis*, 2nd ed. (London: Routledge and Kegan Paul, 1973).

[42] Cynthia M. Grabo, *Anticipating Surprise: Analysis for Strategic Warning* (Lanham, MD: University Press of America, 2004).

[43] Alain Franqu, "The Use of Counterintelligence, Security and Countermeasures," in Craig Fleisher and David Blenkhorn (ed.), *Managing Frontiers in Competitive Intelligence* (Westport CT: Greenwood, 2001).

[44] Robin W. Winks, *Cloak and Gown: Scholars in the Secret War* (New York: Morrow, 1987), 328.

[45] Godson, *Dirty Tricks or Trump Cards*, 231.

[46] Frank Santi Russell, *Information Gathering in Classical Greece* (Ann Arbor: University of Michigan Press, 1999), 190.

[47] Lock K. Johnston, "A Theory of Strategic Intelligence," 50.

[48] Henry Prunckun "The Paradox of Fiction and Terrorism's Overshadowing of Organised Crime as a Law Enforcement Concern," *Salus Journal* 4, no. 2 (2016): 65–66.

[49] *Information security* should not be confused with *computer security*. Information security is used in this book in its widest form; that is, documents and papers, electronic data, software, knowledge, and artifacts.

[50] See, for example, Andrew Fowler, *The Most Dangerous Man in the World.*

[51] For in-depth examples and case studies involving deception, see, for instance, Thaddeus Holt, *The Deceivers: Allied Military Deception in the Second World War* (London: Phoenix, 2005), and Jon Latimer, *Deception in War* (Woodstock, NY: The Overlook Press, 2001). See also, Melrose M. Bryant, *Deception in Warfare: Selected References from Air University Library Collection, Special Bibliography No. 275* (Maxwell Air Force Base, AL: U.S. Air Force, 1985).

[52] Winks, *Cloak and Gown*, 342–43.

[53] William Stevenson, *A Man Called Intrepid: The Secret War 1939–1945* (London: Book Club Associates, 1976).

[54] W. J. R. Gardner, ed., *The Evacuation from Dunkirk: "Operation Dynamo," 26 May–4 June 1940* (London: Frank Cass Publishers, 2000).

[55] Prunckun, *Scientific Methods of Inquiry for Intelligence Analysis*, 10.

[56] Winks, *Cloak and Gown*, 422.

[57] Prunckun, *Scientific Methods of Inquiry for Intelligence Analysis*, 2.

Chapter 4

Tenets of Defensive Counterintelligence

Defensive counterintelligence is concerned with *deterrence* and *detection*. Translating these concepts into actions is done through various *risk treatment options*, or in intelligence parlance, *countermeasures*. Applied in an intelligence context, countermeasures have a somewhat narrower connotation than is commonly found in the mainstream intelligence studies literature. In its application here, countermeasures are an umbrella term for actions that includes either passive defensive or active offensive measures.

This chapter discusses seventeen tenets of defensive counterintelligence.[1] Even though these tenets are the handmaidens for counterintelligence planning (chapter 5), defensive counterintelligence is not the end state; it facilitates the offensive work of the craft—counterespionage. Goal keepers are important to sporting teams because they prevent the opponent from scoring, but a team will never win the game without its offensive side.

Although defensive counterintelligence is not by definition part of the active measures employed in offensive operations, security operations offer concealment for aggressive action—"an effective security program often can do much to mislead or deceive the intended victim of attack even if no more sophisticated measures are undertaken. Although security along will not normally lead the adversary to undertake the *wrong* preparations or to misdeploy his forces, it may lead him to undertake very inadequate countermeasures of even to fail to alert his forces at all, if security is totally effective."[2]

This chapter, as well as the following chapter on planning, serves, assists, and complements offensive counterintelligence.

Tenets of Defensive Counterintelligence

Tenet 1—Executive Responsibility

Of the tenets of defensive counterintelligence, the highest order tenet is that of executive governance. Although it might seem to some as somewhat self-evident, it is worth stating this tenet for clarity. The responsibility for security in all its forms rests with the head of the agency. Although the agency head will rarely be involved in any of the day-to-day security issues, he or she has responsibility for creating and maintaining a security program to guard the agency's confidential information and secret operations. To this end, this functional responsibility is therefore delegated to subordinates (or a committee), and, depending on the size of the agency, there may be several such delegations flowing down the chain of command. Nevertheless, the point is that the ultimate responsibility for orchestrating these activities rests with the agency head, and the importance placed on security within the agency is driven by the commitment of that person.

Tenet 2—Executive Support

For security to be effective the agency head must be willing to promote security so that all employees understand and accept it in the most favorable light. The image of security within the agency must be positive. Staff's attitudes must be cultivated to respect its purpose and, consequently, accept its associated policies and practices.

. . . .

The main hazard to information is complacency regarding its security.

. . . .

Tenet 3—Ethical Symmetry

One of the key issues for security acceptance is that staff view the security regime as one that is in harmony with the prevailing social norms—that is, it does not seek to recreate the model of a dictatorial state to deal with procedural compliance. Nor should it implement countermeasures that are illegal or unethical; for example, barriers that are electrified to a lethal level, or air-locks that fill with poisonous gas.

Tenet 4—Need-to-be-there

The rationale for allowing people to access an area where sensitive information is being processed, analyzed, or stored needs to be established. Although the doctrine's relation to access to information—known as the *need-to-know*[3]—is discussed in more detail in tenet 5 below and in chapter 8 (Defensive Counterintelligence: Information Security), it is important to illustrate the basis for this tenet. Known as *friendly access*, this is a means where the opposition attempts to gain access by deception rather than force. Therefore, access to an agency's offices should be limited to employees and visitors who are known or have appointments. All other visitors should be carefully screened, and their identities verified prior to entry. People making deliveries, including mail deliveries and maintenance workers, should be handled in the same manner. Access to all areas of the agency should be on a restricted *need-to-be-there basis*. If an agency's visitor/staff traffic is heavy, a system of custom-designed identity cards worn on employees' outer clothing can be an efficient method of quickly establishing *friend or foe*.

Tenet 5—Need-to-know

Much of what is considered regarding defensive counterintelligence could be redundant if the opposition was never aware that sensitive information existed. This means that the first breach of security occurs when the opposition becomes aware that information worthy of targeting exists. If one uses the metaphor of a genie, it is at the point when the opposition knows about the information that the proverbial genie has been let out of the bottle and there is no way of returning it. All that can be done at that juncture is intensify the defensive counterintelligence measures and/or conduct an offensive counterintelligence operation. So, if an agency holds information with some degree of sensitivity, its existence needs to be kept confidential to all but those with a need-to-know.

Tenet 6—Counterreconnaissance

This tenet is associated with tenet 5—not allowing the opposition to know of the information or operation in the first place. This tenet seeks to prevent *reconnaissance*.[4] In this sense, it is more than preventing a reconnoitering of a physical target, as the case would be for the location of a piece of critical infrastructure. It is preventing *environmental scanning*—that is, hunting for leads that could indicate the agency is inactive in perusing certain developments. For instance, strategic intelligence analysts use a method known as environmental scanning to investigate issues of value. It seeks to obtain data at the macro level. If in analyzing these data the analysts conclude that there are indicators that the opposition may be involved in activities that they would like to know about, the proverbial genie has been let out of the bottle.

Tenet 7—Realistic Policies and Procedures

Countermeasures need to be flexible and need to correspond to the risk. They should not become a rigid set of policies and procedures. Rather, they need to be fluid and adaptable to changes in the agency's requirements for security. No doubt practitioners will need to consider many factors before implementing countermeasures. Nevertheless, important issues need to be weighed when establishing, or improving, a defensive counterintelligence program. These include, but are not limited to, financial constraints and the willingness of staff to follow proposed procedures. For instance, in the business and private sectors, there is little sense in spending large sums of money on safes and intruder detection systems if the utility is not justified, or it pushes the budget toward insolvency. Likewise, staff may be tempted to bypass security procedures if they are overly complicated or time consuming.[5] Physical security, employee vetting, information handling policies, classification schemes, and the like are only backstops for contest of wits that is at the center of counterintelligence; that is, the offensive stratagems.

Tenet 8—Synergistic Approach

Countermeasures should be modular, that is, able to be adapted either in whole or in part, depending on the results of the counterintelligence planning process that are described in the next chapter (chapter 5, Defensive Counterintelligence Planning). The important issue is that the tenets of defensive counterintelligence are observed and that periodic inspections are carried out to check on the standard of security practiced. Countermeasures can therefore be seen in a synergistic way—the combination totaling more than the sum of the individual components.

Tenet 9—Early Detection

Break-ins and burglaries are not an uncommon occurrence for government agencies or businesses to experience. However, in June 1972 the Watergate affair brought home the reality that break-ins are not only a method for acquiring cash and valuable physical assets, but they are also a technique for information gathering.[6] In intelligence work this technique is referred to as a *black bag operation*.[7] Surreptitious entries are used to plant surveillance devices or to carry out other covert intelligence-gathering activities. Short of creating a mini-fortress, there is nothing that will make an office 100 percent burglarproof—even Buckingham Palace has had its intruder. Ideally, this tenet dictates that an alert is sent to the counterintelligence officer that a penetration has occurred at the time it took place. This facilitates several things: an immediate notification shortens the time the perpetrator has to access information, as well as places the perpetrator under pressure, thus increasing the chance of errors. Errors could also result in trace evidence being left behind. If it is not possible to design an immediate alert facility, then the time between penetration and detection needs to be as short as possible. Detection also increases the deterrent effect of the system.

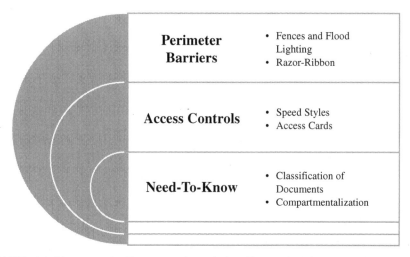

FIGURE 4.1 Diagrammatic Representation of the Tenet of Defense-in-depth. *Source:* Courtesy of the author.

Tenet 10—Defense-in-Depth

The tenet of early detection (tenet 9) is integral to this tenet—that of delay. Namely, once detected, countermeasures should be directed to delaying the perpetrator so that security guards or police can arrive and apprehend the offender. This requires a system of barriers to be installed. Barriers can be any device that separates two spaces. They can range from reinforced walls and doors to transparent glass partitions. Barriers also act to cause the perpetrator to leave behind evidence of how they tried to penetrate the barrier, thus providing a potentially rich source of forensic evidence for counterintelligence investigators. In this regard, the barrier system needs to consist of several barriers to form layers—termed *defense-in-depth*. The theory behind defense-in-depth is that perpetrators will lose momentum as they encounter each barrier. If there was one single defensive barrier, although difficult to penetrate, once breached, the target data is immediately vulnerable. This is known as single point of failure, or a single path to failure (Figure 4.2).[8]

The layering of barriers applies equally to the building obstacles in physical world and to creating the same in the cyber-sphere. The strongest barrier in a defense-in-depth system needs to be located closest to the targeted data. This is discussed in tenet 12.

As to how many layers are needed for security-in-depth to be effective depends on the agency's risk threshold, its security budget, the value of the data it is holding, and for what period these data items need to remain secret.

Allied to the tenet of defense-in-depth is the central pillar of personnel security (see chapter 7). This pillar states that, to ensure that staff who work for the agency do not inadvertently disclose secrets, some form of "protection" needs to be in place. Although not a physical barrier as such, the protection afforded is a barrier nonetheless. This protection takes the form of background investigations. For instance, to guard against people who may seek to intentionally reveal classified information and those who may be so indiscreet that they may unintentionally reveal secrets if employed, a vetting process needs to take place.

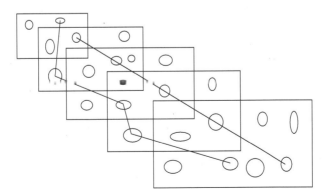

FIGURE 4.2 Swiss Cheese Analogy: The Left-hand Path Avoids the Uninterrupted Route Seen in the Right-hand Path, which Offers No Resistance. *Source*: Courtesy of the author.

Another set of pillars that is associated with the tenet of defense in depth are the three pillars of information security (see chapter 8). These pillars include confidentiality, integrity, and availability. Confidentiality is concerned with the prevention of unauthorized disclosure; integrity is concerned with being able to detect if, and when, information is modified; and availability is concerned with ensuring that the data can be accessed by those with a need-to-know when required.

Tenet 11—Unpredictability

If the agency's barrier defense system could incorporate a feature that causes the perpetrator to be startled or confused as they encounter each barrier, this will add to the overall robustness of the barrier system. A barrier that is predictable can be overcome more easily than one that has several possible outcomes when trying to breach it. Again, early detection and time delay are the overall goals of these related tenets.

Tenet 12—Core Hardening

Following on from the tenet of defense-in-depth (tenet 10), the target data needs to have the strongest barrier around it in the immediate vicinity. And, the risk associated with protecting these target data also needs to be reduced to the smallest possible physical profile. Spreading the risk over a large area (say a floor of an agency's building) weakens the countermeasures established to protect it. Having said that, a security plan needs to avoid placing the target data in a position that makes it susceptible to a single vulnerability. It is therefore

PHOTO 4.1 "Information" Can Also Take the Form of a Physical Artifact. *Source*: Photograph by Airman Daniel Garcia. Courtesy of the U.S. Air Force.

important that the system that is set up to protect the data in the core location of the defense-in-depth plan is not only small in profile but is itself protected. Examples of this type of self-protection system can be seen in physical protection measures that prevent intruder alarms from being tampered with, or an automatic logging system that occurs when users log on to a computer system.

Tenet 13—Delineate and Prioritize

It follows that, if a defensive counterintelligence program needs to harden the protection it has for sensitive information items, then an agency must first identify what these items are. This is of pivotal importance—there is an undeniable need to delineate and prioritize those bodies of information that warrant counterintelligence protection. Concomitantly, the systems, processes, institutions, and individuals in which such information resides need to be prioritized also.[9] Kenneth deGraffenreid once stated: "A country must first know what it is trying to protect. What are those values, secrets and institutions that it needs to protect? In a free society there are lots of them. Given the finite nature of its counterintelligence resources, what are its most precious secrets? This requires analysis and decision."[10]

Tenet 14—Quality over Quantity

As in many of life's endeavors, quality is more important than the quantity or efficiency, and this is the same when it comes to defense-in-depth. This is particularly

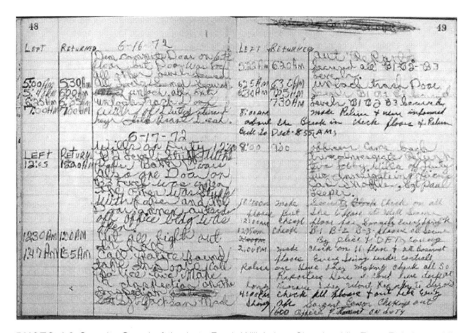

PHOTO 4.2 Security Guard of the Late Frank Wills's Log Showing His Entry Relating to His Discovery of the Break-in During the Night of June 17, 1972, at the Democratic National Committee's Offices at the Watergate Office Complex, Washington, D.C. *Source:* Courtesy of the U.S. National Archives and Records Administration.

demonstrated when it comes to those elements of the system that involve people. Security guards come to mind in this regard. A small cadre of well-trained and motivated security guards who take their time in performing their tasks well is far more valuable than abundant, but poorly trained and lackluster sentinels who rush through their jobs. It took only one observant and responsive security guard to expose the illegal intelligence operation that was eventually traced back to the Nixon White House,[11] with the ultimate result of Richard M. Nixon resigning as president of the United States (see Photo 4.2). In the words of the former director of Central Intelligence, the late Richard Helms, "Efficiency and [quality] security are absolutely incompatible concepts."[12] Counterintelligence units need to recruit talented specialists who not only understand the defensive side of the craft, but the offensive side, because, after all, the offensive side is the "main game."

Tenet 15—Cooperation

As security is usually agency specific, this tenet states that there is a need for cooperation between counterintelligence personnel and external law enforcement agencies. This involves liaising with police and neighboring firms with crime prevention strategies, as well as a formal reliance on law enforcement agencies to effect arrests[13] and to prosecute cases through the courts.

Tenets 16 and 17—Reduction and Complicity

Finally, there are two integral tenets that, although complementary upon first examination, can also be seen as mutually exclusive. Tenet 16 is that the security strategies need to be able to reduce the list of suspected perpetrators to the smallest possible pool. The ability to do this serves as a deterrent, as well as signals that there will be detection. However, if the security countermeasures can be designed to ensure that no single person can breach the safeguards, then this will ensure that more than one person will be involved in any attempt to acquire sensitive data. Tenet 17 could be called the tenet of complicity. Complicity ensures that, to penetrate the security arrangements, it will require two or more people. Having multiple perpetrators increased the chance that errors will be made. The intent here is that the perpetrators' arrangements will be compromised. It also creates a potential trail of link evidence for counterintelligence investigators. If a perpetrator is forced by security arrangements to enter into a complicit arrangement, it acts as a deterrent and provides valuable leads of detection.

Review of Key Words and Phrases

The key words and phrases associated with this chapter are listed below. Demonstrate your understanding of each by writing a short definition or explanation in one or two sentences.

black bag operations   detection
defense-in-depth   deterrence

environmental scanning
friendly access

friend or foe
reconnaissance

Study Questions

1. List the seventeen tenets of defensive counterintelligence.

2. Describe how the opposition might use *reconnaissance* to gain an awareness of, say, an agency's headquarters' critical infrastructure and then contrast this to how it might conduct an *environmental scan* to detect the existence of desired information. Although they are different, are there also similarities? If so, explain what the similarities are.

3. Describe the purpose of tenet 10, defense-in-depth. Give an example of how this tenet could be applied to an office area in which you have recently worked.

4. In relation to tenet 11, devise a barrier system that could provide some degree of unpredictability, thus affording delay to any penetration attempt. As this is a notional example, you can use any barrier to demonstrate your unpredictable system enhancement.

Learning Activity

Consider the tenets of reduced pool of perpetrators (tenet 16) and complicity (tenet 17). Using either your current workplace or a notional one, think of a small collection of sensitive data. These data can be hardcopy documents or electronically stored files. Now brainstorm three strategies that would enable counterintelligence investigators to reduce the list of suspects who have attempted to obtain these data to the smallest possible pool. Finally, think of a countermeasure that could complement each of the three strategies so that it ensures that no single person would be able to breach the strategy to protect the sensitive data.

Notes

1   Many of these tenets were adapted from security-related considerations espoused by Hamilton (1979) but have been specifically crafted to help explain and underpin the concept of defensive counterintelligence. See Peter Hamilton, *Espionage, Terrorism and Subversion in an Industrial Society* (Surrey, UK: Peter Heims Ltd., 1979), 164–74.

2   Cynthia Garbo, *Handbook of Warning Intelligence* (Lanham, MD: Rowman & Littlefield, 2010), 286.

3   There are two principles relating to access to information—*need-to-know* and *right-to-know*. Closely tied to the need-to-know principle is that of *need-to-share* as well as the *responsibility-to-provide*.

4   In this sense, the term "reconnaissance" is used in a way slightly different from the usual meaning—that is, scouting ahead of a main force (Henry Prunckun, *How to Undertake Surveillance and Reconnaissance*). But, *environmental scanning* is in a way related as the person scanning is seeking information about the issues under investigation ahead of the main research effort.

5 Government agencies, or contractors who do work for government agencies, may have a legislative requirement to employ certain levels of security, or certain classes of security devices, or use certain procedures, and these may not be able to be varied.

6 In the case of Watergate, this could be considered as private political espionage as the operation was conducted outside the Constitutional functions of the Executive Office of the President.

7 See, for example, Carl Roper, *Agent's Handbook of Black Bag Operations* (Cornville, AZ: Desert Publications, 1978).

8 Paul Betts, personal communication, October 21, 2016.

9 This tenet stems from discussions with Dr. Petrus "Beer" Duvenage (State Security Agency, South Africa), personal communication, January 23, 2012.

10 Kenneth DeGraffenreid, "Counterintelligence," in Roy Godson (ed.), *Intelligence Requirements for the 1990s: Collection, Analysis, Counterintelligence and Covert Action* (Lexington, MA: Lexington Books, 1989), 151.

11 See chapter one in Richard Helms with Hood, *A Look Over My Shoulder.*

12 Richard Helms with Hood, *A Look Over My Shoulder*, 379.

13 It is worth recalling that in some jurisdictions all citizens have the power of arrest, not only police officers. This is usually predicated on the requirement that the person making the arrest has observed firsthand the commission of a felony (in some jurisdictions a *felony* is termed an "indictable offense") or it may be a summary offense (i.e., a misdemeanor), but these are usually related to property damage or offenses against a person. Laws that allow for a *citizen's arrest* also usually stipulate that the arresting person can use coercive force to apprehend the alleged offender, but once restrained the arrestee must be delivered to the police without delay. For example, in U.S. capital, the District of Columbia Code, Section 23–582(b) provides for arrests without warrant:

(b) A private person may arrest another

(1) who he has probable cause to believe is committing in his presence

(A) a felony; or

(B) an offense enumerated in section 23–581(a)(2); or

(2) in aid of a law enforcement officer or special policeman, or other person authorized by law to make an arrest.

(c) Any person making an arrest pursuant to this section shall deliver the person arrested to a law enforcement officer without unreasonable delay.

And, in Australia section 3Z of the Commonwealth Government's Crimes Act, 1914 gives every citizen the power to arrest for an indictable offense:

(1) A person who is not a constable may, without warrant, arrest another person if he or she believes on reasonable grounds that

(a) the other person is committing or has just committed an indictable offence; and

(b) proceedings by summons against the other person would not achieve one or more of the purposes referred to in paragraph 3W(1)(b).

(2) A person who arrests another person under subsection (1) must, as soon as practicable after the arrest, arrange for the other person, and any property found on the other person, to be delivered into the custody of a constable.

Chapter 5

Defensive Counterintelligence Planning

"In preparing for battle," Dwight Eisenhower advised, "I have always found that plans are useless, but planning is indispensable."[1] As Supreme Commander of Allied Expeditionary Forces in Europe during the Second World War, his observation draws attention to the fact that once the shooting starts, plans lose relevance quickly. His sage words are as applicable to intelligence operations as they are to armed combat. Although it is not possible to predict the future, planning does allow for processes and procedures to be put in place that can anticipant an approximation of the future. This allows for systems to be set up to manage events when they do not go to plan.

Defensive counterintelligence planning is about *denial*. Offensive counterintelligence planning is about *deception*. "While 'denial' and 'deception' are separate terms that can be distinguished conceptually, they are closely intertwined in practice. Almost by definition, deception must include denial: in order to induce an adversary to accept a cover story, information that would reveal the true state of affairs must be denied him."[2]

Rationale for Planning

Plans develop from a cogitative process that results in a strategy. Strategy should lead to the achievement of a goal. It should also include the mechanical process for producing some form of document that records this thinking. In terms of a defensive counterintelligence plan, the goal is to make secure information available to only those with a need-to-know.

Why plan? Without a plan it is difficult to apply the limited resources at the disposal of the counterintelligence coordinator across the spectrum of information that lies within the agency that may require protection, and to do this across all the weeks of a year. In this sense a plan is a document that logically and progressively takes its reader from the general to the specific, and explains how the conclusions drawn were reached. The term *transparency* is used in this context—the reader can see and understand the rationale and logic used to do what is being suggested. Plans contain many elements, or sections, and each is designed to step the reader through the thinking of the planner.

The seventeen tenets discussed in the previous chapter should form the basis for considering the key issues in the counterintelligence planning process—threat, vulnerability, and risk. Recalling Proposition 8 (Synergistic Approach), countermeasures should be modular so that they can be adapted in whole or in part, depending on the findings of the counterintelligence planning process. To develop a plan for an agency's defensive counterintelligence needs, the first step is to conduct a threat analysis.

The two subsequent phases are vulnerability analysis and risk analysis. The results of these three pieces of analytic work lay the groundwork for crafting a plan that addresses *prevention, preparation, response,* and *recovery* (PPRR). In other words, all the methods contained within this chapter are intrinsically linked, acting as building blocks for the systematic development of a plan. Without a plan, an agency's resources may be allocated to areas of low risk and/or low impact, leaving high-risk and/or high-impact areas exposed.

The steps in developing a counterintelligence plan are the following:

1. Identify and locate sensitive information that requires protection;
2. Identify the threat-agent(s);
3. Explore vulnerabilities to the threat(s);
4. Gauge the likelihood that the threat(s) will eventuate;
5. Assess the consequence the threat(s) will have; and
6. Construct a PPRR plan.

Consider the following example of how these steps are applied in practice:

1. Classification—Identify all sensitive information and assign a classification level to these data;
2. Threat—interception of signals at an overseas embassy in an unfriendly country;
3. Vulnerability—the agency's wireless communications located within the embassy;
4. Likelihood—greater than 90 percent probability;
5. Consequence—moderate to severe compromise of classified data; and
6. PPRR—develop a plan that does four things: attempts to prevent such an interception (prevention); prepares the agency for such an interception if prevention measures fail (preparedness); guides the agency in the actions it needs to take to respond to an interception that is underway or has occurred (response); and suggests what needs to be done to aid the agency's client in recovering once the interception incident has passed (recovery). Recovery could be thought of also as a business continuity plan; but with information, this will be in the vein of a "damage control" plan too.

Although discussed here as a packaged approach to counterintelligence, any one of these analyses can be carried out on its own or applied to problems other than protecting secrets. For instance, a risk assessment could be conducted in relation to a person or group acting criminally.

Identify Sensitive Information

One of the most important considerations in developing a defensive counterintelligence plan is identifying the information that needs to be protected along with the places these data are held. In chapter 8 the classification process is discussed, as are the types of information that require protecting and the levels of security that can be assigned to each data item. A reading of chapter 8 is recommended to understand the concerns involved in this issue.

Nevertheless, guarding sensitive information is at the heart of the defensive planning process, and the ability to apply countermeasures (i.e., risk treatment options), which will be discussed later in this chapter, requires that all sensitive information be identified in the first instance. This simple argument sums up the situation: (1) if data are not identified and classified, treatment options cannot be applied to protect them; and (2) if sensitive data are unprotected, the information is as good as in the hands of the opposition.

Threat Analysis

In some agencies the term *threat* has been used loosely to mean *risk* or *hazard*," so some clarification is needed. Essentially, a threat is one person's resolve to inflict harm on another. Threats can be made (by a *threat-agent*) against most entities—people, organizations, and nations. Threats can be benign or malicious. In the case of the latter, the harm can be in many forms and can be suffered either physically or emotionally/mentally. A threat-agent does not have to openly declare its resolve to cause harm to constitute a threat, though explicit words or actions make it easier for field operatives to identify the threat-agent and for analysts to assess the threat.

So, threats are projected by threat-agents, whereas *risks* are the function of likelihood and consequence, and a *hazard* is a nature-induced event or naturally occurring danger. It is important to note the difference and not be tempted to blend the terms as if they were synonymous, especially when writing plans.

Threat analysis acknowledges two factors—that there needs to be a threat-agent (which could be anything from a physical substance to a person or a body corporate/organization) and an object of the threat (i.e., the target, which does not have to be a material target—such as a shopping mall or an individual—but can be an intangible such as a threat to national security or the security of a particular jurisdiction or an event). Stated another way, a threat-agent who has intent and capability must be able to harm something. By way of example, a threat-agent could be an employee who is intent on and capable of passing on classified trade information to a business competitor. Or, like the group Russian *sleepers* who were expelled from the United States in 2010 for spying (Photo 5.1).[3] The group were found to be carrying out long-term, deep-cover

PHOTO 5.1 Russian Federation Deep-cover Operatives. *Source*: Courtesy of the U.S. Marshals Service.

assignments for the Russian Federation and that they had intent and capability to obtain sensitive strategic information.[4]

Identifying Levels of Threat-Agents

Listed below are three broadband sources of threat-agents. This list is intended to present an illustrative hierarchy of typical threat-agents that an agency may confront during conducting its "business." Steps taken to thwart intelligence collection from, for example, a Level II threat-agent would be sufficient to guard against any attempt by the inferior Level III threat-agent, but not the reverse. This is an important factor to remember. It is critical for agencies to determine where their threat vectors originate before deciding on the range and depth of countermeasures they will require. Furthermore, an agency's threat-agent level may change from time to time due to the dynamics of its operations. Consequently, an agency's security needs will also need to either escalate or abate in response to these changing conditions.

- Level I Threat-Agent. Surveillance by a foreign government's security or intelligence agency, or surveillance by an investigation company staffed by former law enforcement or intelligence personnel.
- Level II Threat-Agent. Surveillance by an organized criminal group, a well-financed terrorist or extremist group, a foreign or domestic business competitor employing a "spy-for-hire," a private investigator acting on behalf of a party interested in the affairs of the agency, or other professional fact finders such as an investigative journalist.
- Level III Threat-Agent. Nonprofessional surveillance by, for example, an employee, a business associate or competitor, or another interested individual or group acting on their own with no formal training in investigation or information gathering, or an unsophisticated criminal.

Logical Model for Threat

When counterintelligence coordinators assess a threat-agent, they are gauging whether the agent has *intent* and *capability* to harm a target. To determine whether the threat-agent has intent and capability, analysts need to establish two elements for each of these factors: *desire* and *expectation* (or *ability*) for intent, and *knowledge* and *resources* for capability. These considerations are shown diagrammatically in a logical model in Figure 5.1 below. Threat can also be expressed as an equation in the form of

$$threat = (desire + expectation) + (knowledge + resources).$$

It is important to note that threats can only originate from a threat-agent acting in an offensive role—that is, humans (but can include organizations in the broad sense of the term as these entities are controlled and directed by humans—for example, nation-states, armed forces, corporations, etc.). Threats, by definition, cannot originate from a nonhuman source, such as fire, flood, storm, wind, earthquake, and other forms of nature-induced events, as well as events caused by accident, mishap, misfortune, coincidence, and chance. These are *hazards*. Hazards need to be considered as part of any counterintelligence plan, but this is done at the risk assessment phase.

Turning to intent and capability in detail, desire can be described as the threat-agent's enthusiasm to cause harm in pursuit of his or her goal. Expectation is the confidence the threat-agent has that they will achieve their goal if their plan is carried out. Knowledge is having information that will allow the threat-agent to use or construct devices, or carry out processes that are necessary for achieving their goal. Resources include skills (or experience) and materials needed to action their plan.

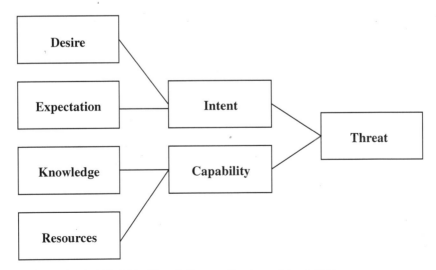

FIGURE 5.1 Logical Model for Threat. *Source*: Courtesy of the author.

The conduct of a threat analysis will vary from agency to agency because each agency's mission will be different. Nevertheless, a step-by-step process might look something like this:

1. Identify the categories from which threats may manifest. These can be called *threat communities*, and this concept is discussed later in this chapter. Examples of possible threat communities could be along these lines: internal and external, with each of these categories being broken down into subcategories—internal may be permanent employees, contract agents, ancillary staff, temporary staff, and others. The same can be done for the external category. The best way to create such a list is to either brainstorm using a small group of knowledgeable people or, if working alone, by using a mind map.

2. Collate the categories and subcategories into a list using headings and subheadings for ease of handling.

3. The lowest level of headings in the collated list (in the above example, it would be subheading) will be the areas that the threat assessment will need to examine. If the subheading of *temporary staff* is selected as a starting point, the counterintelligence investigator would then take each of the four criteria (desire, expectation, knowledge, and resources) and gauge whether that subcategory contains evidence of any of these four factors. If the answer is yes, but only to one or two factors, then the subcategory can be said not to pose a threat. If the assessment shows evidence that three factors are present, then it might be placed on a "watch list" in case the situation changes. If all four factors are present, then, by definition, it poses a threat and a closer look is warranted. But, having said that it is a threat does not mean it is. The assessment is merely an analytical method for helping counterintelligence investigators focus their efforts, and their agency's resources, where they are most beneficial and, hence, the next step.

4. Inquiries will need to be conducted to gather information about whether each of the four factors is of such a magnitude that a reasonable person would draw this conclusion. It is important that all information is weighted in this process and not "cherry-picked" to include only information to support a point of view—this is both unethical and operationally dangerous. A balanced view needs to be formed so that the correct conclusion can be drawn. If, on balance, the evidence does not lead one to draw such a conclusion, a watching brief may be raised. Sources of information can be both primary and secondary, and they can be from either the public domain, private sector, or confidential/classified. An appropriate information collection plan and research method for analyzing these data needs to be crafted as per any intelligence project. A good text for guiding the counterintelligence investigator through this research process is my book *Scientific Methods of Inquiry for Intelligence Analysis.*[5]

Once the formal assessment process is complete, a summary can be created using a simple table that shows the results. This is a handy way for displaying the results, so decision makers can understand the outcome of the assessment without burdening them with large amounts of narrative. A model for calculating threats might look something like Table 5.1.

Although models do not eliminate subjectivity, using a model requires counterintelligence investigators to be transparent about how they calculate threat and, in doing so, positions them to defend their conclusions. You will note that there are no conditions assigned to what constitutes a high level of intent. That is because this needs to be developed in the analytic process that leads to the assignment of the coefficient. Ideally, some form of conditioning statement

TABLE 5.1 Example of a Threat Summary: Threat Community Summary for Former Employees of Manly Pharmaceutical Corporation

Scale	Scores	Tally
Desire		
Negligible	1	
Minimum	2	2
Medium	3	
High	4	
Acute	5	
Expectation		
Negligible	1	1
Minimum	2	
Medium	3	
High	4	
Acute	5	
Total Intent		**3**
Knowledge		
Negligible	1	
Minimum	2	
Medium	3	
High	4	4
Acute	5	
Resources		
Negligible	1	
Minimum	2	
Medium	3	
High	4	4
Acute	5	
Total Capability		**8**
Threat Coefficient		**11**

would be attached to each of these categories so that the decision maker knows what is meant by high intent, low intent, and so forth. An example of how such a conditioning statement scale could be constructed is shown in Table 5.5.

In addition, models do not eliminate miscalculations because of inadvertent skewing. Note in Table 5.1 that intent is calculated by adding desire with expectation, and, in turn, this sum is added to the sum of knowledge and resources (and will range from a low of four to a maximum of twenty). The process of adding limits the spread of values, whereas the process of multiplying any of these scores would increase the values. For instance, if all scores were multiplied—that is, substituting multiplication for addition—as per the equation, the range would be spread from 1 to 625.

The precision of this wide range of values diminishes the counterintelligence investigator's ability to accurately determine either intent or capability. Therefore, it is suggested that adding all values rather than multiplying them will reduce the spread and, therefore, maintain the threat coefficient as an *indicator*, rather than promote it as a reflection of its absolute condition. (Even if the counterintelligence investigator multiplied desire and expectation, and knowledge and resources, but added the resulting sums, it would still yield a very wide spread—from two to fifty—as would the opposite, that is, multiplying the sums that comprise intent and capability—from four to hundred.)

Having said that, two additional issues need to be noted: (1) there is still a need to provide conditioning statements so that the reader of the assessment understands what is meant by a medium threat intent and capability (e.g., along the lines of Table 5.5); and (2) "unknowns" are not accommodated in this model.

The threat coefficient obtained from this analysis is then compared against a reference table to gauge where it sits on a continuum of danger. The scale suggested in Table 5.2 can be varied with additional qualifiers or it can be collapsed if the number is deemed too many. Likewise, how the incremental breakdown of coefficients is determined will depend on whether the agency is willing to accept the risk that a threat-agent may slip under its gaze by raising the categories of negligible and minimum. In the end, their number and their descriptors need to make sense in the context of the asset being protected. That is, each of the descriptors needs to have a conditioning statement attached to

TABLE 5.2 Example of a Threat Coefficient Scale

Threat Level	Coefficient
Negligible	4–6
Minimum	7–10
Medium	11–15
High	16–18
Acute	19–20

it to define what is meant by negligible, minimum, medium, high, and acute. See Table 5.5 as an example.

Threats are context dependent, and what forms a threat in a business setting does not necessarily form a threat in a military or national security setting (though the opposite may be true). Bearing this in mind, an example from national security will be discussed to illustrate the threat analysis method.

In a military situation, say, a low-intensity conflict, threats can range from spontaneous street demonstrations by the local population, at one end, through to terrorist bombing and confrontations with insurgent or guerrilla units at the other end. The techniques for assessing the elements of a threat can vary depending on the issue under investigation and the counterintelligence investigator's personal preference or the agency's policy.

Nevertheless, the approach is to weight each element using some verifiable means that is open to third-party scrutiny. For instance, an analyst may use a force field analysis to judge whether there are threats in Country Q associated with a low-intensity campaign being prosecuted by friendly military units. Likewise, the nominal group technique could be employed not only to assess the four elements of a threat (i.e., desire, expectation, knowledge, and resources), but to generate a list of possible threat-agents (i.e., belligerents) to compare the elements against each other. Participants for such a group could be drawn from subject experts or operational specialists, or a mixture of both. Some of the other analytic techniques discussed in chapter ten of my book on intelligence analysis[6] can also be used, but there is no firm rule on how this analysis should be done.

One way of considering the context for threats is to conceptualize it as *threat communities*. Some examples of threat communities in the realm of malicious human threats include

External

- competitors;
- common thieves;
- criminals and criminal groups;
- international or transnational terrorists;
- domestic terrorists;
- insurgents and guerrillas;
- anarchists;
- cyber-criminals and cyber-vandals;
- rights campaigners;
- spies-for-hire (i.e., former law enforcement, security, or intelligence personal who have turned private operatives); and
- foreign government intelligence services.

Internal

- principals of the business or agency;
- associates;

- current employees;
- former employees;
- temporary staff; and
- contractors.

These threat communities can be subdivided into more distinct groups if there is a need—for instance, rights campaigners can be classified into political activists,

TABLE 5.3 Threat Profile for the Omen Martyrs Faction

Summary Type	Observations
Organization	
Organization	Well organized but not hierarchal.
Affiliation	Autonomous.
Recruitment	Ethnic population centers.
Financing	Extortion and kidnapping the wealthy.
International connections	Training and ideological support.
Behavioral	
Motivation	Radical religious ideology.
Intent	Extensive destruction.
Tolerance to risk	High.
Self-sacrifice	Very accepting.
Willingness to inflict collateral harm	Extreme.
Operational	
Planning	Based on target acquisition intelligence through fixed and mobile surveillance, informants and open-source data.
Targets	Objects that represent Western values or people who do not ascribe to their interpretation of their faith (including other believers).
Target characteristics	Symbolic and iconic objects that afford high visibility and hence high media coverage.[1]
Tactics	Targets mass gathering, critical infrastructure, communications, mass transport, and distribution chains.
Weapons	Improvised explosives and small arms.
Resource Summary	
Skills and Knowledge	Attack vector dependent: Computer-based—low; Electronic/communications—moderate; Small arms—high; and Explosives—high.

[1] Regarding this factor, see Stratfor, *How to Look for Trouble: A Stratfor Guide to Protective Intelligence* (Austin, TX: Stratfor, 2010), 127–31.

religious activists, and single-issue activists (e.g., anti-taxation, anti-whaling, animal rights, antiabortion, etc.). But bear in mind that membership in one threat community (or subcommunity) does not exclude that person from being a member of another, or several other, threat communities.

....

When compiling a threat profile, targets should be considered in terms of their criticality, cost (either as a direct loss, or an indirect, or consequential loss due to disruption), and sensitivity (e.g., compromised information). This is because targets that do not possess any of these attributes may not be considered as threat-agents with the same weight.

....

To better understand the "who" that comprise a threat community, counterintelligence investigators need to compile a *threat profile*. The profile needs to be adequate (perfection is rarely, if ever, obtainable) to understand the threat environment, which aids the next phase in the analytic process—that is, vulnerability analysis. In the meantime, consider the threat profile shown in Table 5.3 as an example that demonstrates the important aspects of a fictitious threat-agent (the order can be rearranged to suit the counterintelligence investigator's research project and other factors can be added if these are deemed inadequate to communicate the message).

Vulnerability Analysis

In short, *vulnerability* is a weakness in an *asset* that can be exploited by a threat-agent. The term *asset* is being used in this context to denote a resource that requires protection and can be places and objects as well as people. In the context of counterintelligence, we are talking about information resources that require protection. Viewed another way, vulnerability can be described as an asset's capability to withstand harm inflicted on it by a threat. Harm can be anything from experiencing a minor nuisance event to a situation that is catastrophic.

Vulnerability is a function of several factors—attractiveness of the targeted information, feasibility of carrying out a penetration, and potential impact if released. This model is shown diagrammatically in Figure 5.2. Usually, these factors entail such considerations as status of the targeted information, potential for the penetration to succeed, potential for the threat-agent to get away with the penetration, and potential to inflict loss (i.e., capitalize on the information obtained). These factors can be weighed against measures to mitigate loss and to deter or prevent penetration of an asset (e.g., say, through a force field analysis).

Formulae-based analyses are popular among law enforcement and security agencies engaged in information protection, and, although these vary from agency to agency, they all follow a basic stepwise formula:

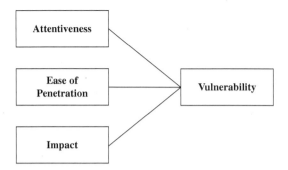

FIGURE 5.2 Logical Model for Vulnerability. *Source:* Courtesy of the author.

1. Define what constitutes an information asset (corporate website, research reports, servers holding classified data, along with others);
2. Sort these assets into categories;
3. Assign a grade or level of importance to each asset; and
4. Identify potential impact on the asset if it suffers harm (i.e., unauthorized access/dissemination).

As there is no one single criterion for calculating vulnerability because each class of information asset may require special considerations to be considered (and there may also be agency protocols that take precedence), one general approach is to use a model such as

Vulnerability = target information attractiveness + ease of penetration + impact

To operationalize the variable *attractiveness*, the counterintelligence investigator could ask questions along the following lines and tabulate the results to insert into the model:

* Could obtaining the target information cause harm and therefore be of value—symbolic, monetary, or strategic? For instance, when the former Soviet Union paraded the CIA's U2 pilot Gary Francis Powers, who was shot down while conducting a reconnaissance mission in 1961, before the world's media, this was of great symbolic importance (as well as having other strategic advantages). This was because obtaining proof that the United States was conducting surveillance of the Soviet Union brought that program to an end (though it was simply displaced by satellite reconnaissance, which the Soviets engaged in also).
* Is the target information readily obtainable? Rather than answer this question in a dichotomous way (i.e., using nominal data—yes/no), ordinal data could be used to give greater precision to the overall vulnerability indictor. For example, is the information obtainable on the Internet? Or are the data obtainable through library research but only held in special collections in a handful of libraries? Or are these data held in security containers with physical security measures?[7] These ordinal type indictors can also be applied to the concept of harm discussed directly above.

Attractiveness needs to be placed in context with the threat-agent. For instance, a business competitor of an arms manufacturer may see the scientific papers published by the company's scientists as very attractive.

To operationalize the concept *ease of penetration*, the analyst could ask these types of questions:

- How difficult would it be for the threat-agent to gain access to the target information? A scale from certain (as in the case of published data) to very difficult (in the case of data contained and protected by armed guards) could be constructed as in the examples cited about attractiveness, above.
- Are there security measures in place (e.g., calculated on a scale of low to high deterrence, or low to high prevention)?

Questions that probe the existence and extent of controls (or lack thereof) can also be asked to gauge ease of penetration. On one hand, if there is a high degree of control effectiveness, this will usually reduce ease. On the other hand, if there is a low level of control effectiveness, it will increase ease. Counterintelligence investigators should be mindful that, with some sensitive information, even a small reduction in control effectiveness can result in a disproportionate increase in ease of penetration. *Impact* could be operationalized by questions like the following:

- What is the basis of harm which could result as a consequence of disclosure? This is akin to attractiveness. It may be context specific, as well as graded as to the person(s) or opposition agency that the information is made available. Again, a scale for context and degree of harm could be constructed.
- In dollar terms, what would the financial impact of an unauthorized disclosure be if the information was simply obtained, but not used by the person (e.g., if the person was apprehended shortly after obtaining the data but before they were able to pass it onto others), through to a complete handover of the information and debriefing? Or it could be put in terms of days/weeks of having to reengineer business practices or operational plans because of the disclosure, or lost units of production, and the like.

Impact should not be predicated on an assumption that all penetrations are designed to result in immediate or visible harm. This may be true of an organization such as WikiLeaks, which publicly stated that its intention was to bring "important news and information to the public [via] . . . an innovative, secure and anonymous way for sources to leak information."[8] But it would not be true of an opposition that wants to use the information, say, in its own counterintelligence program. A template for calculating vulnerability might look something like the one shown in Table 5.4.

The vulnerability coefficient derived from this analysis is then compared with a reference table to gauge where it sits on the continuum of exposure or susceptibility to penetration. The scale can be increased with additional qualifiers or it could be collapsed if the number is deemed too many. In the end, the

TABLE 5.4 **Vulnerability of Company's Scientific Research Expertise**

Scale	Scores	Tally
	Attractiveness	
Negligible	1	
Minimum	2	
Medium	3	
High	4	4
Acute	5	
	Ease of Penetration	
Negligible	1	
Minimum	2	
Medium	3	
High	4	4
Acute	5	
	Impact	
Negligible	1	
Minimum	2	
Medium	3	
High	4	4
Acute	5	
Vulnerability Coefficient		**12**

number and their descriptors need to make sense in the context of the information being protected (the left-hand and center columns of Tab!e 5.5). Qualitative descriptors (i.e., conditioning statements) can be added for each category as shown in the right-hand column of Table 5.5.

Note that *consequence* is not a factor that is considered in a threat assessment. It is, however, considered in a risk assessment (see below).

Risk Analysis

Risk is a function of two factors: *likelihood* and *consequence*. In some agencies the term *probability* is sometimes used instead of *likelihood*, and both are acceptable. A risk assessment can be carried out in relation to almost any situation; it is not just for issues of grave concern. Nor is risk management solely task for counterintelligence; risk analysis techniques can be applied to situations or targets that are not associated with sensitive information—for instance, counterterrorism. Nevertheless, analyzing risk allows counterintelligence investigators to recommend measures that will provide decision makers with the ability to

TABLE 5.5 Examples of Vulnerability Coefficients

Vulnerability	Coefficient	Qualifier
Negligible	1–3	• Can only be penetrated successfully if the threat-agent has an acute threat coefficient; or • Has little or no importance; or • The range of security measures makes penetration very difficult; or • If penetrated, the information has little utility to cause harm.
Minimum	4–6	• Can only be penetrated successfully if the threat-agent has a high coefficient (or greater); or • Has limited importance; or • The range of security measures makes penetration difficult; or • If penetrated, the information has only some utility to cause harm.
Medium	7–9	• Can only be successfully penetrated if the threat-agent has a medium coefficient (or greater); or • Has reasonable amount of importance associated with it; or • The range of security measures makes penetration moderately difficult; or • If penetrated, the information has a moderate level of utility to cause harm.
High	10–12	• Can only be successfully penetrated if threat-agent has a minimum threat coefficient (or greater); or • Has a sizeable amount of importance associated with it; or • The range of security measures makes penetration undemanding; or • If penetrated, the information has a high degree of utility to cause harm.
Acute	13–15	• Can only be successful penetrated if threat-agent has a low threat coefficient (or greater); or • Has a very high level of importance associated with it; or • The range of security measures is nonexistent; or • If penetrated, the information will cause immediate and/or extreme harm.

- accept the risk as is or
- treat the risk (which includes such decisions as to avoid the risk altogether, mitigate the risk, or defer the risk for another person or agency to deal with).

In counterintelligence, investigators can focus on a wide range of risks. These can vary from the minor—say, the release of noncritical information to the public—to risks that are faced by liberal democratic nations from penetrations by the likes of corrupt governments, rogue states as well as organized criminals, and radical ethnic, racial, and religious groups, including ultra-right-wing political groups.

Internationally, risk analysis is the subject of a standard. The Swiss-based International Organization for Standardization (ISO) has published a document that puts forward a common approach for dealing with risk by providing generic guidelines in relation to the principles for how risk is managed.[9] This document is applied by nonprofit organizations, community groups, and individuals.

Some of the key terms in risk management include the technique that is considered here—*risk analysis*—as well as *risk*, *risk assessment*, and *risk management*. According to ISO 31000:2009, risk is "the effect of uncertainty on objectives."[10] Risk assessment is the "overall process of risk identification, risk analysis and risk evaluation";[11] and risk management is the "coordinated activities to direct and control an organization with regard to risk."[12]

Understanding these terms helps distinguish the process of managing risk from the analytic process of assessing risk using the equation:

risk = likelihood + consequence

Likelihood refers to the probability of "a specific event or outcome, measured by a ratio of specific events or outcomes to the total number of possible events or outcomes." *Consequence* is defined as the "outcome of an event affecting objects."[13] Likelihood and consequence are evaluated in the analysis phase of the risk management cycle. This analytic cycle comprises five phases shown diagrammatically in Figure 5.3.[14]

The three analytic phases of the risk management cycle comprise the following steps:

1. the use of two analytic techniques—in the form of scales—to evaluate the information target's risk rating (e.g., a database on a corporate server). These two scales consist of a likelihood scale (Table 5.6) and the consequences scale (Table 5.7).
2. The results of these two assessments are then injected into a risk-rating matrix (Table 5.8) that returns a risk-rating coefficient.
3. Finally, the counterintelligence investigator looks up the risk-rating coefficient on the risk evaluation scale (Table 5.9) to determine what actions (if any) are required.

In addition to the descriptors listed in the Tables 5.7 to 5.9, there may be a need to include a set of conditioning statements, along the lines of those contained in Table 5.5. This also applies to the descriptors contained in Table 5.7. Examples of low-risk events include

- an event that would occur rarely and would result in insignificant consequences (reflected in Table 5.8 as E1); or
- an event that is unlikely to occur and would result in minor consequences (reflected in Table 5.8 as D2).

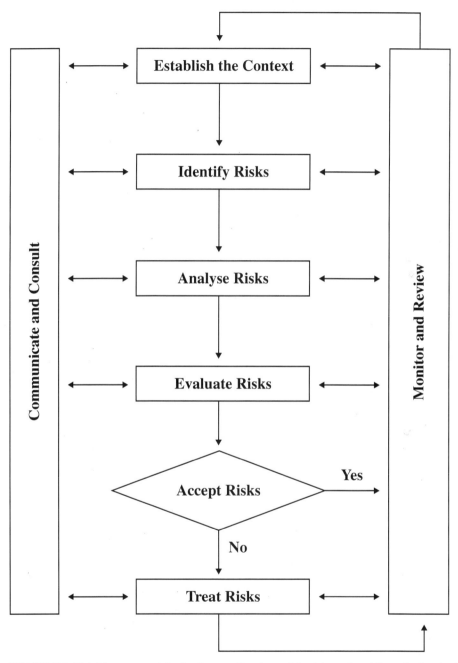

FIGURE 5.3 Risk Management Cycle. *Source*: Courtesy of the International Organization for Standardization.

TABLE 5.6 **Example of a Likelihood Scale**

Rank	Likelihood	Descriptors
A	Almost Certain	The situation is expected to happen
B	Likely	The situation will probably occur
C	Possible	The situation should occur at some time
D	Unlikely	The situation could occur at some time
E	Rare	The situation would only occur under exceptional circumstances

Examples of high-risk situations include

* an event that would occur rarely but result in catastrophic consequences (reflected in Table 5.8 as E5); or
* an event that is likely to occur and have minor consequences (reflected in Table 5.8 as B2).

Treating Risks

Once each risk is assessed in this way, they can be positioned on the risk-rating matrix (Table 5.8) so they can be compared with each other to prioritize treatment options—or in the language of intelligence, *countermeasures*. Take for instance the following events considered by troops stationed in Country Q.

* The risk posed by a local citizen employed to remove rubbish around a forward command post, and who hence gained access to sensitive operational information, was assessed at C5 (possible with catastrophic consequences and, therefore, an extreme risk); or
* harm because of inadequate shredding of some routine sensitive documents could be located at B4 (likely with moderate consequences, so the risk is high).

TABLE 5.7 **Example of a Consequences Scale**

Rank	Consequence	Descriptors
1	Insignificant	Will only have a small impact
2	Minor	Will have a minor level of impact
3	Moderate	Will cause considerable impact
4	Major	Will cause noticeable impact
5	Catastrophic	Will cause systems and/or operations to fail with high impact

TABLE 5.8 Example of a Risk-Rating Matrix

Likelihood	Consequences				
	1 Insignificant	2 Minor	3 Moderate	4 Major	5 Catastrophic
A Almost Certain	Moderate	High	Extreme	Extreme	Extreme
B Likely	Moderate	High	High	Extreme	Extreme
C Possible	Low	Moderate	High	Extreme	Extreme
D Unlikely	Low	Low	Moderate	High	Extreme
E Rare	Low	Low	Moderate	High	High

The scale provided in the risk-rating table (Table 5.9) is useful for judging whether the counterintelligence investigator recommends accepting the risk or treating the risk (and, if so, to what extent). Without the risk assessment process, the recommendations of the investigator could be called into question as an overreaction or, equally, deemed an underestimate of the seriousness of the situation. These models curb subjectivity to some extent by providing transparency about how counterintelligence investigators make their calculations.

Although the risk rating (Table 5.9) shows what is a generally accepted distribution of risk levels,[15] counterintelligence investigators will need to make

TABLE 5.9 Example of a Risk Evaluation Scale

	Risk Rating and Suggested Actions for Treatment
Low Risk	Manage using standard operating procedures.
Moderate Risk	Outline specific management actions that need to be taken.
High Risk	Create a business contiguity plan and a response plan (test annually).
Extreme Risk	Urgent actions are necessary (in addition to those per high risk).

their own judgments as to where these transition points occur. Many times, this will be a topic for discussion with the employing agency or a matter set by policy. But, by using a systematic approach to risk management, investigators can reduce the likelihood, and lessen consequences, through the application of technology, science, or personal or collective effort.

. . . .

According to Emergency Management Australia (EMA), some treatment options include: awareness and vigilance, communication and consultation, engineering options, monitoring and review, resource management, security and surveillance, and community capability and self-reliance.[16] Although these treatment options are discussed in relation to critical infrastructure, they can be adapted for use in treating risks in relation to sensitive information.

. . . .

PPRR Planning

There are four elements to PPRR policy development—prevention, preparation, response, and recovery. Prevention considers the risk and tries to implement ways that could prevent it from happening. Preparedness acknowledges that, despite preventative measures, the event may still occur, and asks how one can prepare for it. If it does occur, response is that part of the plan that deals with how agencies will mobilize and act (and what type of action, etc.). The final element provides guidance for how a recovery operation will take place. This anticipates the worst-case scenario; that is, preventative measures have failed, preparation measures may have mitigated the impact to some degree, but it still occurred; response has contained and brought the event to an end, but it is now time to recover from the event's effects.

Even though this chapter addresses PPRR from a counterintelligence point of view, it should be borne in mind that, when planning for one type of event, it is prudent to consider actions to cover what is termed *all hazards*.

For instance, if a counterintelligence investigator is considering the impact of, say, a penetration by an opposition agent, then why not consider the same (or like) event occurring because of inadvertent leakage or by chance or accident?

When compiling a defensive counterintelligence PPRR plan, try to avoid constructing the plan in such a way that each element forms either a conceptual or real barrier between them—there is usually no clear delineation between the elements though they may be expressed in these terms. Also, bear in mind that each element will not necessarily carry the same weight of importance—the four elements may not be equal. In fact, some elements may not have any strategies or treatments, or few, or minimal.

Further, although the elements are cited in a sequence—PPRR—they may be accomplished at the same time; for instance, response and recovery can (and should) start at the same time as they are inextricably linked (see Figure 5.4).

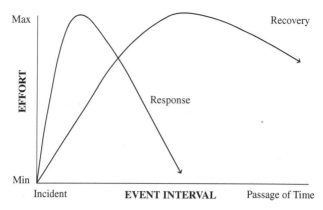

FIGURE 5.4 Comparisons of Response and Recovery Efforts. *Source*: Courtesy of the author.

Finally, though the language appears to contain action-oriented terms, the treatment options do not have to be physically based options. Options involving social dimensions are also needed because, arguably, it is through people that the opposition will gain access to sensitive information. Counterintelligence investigators should try and keep their thinking about treatments broad and innovative. The Australian Institute of Criminology has suggested a 5Is model for solving crime-related issues, and this model could be adapted to counter-measure for defensive counterintelligence.

> This involves the gathering and analysis of information on the specific crime problem (*intelligence*), selection of the full potential repertoire of responses to address proximate and distal causes of the problem in question (*intervention*); action to convert interventions into practical methods (*implementation*); mobilization of key stakeholders and agency participants (*involvement*); and evaluation of outcomes (*impact*).[17]

Review of Key Words and Phrases

The key words and phrases associated with this chapter are listed below. Demonstrate your understanding of each by writing a short definition or explanation in one or two sentences.

all hazards

attractiveness

capability

coefficient

consequence

desire

ease of penetration

expectation

impact

intent

knowledge

likelihood

PPRR

resources

risk

threat

threat-agent

threat communities

threat profile

treatment

vulnerability

Study Questions

1. What are the elements that comprise a threat analysis? Describe each and explain why each is important to understanding a threat.

2. What are the elements that comprise a vulnerability analysis? Describe each and explain why each is important to understanding the concept of vulnerability.

3. What are the elements that comprise a risk analysis? Describe each and explain why each is important to the understanding of risk.

4. What are the elements that comprise a PPRR plan? Describe each and explain why each is important to defensive counterintelligence planning.

Learning Activity

Suppose that you are asked to conduct a threat assessment for a business that is researching a new armored vehicle. The information relating to the new vehicle is currently in the form of a research proposal and the document is in the company's safe within the office of the chief researcher. Conduct a threat assessment and a vulnerability assessment regarding that piece of data using the processes discussed in this chapter.

Notes

1 Dwight Eisenhower cited in Richard M. Nixon, *Six Crises* (New York: Doubleday & Co., 1962), 363.

2 Shulsky, "Elements of Strategic Denial and Deception," 17–18.

3 Top row (L to R): Vladimir Guryev (Richard Murphy), Mikhail Anatolyevich Vasenkov (Juan Lazaro), Mikhail Kutsik (Michael Zottoli), Andrey Bezrukov (Donald Heathfield), and Mikhail Semenko. Bottom row (L to R): Anna Chapman, Vicky Peláez, Yelena Vavilova (Tracey Lee Ann Foley), Lidya Gureva (Cynthia Murphy), and Nataliya Pereverzeva (Patricia Mills).

4 U.S. Federal Bureau of Investigation, *Ten Alleged Secret Agents Arrested in the United States—Media Release* (Washington, DC: Office of Public Affairs, Department of Justice, June 28, 2010).

5 Prunckun, *Handbook of Scientific Methods of Inquiry for Intelligence Analysis.*

6 Prunckun, *Scientific Methods of Inquiry for Intelligence Analysis,.*

7 These are only a small set of categories that could populate a scale-like arrangement of options from open and accessible in minutes to well-protected arrangements using state-of-the-art techniques and equipment.

8 WikiLeaks, "About."

9 International Organization for Standardization, *ISO 31000: Risk Management—Guidelines on Principles and Implementation of Risk Management* (Geneva, Switzerland: ISO, 2009).

10 International Organization for Standardization, 2009, 1.

11 International Organization for Standardization, 2009, 4.

12 International Organization for Standardization, 2009, 2.

13 International Organization for Standardization, 2009, 5.

14 International Organization for Standardization, 2009, 14.

15 Queensland Government and Local Government Association, *Local Government Counter-Terrorism Risk Management Kit* (Brisbane: Queensland Government and Local Government Association, 2004), 16.

16 Emergency Management Australia, *Critical Infrastructure Emergency Risk Management and Assurance*, 2nd ed. (Canberra: Attorney-General's Department, 2004), 43.

17 Adrian Cherney, "Problem Solving for Crime Prevention," in **Toni Makkai** (eds.) *Trends and Issues in Criminal Justice* (Canberra: Australian Government, May 2006), 2.

Chapter 6

Defensive Counterintelligence: Physical Security

The pearls had "little knots in between so if they broke, you only lost one. I wished my life could be like that, knotted up so that even if something broke, the whole thing wouldn't come apart."[1] In intelligence work, defensive counterintelligence are the knots for protecting secret operations. The knots comprise *deterrence* and *detection* and manifest themselves in the form of physical security—the bedrock preventing the "whole thing" from "coming apart."

Though physical security cannot act as an absolute shield, the seventeen tenets of defensive counterintelligence discussed in "chapter 4" predicate it. These tenets need to be used as the basis for assessing threat, vulnerability, and risk, which was discussed in "chapter 5."

Physical protection is an important part of protecting secrets, but it is only part of counterintelligence practice. The other aspects of counterintelligence—neutralization and deceptions—are at the center of the enterprise. In the main, defensive counterintelligence is used to support the offensive side of the contest.

This chapter presents the key physical security countermeasures and their tactical application. Although these countermeasures are described in terms of their potential application, it should be noted that some government agencies, or contractors who do work for government agencies, may have legislative requirements to provide a certain level of security and/or to comply with certain security standards. In these situations, offering lower levels of security, or opting-out of certain security procedures, may not be negotiable. For instance, in Australia the *Protective Security Manual* "facilitates and promotes a consistent approach to security across all Australian Government agencies. . . . It is also the minimum security standard for State and Territory Government agencies which access Australian Government [classified] resources."[2] Other Five Eyes intelligence alliance countries have similar requirements.

Barrier Controls

Perimeter Fencing

A perimeter fence serves several purposes. It first stands as a symbolic division between an area where one is allowed to be and an area where access is controlled. Its physical presence signals to those contemplating crossing that such an act will bring consequences. The important aspect of a perimeter fence is that it can make crossing difficult. Note that it needs to be difficult, as attempting to make it impenetrable may be wishful thinking. Even the Maginot Line failed to keep the Nazis from invading France during the Second World War. What a perimeter barrier will do is declare a "no-go-zone," provide warning if breached, and cause delay if entry is attempted.

Having a declared area that is off-limits gives security guards the ability to detain and question personnel found within the area. A delayed entry will give security officers time to detect and respond.

The configuration of a perimeter fence can vary greatly, and, even though the term *fence* is used here, the barrier can be a wall, a series of bollards, moat, or other construction design. Barriers are often viewed as physical obstructions, but barriers can be devices, such as passwords, security clearances (e.g., secret or top secret), or classifications placed on documents, and so forth.

In contrast, ram-raid or cash protection barriers are not contemplated in the context of perimeter fencing. These types of barriers are designed to absorb high levels of energy—such as that from a vehicle driven into the barrier. Perimeter-fencing standards are usually specified in terms of time to breach the barrier. Features that increase delay include barbed wire or razor ribbon (see Photo 6.1),

PHOTO 6.1 Example of a Barrier Fortified with a Combination of Spikes, Coiled-razor Ribbon, and CCTV. *Source*: Courtesy of the author.

or nonlethal electrification. Some installations feature two or more sets of fencing with cleared areas in between to further cause delay, as well as other variations such as vertically stacked coils of razor ribbon or pyramid-stacked arrays, or other configurations. Perimeter barriers can also be augmented by dog patrols and/or CCTV monitoring or motion detection alarms.

Some issues that should be considered in designing new perimeter barriers, or for assessing the adequacy of existing barriers, are listed below. Although this is not an exhaustive list, the questions are indicative of the types of issues that should be considered.

- Is the height of the barrier in relation to the surrounding space appropriate?
- If chain link, is the gauge of the wire and construction of the pole supports adequate?
- Is there barbed wire or razor ribbon at the top of the fence?
- Is the perimeter fence adequately united with any building or structure that might form part of the perimeter (e.g., by increasing the height of the fence where it joins a building)?
- Is the clear space on either side of the barrier sufficient to notice any attempt to breach the barrier?
- Is the area on either side of the barrier a car parking area or used to store material that could be used to breach the barrier?
- Are there any utility tunnels or sewer or water channels that run under the perimeter, and, if so, are they secure?
- Are the number and location of gates along the barrier adequate for access, including the need for evacuation in case of an emergency or to allow emergency services to enter?
- Are the locking devices used commensurate with the strength of the barrier they are installed in?
- Is there a system of key control for the gates and other secured penetrations in the barrier (e.g., workers access holes)?
- Is the barrier posted with "no trespassing" signs at regular intervals?
- Is the barrier's perimeter checked by patrols, dogs, or CCTV to detect attempts to breach the barrier and to act as a deterrent?

Tangle-Foot Wire

This is either barbed wire or razor ribbon that is used to construct an obstruction to tangle intruders' feet. It can be constructed outside a facility's perimeter fence or in the area formed between a set of double fences. In the latter case, it adds greatly to the deterrent effect. The barbed wire or razor ribbon is usually supported by short, metal stakes driven into the ground and secured at irregular intervals. The height of these support stakes should be less than the height of the wire coils, so intruders cannot use them as balance points. If the barbed wire or razor ribbon is laid in a cross pattern it adds to the obstacle's overall effectiveness by making the pattern more complex to negotiate.

Perimeter Beams

If the outermost defensive measure is the perimeter fence, then an additional fortification is an electronic "trip wire" known as a *perimeter beam*. These devices are usually mounted to a structure inside the fences to help reduce defeat by tampering. Although intruders can see these devices, the difficulty of avoiding triggering them is not trivial. As such, their use presents a high level of deterrence. However, in terms of detection, they are known to present false positives—that is, they can be prone to triggering by wind-blown vegetation, debris, the movement of animals, and even spider webs. Certain zones will need to be deactivated when patrols are conducted or if dogs are used, and then reset.

Perimeter Towers

Observation towers offer security personnel a way of increasing the viewing range for large or spreading facilities for which they are responsible. If the area under observation is illuminated with floodlights, towers can be used at night as well as during daylight hours. It is important that, if more than one tower is required to cover the area under guard, the towers are placed so that the field of view from each tower has some common area of overlap. Inclement weather may adversely affect the advantages of towers, in which case foot patrols or CCTV may need to be considered as backup measures. It is essential that a primary and secondary method of communication is incorporated in tower design along with a system of sounding an alarm (visual as well as audible). Temporary or mobile towers may also be used for special projects or occasions.

Doors
External Doors

External doors are not only a symbol of strength but one of great practical application. It is the physical barrier that separates the opposition's agents from the areas they seek to access. External doors should be solidly constructed and have three hinges per door. The installation of the additional third hinge contributes greatly to the door's resistance against forced entry. Hardwood doors are better than those constructed of softwood, and solid doors are stronger than ones containing panels. However, wood-paneled doors are more secure than doors containing glazed panels.

It is equally important to have strong door frames to prevent failure during attack. Door frames should be securely fixed to the wall by appropriate bolts. Furthermore, double-cylinder deadlocks should be installed on all external doors. The double-cylinder deadlock needs a key to open it from either inside or outside and, when in use, it prevents an intruder from using the door as an exit after intrusion. The deadlock system also offers a medium to high degree of protection against *lock picking*. There are also multilocking systems that incorporate vertical bolts and rods designed to reinforce the door in conjunction with the deadlock option.

PHOTO 6.2 U.S. Soldiers Breaching External Door in Buhriz, Iraq, November 30, 2010. *Source*: Photograph by Air Force Staff Sergeant Stacy L. Pearsall. Courtesy of the U.S. Army.

External doors can be fortified by the addition of security grilles or an outer set of security doors that feature a mesh or grille construction. Such a feature adds both deterrence and delay for those determined to breach the barrier. A fortified external door is shown in Photo 6.2. The sizable amount of force needed to break down this door can be seen in this photograph. The noise generated in the breach would no doubt give alarm to the occupants, thus providing time to destroy any confidential information that might be sought by those searching.

Flush bolts are used to secure the inactive half of a set of double-leaf doors. These bolts are fitted to the top and bottom of the inactive door as close as practicable to the leading edge to strengthen its resistance forced entry. The length of the bolt and the gauge of the bolt itself is key in determining the strength the bolt can withstand in an attack. Generally, the longer and wider the bolt, the more strength it has. Balance needs to be applied in fitting flush bolts to ensure the aesthetics of the architectural design of the doors is maintained. If this proves inadequate, the design of the doors may have to be revisited with the architect to design a door system that provides both security and a pleasing visual look.

Internal Doors

Depending on the application, internal doors can be as plain as a solid panel or as stylistic as architectural design glass sliding doors. Steel doors that are common features in banks can also be employed as internal doors. The room in which one of these would be hung would not hold cash or securities, but information or communications equipment carrying classified message traffic.

The main function of internal doors is to define areas that require approved access and to cause delay if a breach is attempted. Digital card readers, swipe card readers, keys, or other means of accessing these areas are the standard. More sophisticated biometric access controls can be used, but this equipment is costly and perhaps warranted for information that is classified at the highest levels of secrecy.

Entry and Exit Control

Speed Styles

Access control to an agency's building, or within areas of the building, can be controlled by *speed styles*. These are not intended as outright barriers, as would be the case with reinforced doors, but a convenient way of triage—that is, separating those with approved clearance to enter and those without. They allow large numbers of staff to enter or exit with convenience and do not slow entry or departure but facilitate control and will alarm security guards to any attempted breach, whether intentional or by error. Access is usually by electronically coded cards. By coding these cards centrally, security staff can reactivate cards without the staffer presenting the card. In practice this means that, if a person is transferred on short notice to a special project in another area, his or her access can be approved via the computerized coding system, thus allowing them their new accesses. Likewise, when they complete their posting in certain areas, their accesses can be removed, and new ones assigned. Being computerized also allows for a log to be generated, which could be used to help counterintelligence investigators in any inquiry relating to breaches.

Electronic Security Access Cards

Security access cards provide a convenient way to triage staffer movements through controlled areas of buildings, car parks, and other zones controlled by the agency. They can be electronically programmed for access, as well as to arm or disarm alarms within designated areas. The more common use is with speed styles (see description in the section above) and to provide an audit trail via the electronic log generated each time the card is used. The physical size and design of the cards can vary depending on the agency, but usually they are the size of a credit card or driver's license. For instance, they can be combined with a photographic ID and can also contain color-coded security classifications.

Technological Improvements in Access Control

The post-9/11 security environment has seen the rapid development of new technologies for screening people for access to public facilities. The first example that comes to mind is access to airports and other transport hubs. The need to triage people with a need to enter these facilities is combined with the need to identify persons of interest so that their location, movements, and associations can be used for intelligence analysis. These same technologies can also be used for defensive counterintelligence purposes—to screen those with a need-to-access a location, and hence the information or people there, and those who need to be directed elsewhere. The technologies that were in use at the time of writing included many biometrics—facial recognition, fingerprints, iris or retinal scan, voice prints, odor, and DNA.[3]

Although these technologies may give the impression that they afford an ironclad system of identification, there are some limitations and, as such, no single biometric device is able to provide 100 percent effectiveness. Some form of triangulation may be needed to ensure authentication.

When planning biometric installations, the following aspects must be considered: whether the access control is fully automated (i.e., not attended by a security guard) or semiautomated (i.e., staffed by a guard); whether the environment is friendly (e.g., the building is located in the agency's home country) or unfriendly (e.g., a hostile overseas location); and whether the subjects who are providing their biometric data are comfortable with the collections methods in relation to their societal, cultural, and religious norms, as well as the ethical standards associated with providing such biometric data, and the hygienic conditions when doing so.[4] These factors are, of course, based on the level of risk and the security level of the information being protected.

Windows

All windows should be protected by a suitable locking device. Keyed window locks provide a high level of security because an intending intruder can cut or smash the glass to reach and open any non-keyed device. Keyed locks also prevent windows from being opened for use as an exit by a successful intruder. Other window security devices include bars and grilles. These are a must for air vents, fan openings, and skylights. Reflective window tinting is another effective countermeasure. Although not intended to prevent entry, reflective tinting provides a high level of protection for staff, equipment, and processes contained within. By denying intruders knowledge of what is inside a building, an agency can increase its level of physical security. An alternative to window tinting is the use of translucent glass.

Glass-Break Detectors

These are devices that activate when glass panes are broken. These devices employ sensors, which are essentially microphones that are designed to trigger an alarm once a frequency of noise or vibration within the range emitted by the breaking of glass is detected. These devices are commonly mounted directly on the glass panes of doors and glass wall partitions. Other variants include thin strips of aluminum adhered to the outer edges of the glass panes; if the glass is broken, it cuts the circuit created by the metal foil, thus activating an alarm. Or, seismic sensors that detect the vibrations generated in the breaking of the glass may be used.

PHOTO 6.3 Computer Workstations in Full Public View. *Source*: Courtesy of a confidential source.

Curtains and Reflective Film

In situations where the contents of an agency's offices can be viewed from public areas (see Photo 6.3) or from adjacent building, the use of curtains, blinds, or reflective film should be considered. Protection from onlookers is especially important during the hours of darkness as the interior of offices are brighter than the ambient outside.

Secure Containment

Strong Rooms and Keeps

A *strong room* is an area within a building that has been constructed to hold items of value. In the business and financial world, these items can include cash, jewelry, precious metals and stones, artworks, guns, pharmaceuticals, and so on. In the world of defensive counterintelligence, it is information contained in documents and digital records that are the concern, although artifacts may fall into this consideration from time to time.

Strong rooms are also known by the terms *keeps* and *vaults*. In medieval Europe, a *keep* was a place with a castle fortress that was heavily defended. As such, these areas held the castle's food and water, as well as the armory; the reason for this was to provide an area to retreat to during sustained attack or siege, thus increasing the inhabitants' chances of survival.[5] Nevertheless, whatever the term used, their intent is the same—to protect the items placed within from unauthorized access and theft. Strong rooms differ from safes in that strong rooms are purposely built into the design of the building, whereas safes are smaller, independent storage devices that can be moved if the need arises.

TABLE 6.1 Window Glazing Types and Indicative Security Ratings

Glazing Type	Indicative Level of Security
Plate glass (also known as *monolithic glass*)	Provides negligible resistance to attack.
Wired glass	Provides a marginal improvement over plate glass, but still in the negligible range.
Laminated glass	The layers of glass that are bonded together provide some resistance to attack.
Shatter resistance film	Used to increase the level of resistance from attack for standard glass types such as plate glass and wired glass. Its effectiveness depends on the product used and how it is applied, but generally only offers a small increase in protection.
Polycarbonate	Resists attack and is a commonly used type of glazing for security.
Bullet resistant glass	This type of glass offers a very high level of resistance from attack, including resistance to ballistic attack. Categories of bullet resistant panel and elements range from 9 mm military parabellum through to rifle rounds, such as 5.56 mm and 7.62 mm, as well as shotgun rounds using full choke and single slugs.
Shielding glass	Not intended to protect from physical attack but from "attack" by an electronic eavesdropper — uses radio frequency shielding to reduce emissions that could be intercepted outside the classified area.

Safes

Safes are intended to offer varying levels of protection for documents and other classified items, for instance, classified electronic devices such as secure two-way radio equipment and secure cell telephones. Safes are generally constructed with an inner and outer casing of hardened steel plate, with the cavity between the two layers filled with steel-reinforced concrete (and other refractory materials to aid the maintenance of physical strength in intense heat). The level of protection from attack is categorized in different ways, but the level designation indicates the amount of force required to breach the safe and/or the time required to affect the breach. For instance, a safe holding a low security level may be breached with hand tools such as hammers, punches, and chisels, by hydraulic prying, or with pressure tools. A safe of a higher security level may require the use of an oxyacetylene cutting torch, a high-speed drill, a diamond-grinding wheel, or explosives. The time frames required to resist attack could range from, say, fifteen minutes to thirty minutes.

Key Control

A system of key control is essential for preventing unauthorized personnel from obtaining or duplicating keys. All existing keys and their corresponding locks should be catalogued. Keys currently issued should be signed for and they should be collected when employees terminate their employment. If a key is lost, the lock or its cylinder should be replaced. It is important not to label keys with their purpose; if necessary, use a color code. The control of keys for an agency's document containers should follow these guidelines.

Illegal Entry

If an agency discovers that its offices have been broken into, the head of counterintelligence is usually called in the first instance, as it is that person who has responsibility for the subsequent reporting and investigation.[6] The agency's policy on security will advise whether the investigation is handled within the agency or by an external law enforcement agency. In any case, notification should happen at once. It is important to secure the area and not disturb evidence that may assist the investigation. A guideline for dealing with instances where information has been compromised is outlined in chapter 8 (Defensive Counterintelligence: Information Security).

Security Lighting

A lighting system is more than just providing adequate illumination to conduct business; it acts to provide deterrence and detection. Without lighting, the countermeasures taken to establish barriers are placed under increased risk of penetration. A good lighting system should be designed to perform four essential functions:

* provide sufficient illumination to deter entry and make detection certain;
* provide redundancy in case of failure of any one of the many single light sources that might otherwise leave a dark area in the coverage area (this assumes there is an auxiliary power source for the installation being protected);
* eliminate heavily shadowed areas; and
* withstand efforts directed at its intentional destruction.

Sensor Lighting

Motion sensors can be wired into the power circuit of a lighting system to surprise intruders through immediate illumination of an area. Although the sensors are visible to intruders, the sudden illumination provided by the sensor switches can place the intruder in a position that subjects them to time pressure to react. It is in the immediacy of the reaction that errors can be made in exiting the area, and, if CCTV recording is used in conjunction with the sensor lights, there is evidence for counterintelligence investigators. Motion sensors can be switched

PHOTO 6.4 Floodlighting at a Building's Pedestrian Gate Entrance. *Source*: Courtesy of the author.

to operate either manually or automatically or switched to the off position. They are suitable for floodlighting (illumination over a large area) or spot lighting (direct light onto a specific location or item).

TABLE 6.2 **Some Positives and Negatives of Motion Sensor Light Switches**

Benefits	Drawbacks
Movement activated, thus providing surprise	Their installation is known to intruders
Can form part of a wider alarm or CCTV installation	False trigger by animals and wind-driven debris
Can save power costs as lights are only switched on when required	Require regular checking for proper operation

Closed-Circuit Television

Over the years there has been steady growth in the development of technologies relating to CCTV. The use of CCTV cameras in crime prevention is well documented in the security literature, and these cameras can now be seen in public places of all descriptions—shopping and business districts of cities and towns; train, tram, and subway systems; retail stores; public buildings; and parking lots.

Research shows that offenders understand that CCTV images can be used to identify them and can be used in the prosecution of cases before the courts. This research indicates that, if an offender understands that the visual evidence from a CCTV system will be used to identify and capture them, they perceive these systems as a credible threat, and they, thus, act as a deterrent.[7]

Because of the range of equipment available commercially and the ways that the components can be configured, it is not possible to review them here. Nevertheless, the key aspects of a good system are visual coverage; quality of the recorded images; monitoring (including remote, delayed, and real-time) and storage of the digital images; export of the images; and flexibility so that authorized third parties can easily view the images. System design should be site specific, and the degree to which the key aspects just cited are incorporated into the system will be based on the level of protection required. That is, the level will be in line with the classification of the data being protected.

Whether a CCTV system is installed inside the agency or outside, the quality and placement of the cameras and their associated components need to be considered carefully. Assume that all video images will be used as evidence in legal proceedings; therefore, the system needs to be of a high standard and installed so that positive identification can be made and recorded. Procedures for handling, copying, or duplicating the video images, and the safe storage of the tapes or disks also need to be considered as any court of law will want to be assured that others did not inadvertently alter the images. This is known as the *chain-of-evidence* or *chain-of-custody* and is an important concept in counterintelligence investigations (see appendix D).

There are several factors that influence an agency's ability to capture high-quality video images that can be used to prosecute a matter in court. First is the quality of the CCTV camera itself—it must be at the upper end of devices that are on the market. Inexpensive equipment may not be robust enough to perform to legal evidentiary standards. Images for use in a court of law need to provide recognition, detection, and movement monitoring and be of high quality.

Recognition

The camera should be installed so that it will provide an image of a suspicious person's head and shoulders. This is usually done as the person enters the restricted area. If a height marker is placed in the entrance way of the restricted area so that it too is recorded in the video frame, this will provide counterintelligence investigators with height, along with identity. The location of CCTV cameras is categorized by purpose; that is, to observe, to detect, to recognize, or to identify. Not all cameras may have the enhancement image resolution to identify, because some cameras may be needed simply to observe the pattern of entry or exit or the movements within an area, and some to provide identification.

Detection

Cameras can provide an image of the person as they move in or around a restricted area and will provide counterintelligence investigators with evidence that the person of interest was within the location of interest (e.g., a safe or filing cabinet, computer workstation, etc.). The position of the cameras in these areas should show the person's presence in the restricted area with a clear image of his or her face as a court will want to satisfy itself that it is the same person that entered the agency's restricted area. Even if these images are not used in court, counterintelligence investigators planning an offensive operation, rather than a criminal prosecution, will need to assure themselves of the same.

Monitoring

If the agency's restricted zones are large areas, such as entrance areas, lobbies, car parks, and queuing lines, cameras that cover these areas need to provide evidence of a person's movements in, out, and around. For instance, if an agency was considering CCTV for its employee car parking area, then cameras should be installed that can monitor the approach to the car park, its entrance, and the parking bays on the lot. These cameras would show vehicles as they entered and exited. Other cameras should then be placed so that they record the license plate numbers of the vehicles and, if possible, the driver's face behind the steering wheel.

TABLE 6.3 Purposes of CCTV Surveillance

Purpose	Image Size
Observe	The target person or vehicle should appear as an image at about 5 percent of the viewing height of the CCTV monitor.
Detect	The target person or vehicle should appear as an image at about 10 percent of the viewing height of the CCTV monitor.
Recognize	The target person or vehicle should appear as an image at about 50 percent of the viewing height of the CCTV monitor.
Identify	The target person or vehicle should appear as an image at about 120 percent of the viewing height of the CCTV monitor. At this resolution the image of the target should be of a quality that will permit counterintelligence investigators to identify the target individual or provide confirmatory details to the level of a vehicle's license plate number.

Image Quality

The clarity provided by CCTV cameras is as important as its mounting location. A dirty lens will distort the images. An out-of-focus lens will also produce image degradation, so maintenance is important. Ensuring the camera is not pointed into floodlights or the sun is critical to avoid the iris of the lens closing down and making the images dark and indistinguishable. Likewise, pointing the camera into dark areas without adequate lighting will produce equally poor results. A constant, yet adequate lighting source is important to image quality.

Signage

To further enhance the deterrent effect of CCTV, the agency should display signs at the entrances of restricted areas indicating that the area is under CCTV surveillance.

Placebo CCTV Cameras

If the agency has assessed the need for CCTV cameras, then it is viewed as false economy, and false utility, to install *placebo cameras* (these are also referred to as *decoy* cameras or *dummy* cameras). A view shared by security contractors is that the extra money associated with installing fully operational cameras is worth more than the marginal advantage, if any, of a decoy camera. Research shows that there may be some deterrence effect, but that it is reasonable for

PHOTO 6.5 Illustration of CCTV Surveillance Camera Signage. *Source*: Courtesy of the author.

a well-prepared intruder to differentiate between a real camera and a decoy.[8] If this happens, the deterrent effect afforded by CCTV could be lost and the agency may become an attractive target because it has less protection than what it projected.[9]

Intruder Detection Systems

Intruder alarms will not prevent the physical entry of the opposition's agent; however, installation of a system could add an exponential level of deterrence. But the focus such a system is not the protection of tangible assets, such as cash, precious metals, artworks, or goods that could easily be converted to cash, but rather the protection of information. Protection of tangible assets may require an alarm system configured differently.

By installing an intruder detection system, the intention is to achieve a level of security in line with the level of sensitivity of the information being protected, not absolute security. It should be kept in mind that the opposition's agent will gain a greater advantage by obtaining the targeted information without the agency's knowledge. It is therefore less likely that entry into an area or document storage container protected by an alarm would be attempted as it would alert the agency to the fact that sensitive information has been compromised. Nevertheless, it is possible that the opposition's agent could disguise such a penetration as a simple burglary targeting property, or even an act of vandalism, hoping to throw any subsequent investigation off the track.

Not all areas of an agency's offices must have a high level of physical security to protect their sensitive digital or documentary information. A particular office or meeting room can be designated as *the* area in which the most sensitive information is held, and other offices can retain lower-level documents used routinely. In this example, only the secure room would need to be considered for an intruder alarm system.

This same principle applies to electronic eavesdropping. An office or meeting room can be reserved for confidential discussions. Likewise, only that room would need to be fitted with an intruder detection system (and possibly sound-proof insulation). If the agency is small and on a restricted budget, such a secure room may be used for both sensitive meetings and the storage of confidential documents (but not labeled or identified confidential for obvious reasons).

Type of Detection Sensors

There are two basic types of intruder detection devices; the *passive infrared* (PIR) and the combination passive infrared and microwave (*dual technology* or DT). PIR devices are designed to detect temperature variations and, in the case of intruders, this would be from the thermal radiation emitted by their body. DT devices can detect both temperature variations and movement. Older versions of these sensors were subject to false positives because of changes in temperatures—heating and cooling. But, the DT sensors monitor temperature variations, as well as movement, through the transmission of microwaves. The microwave component operates on the Doppler principle, like radar.

To activate the alarm, both sensor elements are required to be triggered; thus, the combination acts as failsafe.

Drone Defense

Drone technology has been a boon for many industries. In the outback of Australia pastoralists use drones to check drinking water levels for sheep and cattle over hundreds of miles of grazing property. Before drones, this task could only be done by "jackaroos" in four-wheel drive vehicles. It might take days of driving and having to camp over night before the job was done. With drones, a pastoralist can program her drone to fly a specified route and return with video images of each watering hole. Then, a jackaroo can be tasked to drive the watering point that needs attention. The savings in labor and resources is enormous.

Every week the news media carry stories of new applications of how drones are being deployed for innovative tasks. But, along with these stories are those of how the same technology is being used for nefarious purposes—to steal secrets. What once could be screened or camouflaged from public view can now be laid bare to a drone's camera.

Passive and active countermeasures are available for drone defense. Screening and camouflage are still effective for airborne spying, and examples from history show this to be the case. For a discussion of this, see chapter 13, particularly the sections on decoys and camouflage.

Active countermeasures technology is developing as fast as drone technology. The crux of these technologies is an attack on the electronics that maintain and guide flight. Like warships defending themselves from incoming missiles, a ground facility can use similar technology to jam the guidance systems of drones or interfere with its internal circuits to cause it to crash. There are a number of commercial companies offering these devices and no doubt many radio engineers who are freelancing in this market for clients who want to keep a low-profile.

Although there are capture devices that operate by shooting a net at the drone to ensnare it and bring it to the ground, these have inherent issues. Chief among the problems is the device itself—the like man-portable anti-tank rocket launcher. Its mere appearance is likely to cause concern if deployed on any site other than a military base or a law enforcement facility. But, radio jamming equipment is another matter. The appearance of small radio antennas is very unlikely to raise an eyebrow yet is likely to be more effective because there is no need to have trained personnel on standby to use the net-thrower. Any staff can "flick a switch."

Computer Physical Security

Computer security is a complex issue. It is comprised of several areas of concern, from the physical security of the hardware and their installations to the way the software applications run on these systems and the way data is sent to and received from remote computers and other networks. Here, defensive

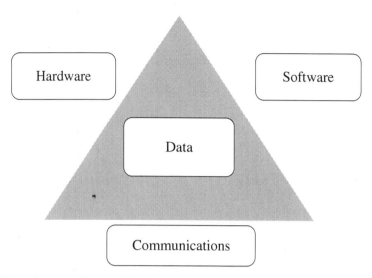

FIGURE 6.1 Computer Security's Three Main Areas of Concern—Hardware, Software, and Communications. *Source*: Courtesy of the author.

counterintelligence is concerned with making the nodes, or access points, to these electronic systems and, hence, data they hold secure from unauthorized access by the opposition. This three-sided relationship is shown diagrammatically in Figure 6.1.

As there are numerous hardware configurations based on a wide range of manufacturer models and industry standards, it is not possible to canvass these in detail here. Nonetheless, it is possible to talk in general terms about the essential countermeasures that will provide high levels of computer physical security. Here is what could be argued to be the top eleven countermeasures:

1. Lock the computer base unit to the workstation or, if it is a server, lock the server room. This applies to the most important network devices such as the switches, hubs, and routers, as well as the modems, gateways, and firewalls. The cases for many desktop computers come with quick-release fasteners to aid technicians making repairs, but these will also allow quick access to the computer hard disk drive by unauthorized persons. Cases should be locked closed.

2. Mount all computer and communications devices within the server room in racks. This adds an additional layer of security, especially if the cabinets are themselves locked and the devices mounted in the racks are bolted to the frames rather than fastened with quick-release hardware.

3. Require a log-in for desktop computer terminals and log entry into and exit from server rooms. If the computer terminal is in a public location like a reception area, require card access or biometric log-on, in addition to password protection. Position computer monitor screens in a way to prevent viewing from windows, doorways, or glass partitions, as well as by any nonauthorized persons in, say, a reception or waiting area.

4. Install CCTV surveillance in the server room so that it digitally records images of all who enter and leave, in addition to their movements within the room.

5. Disable computers that are not in use. Equip computers that must remain in open areas, sometimes out of view of employees, with smartcard or biometric readers so that it is more difficult for unauthorized persons to log on.

6. To limit the possibility of staff copying data to removable media such as CDs, DVDs, or USB drives, disable these drives and ports. There are commercial products that will physically disable these drives and ports and there are software solutions to do the same.

7. Portable computers, such as notebooks and netbooks, present concerns, as these devices are taken away from the security of an agency's buildings where, under the tenet of defense-in-depth (tenet 10 of defensive counterintelligence), physical security is high, and into the field where hostile threats exist. For instance, the portable computer can be stolen along with all the data it holds. If the computer is programmed for agency network access, these data will be stolen also. Therefore, the hard disk drive needs to be protected with a high level of encryption so that access would require years to decrypt the partitions, the operating, programs, and data. This is known as *full disk encryption*. Handheld devices need secure storage in safes when not in use. They present the same problems as portable computers and more as they can be inadvertently left by the user in, say, a café, bar, or restaurant.

8. Allow only trusted and qualified technical personnel to service or make modifications to a computer system.

9. Conduct electronic countermeasure sweeps at irregular intervals for "bugs" or wiretaps.

10. Shield cables leaving the server room in metal conduit to prevent electromagnetic radiation, which could be intercepted, and to deter illegal tapping.

11. When disposing of old hard disk drives, use a commercial disk cleaning software package that writes zeros over the entire disk surface. This will leave the disk usable, but no data will be recoverable. If the aim is to destroy the disk, then, after using a software cleaner, drill four holes (e.g., at twelve o'clock, three o'clock, six o'clock, and nine o'clock) through the unit so that each hole punctures the magnetic platter (Photo 6.6).

Finally, the security measures that an intelligence unit adopts to protect its computer systems should not be discussed with anyone outside of the agency. It is acceptable, however, to acknowledge that measures to combat espionage and sabotage are in place, but the specific techniques and procedures should never be confirmed.

Video Display Units

To a large extent, flat screen technology has eliminated the problem that once existed with cathode ray tube (CRT) computer monitors. That is, the older video display units (VDUs) were prone to image *burn-in*. This phenomenon became evident when images of the data being displayed were electronically

PHOTO 6.6 Physical Destruction of a Hard Disk Drive. *Source*: Courtesy of the author.

etched into the phosphor on the inside of the unit's screen during use. There-fore, these older VDUs needed to be inspected for signs of burn-in prior to disposal, resale, or transfer to other more open areas of an agency's office, such as a reception area. If an agency still uses CRT monitors, sound security advice would be to immediately replace these with flat screen technology.

Guarding Services

General Considerations

A *security guard* is usually a person employed to provide protection services for people, property, and valuables. They are sometimes called *security officers*, but, whatever the term used, they should not be confused with *bodyguards*, who are employed specifically to protect a person from direct violence. Although secu-rity guards may have as part of their duty statement the protection of people, such function is usually discharged by alerting them to the need to evacuate in case of fire, providing first aid, or observing and reporting to a law enforcement agency threats posed by people acting criminally.

Guards are usually in uniform and can be hired by the agency itself or by a third party that provides the guards' service to the agency under contract. Their presence is, in the main, to provide deterrence. They also provide compliance with policy, practice, and procedures by detecting breaches and reporting. More importantly, they should act to help educate agency employees by providing polite and helpful instruction about how best to adhere to the agency's security policies.

Although a security guard's function is to observe and report breaches to police, security guards in many jurisdictions that have a legal framework based on common law can make arrests under the doctrine of what is known as a citizen's arrest. Moreover, some jurisdictions have passed legislation that grants all citizens the power of arrest.[10] In some jurisdictions, security officers can be deputized as sheriff's officers or special constables (or other functional titles) to act as agents for law enforcement agencies. This is usually done in a limited capacity within the building's precinct, including the grounds immediately adjacent to the building (i.e., land owned or controlled by the agency).

Security guards prevent breaches to a large degree by their presence. They provide observation via static observation, as well as patrols inside and outside of the agency's buildings. The advantages of guard service are many, but the chief reason is that it places a rational person at a site of high vulnerability or risk who can assess, and respond appropriately to, a particular situation.

Sensitive Compartmented Information Facility

A sensitive compartmented information facility (SCIF, pronounced *skiff*) is an area, or a room, or an installation where sensitive information can be stored, used, discussed, or processed. A SCIF can be a permanent working area or a temporary working space (see Photo 6.7). In either case, the specifications, its construction, those who can access the area, and the procedures for its operation are set out in directives, policy, or technical manuals.

From a counterintelligence point of view, one of the key aspects of its construction, as well as its access, is the attenuation to sound and electromagnetic radiation from the work area. The SCIF is essentially a safe-haven where

PHOTO 6.7 President Barack Obama is Pictured in a Temporary SCIF that was Setup in a Rio de Janeiro, Brazil, Hotel Room. It shows the president being briefed on the revolution in Libya, March 20, 2011. Chief of Staff Bill Daley is pictured on the left and National Security Advisor Tom Donilon is on the right. *Source*: Courtesy of the Executive Office of the President of the United States.

classified work is carried out, so the facility, whether permanent or temporary, needs to be proofed against the inadvertent overhearing by unauthorized persons. The techniques for acoustical protection and sound masking can be simple or elaborate and will vary with each installation. The important consideration is that the acoustical countermeasures are in line with the risk assessment for the users and the level of information being used.[11]

Safe Houses

A safe house is a building that is controlled by the agency. It offers agents and intelligence officers a secure place to meet and stay that is out of harm's way by the opposition. Recall the second underpinning of the theory of counterintelligence—the *proposition of data collection*—which states that the opposition will use various means to collect data on an agency's operations. The safe house is therefore a means for providing a venue that hides operatives and the meetings they have, including pre- and post-covert operational activities.

Safe houses have been used throughout history—from biblical times to the present—to protect participants who were involved in secret operations. Take, for instance, the hiding of the late dictator of Iraq, Saddam Hussein. He was harbored in various safe houses while Coalition Forces searched for him. Finally, he was located on December 13, 2003, hiding in a secret underground "spider hole" (i.e., a one-man, foxhole-like hide) at a farmhouse in the village of Ad-Dawr, which is near Tikrit, Iraq.

At first thought, a spider hole may seem to have been an odd place to consider as a safe house because it employed none of the physical security measures discussed in this chapter—fortified doors, locks, barbed wire, CCTV, and others. But it is the absence of these obvious security treatments that makes a safe house safe. That is, the theory of safe houses is that, if the facility blends in with its surrounds and calls no attention to itself, then it is unlikely that anyone viewing the facility will notice it. *Hide in plain sight* is a phrase often used to describe this technique. The key determinant for a facility to be considered a safe house is secrecy.

Although secrecy may seem an easy requirement to meet, in practice it is not. For instance, if a safe house is being established for the first time, then there will be people who will wonder what the facility is being used for. For example, real estate sales or rental agents will be asking what the buyer or renter has in mind for the property. And, this is only the beginning. Think of all the utility companies that will need to be contacted to organize light, power, water, and gas. With each contact come questions and the production of identification, and so forth. Each contact raises the risk of a breach of secrecy. Accordingly, a well-developed cover story is essential. If the agency has a large budget, safe house establishment and maintenance can be done by dedicated staff whose job is to plan and carry out these counterintelligence support operations.

Sometimes commercial businesses are used as cover for safe house activities. Take, for example, a business that owns a warehouse; this facility could be used to store equipment as the comings and goings of trucks and personnel would look no different from normal trade or commerce. A private bed and breakfast (B&B) could be used as a safe house as "guests" come and go regularly. Operatives could use the B&B as a place to conduct meetings or as a staging point for pre- or post-operations, and so forth because no other guests would be using the B&B; its sole function is to serve the agency's field operatives.

Still, maintaining secrecy of a safe house, even if a commercial cover is established, is also difficult as operatives may be followed to the safe house or the safe house may come under surveillance. As such, consideration needs to be given to countermeasures, which would include policies and procedures for dealing with suspected cases of surveillance and guard against the inadvertent drawing of attention to the safe house. Once the safe house's cover is "blown," it is a time-consuming and expensive task to decommission it and establish a new venue.

Crime Prevention through Environmental Design

Crime prevention through environmental design (abbreviated as CPTED and pronounced *sep-ted*) is the application of architectural design and space management concepts to prevent crime. In this regard the CPTED concept has application to the work of counterintelligence. Although crime prevention theory incorporates other strategies, counterintelligence officers could gain much from studying CPTED principles and practices.

CPTED was coined by criminologist Dr. C. Ray Jeffery in 1971 in his book *Crime Prevention Through Environmental Design*.[12] The purpose of CPTED is to attempt to influence a person's behavior prior to committing an act. Specifically, it looks at prevention of the commission of a criminal act, but, in the case of counterintelligence, this would be the unauthorized disclosure of sensitive information or related disloyal or treasonous acts (which may also be a crime). The basis of CPTED strategies is that it increases the risk of the perpetrator being detected and apprehended. Deterrence is one of the principles of counterintelligence theory, so it can be seen why the application of CPTED is so apt.

There are three overlapping strategies involved in CPTED and these comprise natural access control, natural surveillance, and territorial reinforcement. Although these topics will not be covered in this book, it is worthwhile to briefly examine one of these as a means of demonstrating CPTED's application to defensive counterintelligence. Take, for instance, natural access control. According to the late criminologist Timothy D. Crowe, natural access control includes designs that control movement by directing it in certain ways or restricting it: "Create one-way in and out to promote the perception of potential entrapment for abnormal users of space."[13]

There are complementary strategies for crime prevention that include social crime prevention, situational crime prevention, and community crime prevention and these are worth examining in cursory fashion as a way of rounding off this review of CPTED.

Social Crime Prevention

These are strategies that are aimed at addressing the causes of crime and the dispositions of individuals to offend and engage:

- family-based interventions;
- training and education;
- youth work; and
- employment opportunities.

Situational Crime Prevention

Situational crime prevention includes strategies that focus on the design and management of the physical environment to reduce the opportunities presented for crime and to increase the likelihood of detection.

1. Security measures that remove the opportunity to commit an offense and/or make it more difficult to commit an offense by
   - target hardening;
   - removing the target; or
   - removing the means of committing an offense.
2. Strategies that reduce the incentive for a person to offend while increasing the chances of detection by
   - permanently marking property;
   - formal/informal surveillance; and
   - natural surveillance.

Community Crime Prevention

These are strategies that combine both social and situational crime prevention measures and are aimed at influencing behaviors in order to reverse "decline" in the physical environment in order to increase the capacity of the community (which may include residents and potential offenders) to exert a greater degree of control over this environment and their lives. These strategies may include

- housing policies and
- community development projects and services.

Review of Key Words and Phrases

The key words and phrases associated with this chapter are listed below. Demonstrate your understanding of each by writing a short definition or explanation in one or two sentences.

access cards	floodlighting
chain of custody	flush bolt
CPTED	glass-break detector
dual technology sensors	hide in plain sight

lock picking

no-go zone

passive infrared sensors

perimeter beam

security guard

SCIF

speed style

vaults

Study Questions

1. Describe two goals that perimeter fencing achieves.
2. Describe two situations where glass-break detectors could be used to improve security.
3. Explain why a counterintelligence security officer might consider a dual technology sensor over an infrared sensor.
4. List the four purposes of CCTV surveillance and describe the image size required to facilitate each.

Learning Activity

In the context of your current office environment, take stock of the physical security measures afforded to desktop computers in your immediate area. Then, using the list of the eleven physical security countermeasures (see above), rank the level of security. Do this by drawing up a table with the eleven countermeasures represented in rows. In a column, note whether the countermeasure is complied with, or not. If the countermeasure is not complied with, list in another adjacent column your recommendation as to how best the countermeasure could be achieved and include at the end an estimated cost for implementation. In a fourth column, estimate the costs that would be incurred if the data contained on the desktop computer were "compromised" by not having the countermeasure. That is, what would the estimated value of the information be in the hands of the opposition, or what "damage" could it cause if it was released to the public domain or another metric of "loss"? The object of the learning activity is to demonstrate the value of security by looking at one aspect. This exercise can be conducted for the other defensive counterintelligence countermeasures—barriers, doors, and window treatments, along with others.

Notes

[1] Janet Fitch, *White Oleander* (New York: Little Brown and Co, 1999), 198.

[2] Commonwealth of Australia, *Protective Security Manual* (Canberra: Commonwealth Government Printer, 2005), i.

[3] Anil Jain, Ruud Bolle, and Sharath Pankanti, "Introduction to Biometrics," in Anil Jain, Ruud Bolle, and Sharath Pankanti (ed.), *Biometrics: Personal Identification in a Networked Society* (Norwell, MA: Kluwer Academic, 2002), 16–17.

[4] Jain, Bolle, and Pankani, "Introduction to Biometrics," 16–17.

[5] See, for example, Roger Stalley, *Early Medieval Architecture* (Oxford: Oxford University Press, 1999), 86–91.

[6] Toilets and other out-of-the-way places within an agency's building, whether in a security area or not, should be checked at the end of the day's business for intruders who may be hiding there to launch their attack.

[7] Brandon Welsh and David Farrington, "Public Area CCTV and Crime Prevention: An Update Systematic Review and Meta-Analysis," *Justice Quarterly* 26, no. 4 (December 2009): 716–45.

[8] Ronald V. Clarke and David Weisburd, "Diffusion of Crime Control Benefits: Observations on the Reverse of Displacement," in Ronald V. Clarke (ed.), *Crime Prevention Studies, Volume 2* (Monsey, NY: Criminal Justice Press, 1994), 165–83.

[9] Placebo, decoy, or dummy cameras are intended to give the impression that the area is under surveillance when it is not. As such, some lawyers have argued that the installation of these cameras could create a civil liability. That is, it could create a risk in cases where a person is attacked, hurt, or injured in what would have been the view of the camera had it been operational. Here, a plaintiff could contend that he or she had a reasonable expectation that security would have responded to help. For instance, see Ron Lander, "Cheap Trick: Are Fake Video Cameras Inexpensive Solutions or Lawsuits Waiting to Happen?" *Campus Safety Journal* 10, no. 9 (2002): 16–17.

[10] See note 13 in "chapter 4" for a discussion of this power but note that this is an academic discussion and should not be construed as legal advice.

[11] See, for instance, Director of Central Intelligence, *Directive Number 6/9, Physical Security Standards for Sensitive Compartmented Information Facilities* (Washington, DC: CIA, November 18, 2002).

[12] C. Ray Jeffrey, *Crime Prevention Through Environmental Design*, 2nd ed. (Beverly Hills, CA: Sage, 1977).

[13] Timothy D. Crowe, *Crime Prevention Through Environmental Design*, 2nd ed. (Boston: Butterworth-Heinemann, 2000), 55.

Chapter 7

Defensive Counterintelligence: Personnel Security

History has shown that one of the greatest openings for the opposition to infiltrate an agency and acquire its secrets is through trusted staff. There are two groups of people who fall into this category: those who set out to penetrate the agency from the beginning by trying to get hired and then compromise security, and those who are "turned" at some stage in their careers and then steal classified data.

In the former group are the likes of the Soviet spies Kim Philby, Donald Maclean, Guy Burgess, and Anthony Blunt. In the latter group are those spies who turn against their country for money—Aldrich Ames and Robert Hanssen—or other reasons. The purpose of personnel security is therefore to determine whether a person can be trusted with secrets, or to carry out secret operations and remain loyal in maintaining those secrets. The policies, practices, and procedures discussed in this chapter are in line with the defensive tenets of counterintelligence; particularly, tenet 4 (need to be there), tenet 5 (need-to-know), and tenet 10 (defense-in-depth).

Central Pillar of Personnel Security

The central pillar regarding personnel security is this: Ensure that the staff who work for the agency do not inadvertently disclose secrets, intentionally reveal classified information, or (in extreme circumstances) use that information in violent action against the agency's facilities, processes, or personnel. Take, for instance, the case in July 2011 where a police official used his position of trust and insider knowledge to assassinate Ahmed Wali Karzai, the politically influential half-brother of Afghanistan's President Hamid Karzai, thereby undermining the country's slow progress to democratic rule.[1]

Intentionally revealed information is different from whistleblowing—what is at concern here is the notion of selling secrets for personal gain, or trading secrets for ideological reasons. So, personnel security is not about control per se, but about the management of personnel who generate or use information to support or make decisions. It is about the prevention of poor hiring practices—practices that could lead to the employment of unethical people who may disclose confidential information—and the frustration of any attempt at penetration by an opposition agent.

Types of Harmful Disclosure

The amount of information that one has access to at work is quite sizable. And, every business enterprise has vast amounts of information—whether they are private sector businesses, non-government organizations, or government agencies. Even individuals hold secrets—about their bank details, the money they earn, what they buy, where they go, who they know, what their health is like, what their interests are, and many matters. In most cases these details are benign, but, in the hands of the opposition, these data can be used to devastating advantage.

. . . .

Ask me about my vow of silence. — bumper sticker

. . . .

Hiring Practices

Positions that require security-cleared personnel are those that generate, use, or handle classified data. Take, for example, intelligence analysts: they generate classified reports and use classified information in the process—so they need security clearances. Managers and policy- and decision-makers use classified reports—so they too need security clearances. The list is long but suffice to say that anyone with access to classified data requires a clearance (including janitorial staff, as technically they too have access to data, even if it is indirect through being in the same room as intelligence analysts who are using that data).

Positions that require security classification can be in the military or government service, the private sector, or even those held by individuals who work on contract to any of these agencies. Recall the typology of counterintelligence discussed in chapter 2—national security, military, law enforcement, business, and private. All these employment sectors are environments of security-cleared personnel.

Screening Personnel

The personnel screening process should start at the application stage with the applicant completing a personal history statement (sometimes abbreviated as PHS). The reasoning behind this is to provide counterintelligence screening staff with enough information to verify that the person is who they claim and has the necessary personal integrity to maintain confidences. In addition to the applicant's full name, current residential and business address, and date and place of birth, the PHS can include such sub-histories as

- residential history;
- educational history;
- marital history;
- citizenship history;
- employment history;
- military history;
- financial and credit history; and
- criminal history.

Other details that might be addressed include membership in organizations, and character, professional, and credit references. (See appendix A for an example of a personal history statement.)

When staff review the applicant's personal history statement, they are looking for any inconsistencies, discrepancies, or unaccountable periods of several months or more. If discovered, these should be verified. Even though an applicant may pass this initial screening process, once he or she is hired a probationary period should be set as a contingency for their possible dismissal should there be evidence of them being a security risk. Similarly, when an employee is promoted or assigned to sensitive duties, a screening procedure should be conducted. This screening process should cover the time elapsed from his or her initial hiring to the present. This is to ascertain if any factors during the promotee's recent past could place in jeopardy the confidentiality of the information he or she will be handling.

Nondisclosure Agreement

A standard means of safeguarding sensitive information is by drawing up a nondisclosure agreement. Sometimes these are also termed *secrecy agreements*. These agreements are intended to create a psychological impression on employees, reinforcing the importance of protecting information with which they have been entrusted. These agreements are in effect legal contracts and can be used as evidence in legal proceedings if an employee is found to be in violation of it (see appendix B for an example of a nondisclosure agreement). Nondisclosure agreements should be considered for temporary clerical staff, contract cleaners, indoor plant gardeners, and the like.

. . . .

The U.S. *Intelligence Identities Protection Act, 1982,* makes it a felony for people who have, or have had, access to classified information to reveal the identity of covert intelligence agents.[2]

. . . .

Background Investigations

A background investigation is the gold standard for security clearances. They are conducted to establish an applicant's identity and their ability to reliably hold confidential information that if revealed could adversely affect the agency or the state. The background investigation helps determine who the person is and if there are mature, responsible, tolerant, honest, and loyal. Background investigation look for four factors that are captured in the acronym MICE. MICE is shorthand for the four motivations that influence people betray secrets—money, ideology, compromise (i.e., the person has been compromised/blackmailed), and ego.

The background investigation involves counterintelligence investigators systematically checking the details of the personal history statement and/or a questionnaire, and then contacting former associates, employers, and other individuals listed by the applicant. It needs to be borne in mind that, by and large, people who apply for security-classified positions are honest, law-abiding citizens. These people are fellow citizens who pay taxes, live decent lives, and are worthy of the agency's respect in every way. The background investigation therefore needs to be carried out in the most ethical and respectful manner.

Some applicants, however, have issues or have committed infractions that will preclude them from selection. In conducting a background investigation, the counterintelligence investigator is looking not a singular infraction or an isolated lapse of judgment to "catch a person out," but at a combination of factors that present a clear picture that the person is likely to be unstable—that is, not trustworthy and disloyal. This is a distinction that has not always been made well—"Careers of loyal officers have been destroyed on the basis of suspicion versus facts, assumptions versus proof."[3]

Errors in judgment were evident in the ultra-conspiratorial era when James Angleton headed counterintelligence staff at CIA. It is a fact of tradecraft that the supply of disinformation by the opposition is kept vague so that the recipient can interpret it in several ways—like a horoscope that can be read to imply what the reader wants. That is because disinformation is designed to cripple the recipient's intelligence operations. Opposition forces provide leads that produce suspicions that paralyze—for instance, good officers who as now treated as if they were compromised. "You [only] find out when old colleagues start turning the papers face down on their desks while they're talking to you, not taking any phone calls when you're in the office, pretending not to see you in the corridor, and shying away from you in the men's room."[4] If judgment is not exercised, counterintelligence can become a liability rather than an asset.[5]

Some factors that are considered as part of the MICE approach include personal stressors—martial and family issues, financial difficulties, embarrassing behaviors, or conflict in the workplace (vindictiveness). Other reasons might include simple curiosity or a challenge of wits. Greed is a recurrent theme in cases of betrayal. Then, there psychological reasons such as paranoia, narcissistic personality, having a persecution complex, or the need for gratification (impulsiveness) or attention (self-image), as well as other conditions.

Security Vetting Levels

As an *indicative guide*, below in bullet points are four levels of vetting. These levels and their corresponding classification designators may differ from agency to agency and from country to country. Nevertheless, the point being illustrated is that with each level of vetting a more rigorous investigation is carried out. This is in line with the level of risk posed by the unauthorized disclosure of information. A detailed discussion of security classification levels appears in chapter 8 (Defensive Counterintelligence: Information Security). But, to understand the vetting process, these four levels, taken from the Australian security context, stand as examples.

- *Baseline Security Vetting*—this involves inquiries that will ensure that applicants are who they claim to be, live where they state on the application, and are not working illegally or committing any other form of deception. This level of vetting is considered suitable for accessing sensitive information at Protected (or Confidential) level.
- *Negative Vetting Level 1*—this involves several inquiries that are discussed in the following sections. The number or type of inquires will differ by agency but generally this level of vetting is suitable for information classified at Protected (or Confidential) and Secret.
- *Negative Vetting Level 2*—this level is likely to be as per negative vetting level 1 but may involve inquiries that go back further in time, for instance, ten years rather than five for level 1. As such, it is suitable for personnel needing access to Protected (or Confidential), Secret, and Top Secret information.
- *Positive Vetting*—as this level permits access to the most sensitive types of information, including caveated and code word data, this level of vetting usually requires a more "aggressive" form of inquiry that may include psychological testing, as well as other intrusive inquiries.

Scope of the Investigation

In general, the scope of a background investigation covers the past ten years or until the person was age eighteen, whichever is less. Access to top secret or code word data may require an investigation beyond ten years depending on the agency and country. The length of time that counterintelligence investigators go back is determined by the risk associated with each clearance category—it is proportional. That is, the harm that could be caused by unauthorized release of top secret data is greater than that of secret, so the added expense of probing beyond ten years' background information may be warranted.

National Agency Check

A common check of personnel is that of a national agency check. Counterintelligence investigators may routinely check the applicant's record with police agencies on a state/province level, as well as the national police authority. The reasoning behind this is that the applicant may have lived in other jurisdictions and had adverse details reported against him or her. They may have simply visited other areas of the nation and encountered trouble while there. This is common where the applicant is involved in frequent interstate travel with a former employer.

Personal Interview

The purpose of the personal interview is to allow the applicant to clarify issues in their personal history statement or the questionnaire, if a counterintelligence investigator cannot resolve or reconcile a response with other data. It is also an opportunity for counterintelligence investigators to probe areas of possible inconsistencies that are not overt but hold the potential for hiding or telling half-truths (i.e., education qualifications).

The personal interview is not a "fishing trip" where the investigator asks a stream of questions trying to "catch-out" the applicant. The interview is designed to help the vetting process, not bring it into disrepute by trying to embarrass the applicant. The personal interview is not a modern-day version of King Henry VII's Star Chamber,[6] nor should the investigator present in the persona of Fyodor Dostoevsky's the Grand Inquisitor in his novel *The Brothers Karamazov*.[7]

Birth

The applicant's place and date of birth need to be independently verified as a basis for establishing the individual's identity. This is done by obtaining an original or certified copy of a birth certificate. Such certificates are issued under seal by an office or bureau of vital statistics or a registrar of births for a particular jurisdiction.

This is one of the more important aspects of verifying a person's identity. At one time, false documents were commonly referred to as simply *fake IDs*, and the act of passing-off oneself as another character was known as *paper tripping*.[8] But, at the time of this writing this has become known as *identity theft*. Despite the evolution of the term, make no mistake—these documents remain fake IDs.[9]

It is very easy for criminals to obtain our personal information and our identities. Everything from low-tech to high-tech is readily available. It seems that not a day goes by without hearing about another news story on identity theft.[10]

Citizenship

Verification of citizenship is an important aspect of the personnel security process. This is done for both legal reasons and ideological reasons. Anticipating the worst, if the person subject to the vetting process at some stage in the future discloses information in an unauthorized manner, then having jurisdiction to detain, question, and prosecute the person is an important aspect of the tenets of defensive counterintelligence (tenet 15).

From an ideological point of view, if the person is a citizen of the country hiring him or her, then they may be required to take an oath or swear or affirm allegiance (usually under a specific statute). As strange as it may seem, some people will refuse to provide such an undertaking, thus bringing to a head a potential security issue. It is simple, but effective. The applicant's immediate family members should be verified also. Immediate family members are usually those living with the applicant or who the applicant has care and control over. For instance, these people may include a wife, husband, or partner, children, and parents or other relatives living with the applicant.

If the applicant has a foreign-born family member in this category, then their citizenship needs to be verified also. The rationale is simple: if the applicant discloses confidential information to these unauthorized people, then counterintelligence investigators will want to interview them and subject them to the legal procedure of the jurisdiction as they would with the applicant. If they are foreign born, then it is doubly important that they are vetted, as their country of birth may be hostile to the agency or the agency's country and have placed pressure on these individuals to obtain information from the applicant via their family ties. This is, of course, country specific—some countries are openly hostile to others; some have strained relationships; and others are close friends and allies. So, the country context needs to be considered when considering this factor. It may or may not be an issue of paramount importance.

Educational History

Arguably, this is one of the most falsified areas of a personal history statement. Issues arise when applicants either overstate their academic qualification or fabricate outright the qualifications they hold. There is also the issue involving people who purchase qualifications that appear for all intents and purposes as the ones required by the hiring agency but are issued by non-accredited educational intuitions. Non-accredited colleges and universities that offer these parchments for sale have been described as "diploma mills," and the credentials they issue are bluntly termed "fake degrees" and "worthless degrees."[11]

For instance, if a position within an agency requires the applicant to hold a Bachelor of Arts degree, but the applicant left university in her last semester before graduating, she cannot claim to hold this degree. If she falsely claims this, it raises several related issues: she may not beyond falsely providing other information; she may have a low threshold to other forms of deceit; and her low standard of ethics may apply to other areas of her life—both professional and personal, with the latter potentially impacting, in turn, her professional life (e.g., a gambling addiction that may drive her to sell classified information).

Accordingly, counterintelligence investigators need to verify these details. The most important to verify are those qualifications required for the position, or the highest degree/diploma attained. If the applicant's education or trade qualifications were attained outside of the scope of the period required for the security clearance sought, then the applicant's highest degree or diploma beyond high school is usually the only one verified. For instance, if an applicant claims to have attained a Master of Arts degree and this can be confirmed, then there is little point in confirming that they hold a high school diploma, which may have been issued fifteen or twenty years prior.

Employment History

A person's employment history is a telling source of the applicant's on-the-job performance when it comes to issues of security and confidentiality. Telephone interviews with past supervisors and/or co-workers can help verify whether the applicant is able to maintain confidences relating to sensitive work matters. They are also able to verify that the applicant has not been dismissed for inappropriate disclosure of information or issues that are relevant to a security clearance.

Counterintelligence investigators need to be cognizant that poor work reports by former supervisors may be the result of professional jealousies or animosities that have no bearing on the security clearance process. Very bright and highly capable people often get less capably colleagues offside. This is a fact of work life but should not color the applicant's vetting report as such motivations can be mischievous. Verification of the past two years of employment history is a usual standard and periods of unemployment that exceed sixty days should be verified.

Military History

In the same vein as an applicant's employment history, their military service dates should be verified from records searches or via the registrar. The most important issue here is the type of discharge awarded to the applicant for their service, as it may be a factor in assessing their trustworthiness.

Personal References

These are different from the references who are asked to provide comments on the applicant's ability to perform the tasks associated with the job they applied for. Whether the applicant can perform the job and to what standard is outside the scope of a security clearance. Counterintelligence investigators are tasked security-related issues only. So, regarding personal references, these are people who know the applicant personally and can speak about his or her ethical behavior.

Neighbors

A check of the applicant's neighbors is akin to a personal reference check, except that neighbors are likely to be acquaintances through the neighborhood they share rather than social friends, though this can vary, and they may be both. Interviews with neighbors can confirm any adverse behaviors that may not show up through outer checks—for instance, acts of personal violence, criminal activity, and the like. In the case where the applicant has not been at an address for long enough to contact neighbors (in the case of frequent movers or apartment dwellers), contact with landlords should be considered. However, some caution needs to be exercised with neighbor checks.

Because a person cannot select who lives next to them, personal disagreements are common. As such, the counterintelligence investigator should consider with care any adverse information as it may be wrongful or designed to "get even" with the applicant due to some falling-out over a minor residential issue.

Foreign Contacts and Activities

For some security-sensitive positions it is necessary to assess the applicant's foreign contacts. It is important to identify personal or business contacts in foreign lands who may have the potential to pressure the applicant to compromise classified information. Consideration of issues such as the frequency, intensity, and means of contact (e.g., in person, telephonic, or electronic) will help this assessment process.

Likewise, the applicant's foreign activities may be another indicator of their state of mind and the way they may act in guarding classified information. But just because a person may travel regularly to a place that is at the time seen as hostile to the agency's country does not mean that they are a risk. For instance, there are places in the Middle East, North Africa, and Southeast Asia that could be considered hostile to one country or another. If the applicant has a spouse who enjoys archaeology as a hobby, they may travel to these countries regularly. In such a case, counterintelligence training, rather than eliminating the individual from the employment selection process, may be all that is required.

Financial and Credit History

Verification of an applicant's financial and credit histories is a sound way of establishing grounds for a stable fiscal footing. Research shows that people who are chronically in debt, spend big, or are unable to maintain a budget often find themselves in financial jeopardy. Such a position could pose a risk to the granting of a security clearance. This is because having financial troubles, whether because of spending beyond one's means, gambling, or other compulsions, may place the applicant in temptation's way to sell information as a way solving their problem.

This is a generalization and each case needs to be assessed on the facts, but it is a view shared in many security circles and based on experience as well as research findings. Therefore, asset ownership, income, and liabilities need to be estimated to see if the picture being presented by the applicant is accurate. One way of doing this is using an analysis of net worth.

Net worth is a calculation of the difference between the applicant's assets and liabilities. If the counterintelligence investigator conducts the net worth analysis over a period, say, for the end of each financial year, he or she can compile a picture as to whether the target is growing in worth or is experiencing losses and what the magnitude of these gains or losses might be.

The step-by-step formula for calculating net worth is as follows:[12]

1. Assets—liabilities = net worth;
2. Net worth—prior year's net worth = increase or decrease in net worth;
3. Net worth increase (or decrease) + living expenses = income;
4. Income—funds in known sources = funds from potentially illegal sources

Association History

It is unlikely that any applicant with any intellect would admit on their personal history statement membership in a group that has intent to overthrow his or her government through force or violence. Or, that they now support, or have in the past supported, organizations that have this as one of their goals.

Nonetheless, the counterintelligence investigator should put these questions to the applicant directly at interview or via a questionnaire. Untruthful answers lay grounds for dismissal and/or legal proceedings if detected later, as well as provide leads for further questioning if information from any other sources reveals contrary indicators. Public records and other open-source information are an important source of such information.

Search of Public Records and Open-Source Information

Open-source data is a valuable source of information that can complement the various history checks and interviews mentioned in the above sections. This may be in the form of publicly available records as well as social media.

Government records that show adverse data such as bankruptcy records and civil court judgments are examples. But, as pointed out in chapter 1, the Internet is an information-rich environment where people post personal information many years before they realize the gravity of revealing so much personal information. Once posted, it is sometimes impossible to remove.

There are a host of technical reasons for this and that discussion is beyond the scope of this book, but suffice to say that if a counterintelligence investigator searches the Internet, he or she may find information that suggests the applicant may have been involved in subversive activities at one time contrary to the assertions made on the current application.

Social Networking

In sociology and anthropology, a *social network* is a social structure that comprises a relationship between individuals and/or groups. These relationships can be based on any number of factors including kinship, friendship, shared interests (or dislikes), political affiliations, business arrangements, and so on. Likewise, networks can also be associated with a set of objects or events.[13]

Although social scientists use the study of social networks to explore practical and theoretical questions relating to their discipline, counterintelligence investigators can exploit social networking via website services to complement their investigative sources of data. These Internet-based facilities allow people to meet and maintain contact based on the factors cited by sociologists—kinship, friendship, shared interests, political affiliations, and many others. A report on the social networking service *Facebook* claimed that the much debated[14] "six degrees of separation"[15] between any two people on the globe was, in November 2011, 4.74 using this social networking service.[16]

It is no surprise then that employers use these services as information-rich sources of intelligence—abbreviated as SOCMINT, for *social media intelligence*. For instance, an Australian study found that more than a quarter of

Australian employers used social networking sites to screen job candidates "with almost half of these employers admitting to turning away prospects based on something they've seen on *Facebook* or *Twitter*."[17]

The issue of having personal data freely available online is a problem for security-cleared personnel who should be "keeping a low profile" to avoid contact, however remote, with the opposition. For instance, the issues that a staffer must consider regarding physical and personal information and communications security are weighty. However, these issues are almost cast aside when that person places personal information about themselves on the Internet for others to read (regardless of what "privacy controls" are in place to limit viewing of these data).

From the point of view of the counterintelligence investigator who is vetting a potential applicant, these data can be invaluable. However, online social networking services can be a security worry once the person is granted clearance, as their use becomes a potential weakness in an agency's overall defense. As an example, take the applicant who applies for a position in a covert unit as an operative who will go undercover. But, before joining the agency, that person was a member of a social networking service and posted many facts and comments about herself as well as her photographs at various events. At the time, these were all considered harmless but, now that she is applying for a covert assignment, these data are accessible to society's "global outlaws" and can be used against her and her agency. Recall the case of the chief of Britain's secret intelligence service, MI6, Sir (Robert) John Sawers, who had his personal details along with a few photographs publicly displayed on his wife's *Facebook* page.[18]

When writing blogs, tweets, memoirs, and so on, the questions that an officer or operative needs to ask themselves are the following: What does this information reveal? If I came into possession of these data regarding an opposition operative, what would it tell me, and how could I exploit it? The answer seems obvious; any disclosure can be potentially harmful. Avoiding social media is a wise consideration. So too would be not permitting friends and relatives to post details about you, or uploading photographs of you to social media platforms.

Facial Recognition

If it seems a remote possibility that the opposition will obtain an individual's personal information on the Internet and then make the connection to, say, a covert operative, then consider the following. According to research being conducted at the time of this writing, "outlaws" are using facial recognition to identify undercover operatives. According to research there is anecdotal evidence that indicates outlaw motorcycle gangs have attended police graduations in a specific Australian state. The purpose was to take photographs of the graduating officers because in years to come some of these officers may become undercover operatives.[19] These outlaws purportedly used commercially available facial recognition software to scan the images of the people they photographed (or download from social networking web services) and match these with people who they suspect as being a threat (i.e., potential undercover operatives).

If this is the case, then it is not unreasonable to suggest that other global outlaws may mimic this tactic and photograph, say, the graduates of the world's military academies (e.g., West Point, Annapolis, Duntroon, Sandhurst, etc.) and use the same method to identify clandestine operatives. If this comes about, such a graduate, who is later recruited into a covert unit of an intelligence agency, may find it impossible to explain his or her military service when they turn up at their nation's embassy in some troubled part of the world under diplomatic cover. In such a case the opposition would have a photograph of them graduating from their nation's military academy a few years before, with an unexplained absence from the profession they purport to represent in the interim years.[20]

This technique need not be limited to just graduates of military academies. Any potential pool of personnel can be photographed, because concealable digital cameras make the job so much more efficient. The list of potential data collection sites for images of people's faces is very long—airport and seaport immigration queues, entrances to government buildings or research laboratories, and the list goes on (consider the wealth of photographic data contained in college and university yearbooks as a start).

Although this is an issue for an agency's defensive counterintelligence program, it is also a gold mine of rich information for the agency's offensive counterintelligence program. Because, what can be done to an intelligence agency, that agency can and should return in kind.

Polygraph Examination

Using a polygraph to determine truth is far from an established science.[21] Though the principles are based in science, the human mind is subject to many variables that the polygraph cannot control for—the spectrum of human emotions and sentimentalities. Because these feelings differ from person to person, and vary in intensity, the polygraph cannot establish with a high enough degree of certainty, *truth*.

The polygraph (or *lie detector*) is an instrument that records physiological changes to a person's blood pressure, pulse, respiration, and skin conductivity while questions are put to them. The theory is that telling a lie will cause a person to register changes to one or more of these vital signs, indicating deception manifested by the anxiety or fear felt. But, human physiology being the complex subject that it is, an instrument that registers vital signs cannot account for physiological reactions that are not unique to deception. Nor can it completely account for techniques used by hostile agents who have been schooled in biofeedback methods that reduce anxiety, or the taking of certain types of tranquilizers to defeat or distort the examination's results.

To overcome these issues, the instrument relies on the polygraph's training and skill.[22] Like all technical occupations, these skills vary from operator to operator. Though some agencies have used the polygraph for decades, and consequently have well-trained operators, other agencies are not endowed with such talent.

PHOTO 7.1 Polygraph Interrogation. *Source:* Courtesy of the Federal Bureau of Investigation.

These problems have seen KGB moles like Aldrich Ames pass not only one polygraph session, but two interrogations. Conversely, they have been many reported false-positives that resulted in people who have not violated[23]their secrecy oaths, that "deception [was] indicated."[24] Nevertheless, "a lack of evidence supporting the scientific validity of polygraph testing does not invalidate the polygraph as a security-screening device."[25] Though, even with the best trained operators, the error rate is unlikely to reach zero. This underscores the need to obtain corroborating evidence in cases where the polygraph *indicates* information concealment. Still, the polygraph remains "the best [mass] security-screening device available."[26]

What Should Not Be Considered Adverse

There are two situations that present themselves as issues that should be approached by a counterintelligence investigator with balanced judgment. The first issue is about a person's financial problems and the second involve psychological issues.

Noticing changes in staff behavior may be not only good management, but good counterintelligence practice too. Changes in a person's mood or actions may be an indicator of deeper personal turmoil. If, say, a staffer has become more and more argumentative and his or her discussions with colleagues increasingly heated over time, it may mean more attention needs to be paid to find out why this could be happening. Take for instance the case of the *WikiLeaks* informant, Private First-Class Bradley Manning. Now known as Chelsea Manning, she was convicted by court martial in 2013 for violations of the U.S. *Espionage Act*. Media reports allege that she was suffering from psychological stress before her leaking of some 750,000 classified documents.[27]

The excessive use of alcohol has been identified as one such indicator. This could potentially give rise to temptation or attraction to compromise information in a misguided attempt to solve personal issues (take, for instance, the case of Aldrich Ames who was reported to have had a drinking problem[28]). It is not to say that a personal issue or a drinking problem is cause by itself to not grant or revoke a security clearance, but it does mean that a closer examination is warranted. History has shown that such issues have led, directly or indirectly, to staff disclosing classified information as a way of exacting revenge against the agency, or to bail them out of financial difficulty, or any number of other justifications for these problems (real or imagined).

Getting a person to talk to a counselor who is part of the agency's employee assistance program is a good start to help resolve the problem before it harms the individual or the agency. Such steps are no longer considered in an adverse manner but are the healthy exercise of good judgment, as they seek to maintain a sound state of mind, as well to keep-up work performance. Just because a staffer seeks psychological counseling is not grounds per se for suspicion—it is a sensible move to get life back to normal. By contrast, not seeking counseling may be an indicator that things could get worse.

The same applies to financial difficulties. If a staffer seeks financial counseling or help with debt management, it is a healthy sign that the person is now taking control of their life and trying to manage their way-out of difficulty. Growing debt may give rise to the temptation to, possibly, sell classified information as a way of clearing the debt. But to be upfront and seek help is an honest way of dealing with an embarrassing issue. Recall that a personal situation like this is analogous to the thousands of companies that go into liquidation or bankruptcy each year because management did not seek financial assistance early enough or did not try to manage out of it through denial.

Key Security Obligations of Employees
Fraternization
Interacting with foreign nationals is part of modern-day life. Many of an agency's citizens may even be married or in long-term relationships with people born abroad. This is not usually a problem unless an opponent uses this relationship to exploit the agency's employee.

In the context of fraternization, what is meant is that a single employee should be conscious that an opponent may take advantage of a person's desire for human contact while living far from home, family, and friends by placing before that person an agent in the disguise of a "companion." The term *honeypot* is often used in intelligence parlance to describe this trap.

The case of U.S. Marine Clayton Lonetree is an example of how an opponent can construct a situation where what appears to be a genuinely warm and caring relationship develops, but it is instead an elaborate plot to obtain classified information.[29] USMC Sergeant Lonetree was convicted and sentenced to a thirty-year prison sentence (later reduced to fifteen years but released after nine years) for spying. He was reported to have fallen in love with a Soviet intelligence officer while posted to the U.S. Embassy in Moscow in the early 1980s.[30] This love affair was the groundwork for later blackmail and the revelation of secrets to a foreign intelligence service. Therefore, there is often a "no fraternization" policy in place to guard against these traps.

Although honeypots are clearly applicable to national security and military counterintelligence situations that have been made notable in spy fiction,[31] they can apply in other contexts too. For instance, there have been media reports where law enforcement officers have had romantic relationships with organized criminals and this relationship placed pressure on the officer to provide information and warnings about operations targeting the group.

Contact Reporting

Agencies should have a policy that requires personnel to report any contacts with opposition personnel services for several important purposes. First, it facilitates the dissemination of the content of the contact—whether it was a personal encounter or a conversation via electronic or telephonic means. The person, what position they hold in the opposition agency, what was discussed, the way it was discussed, and future arrangements to follow up on any issue rise, and so on can be vital insights for intelligence analysts who blend these data with many other pieces of information to answer strategic and tactical research questions.

The second aspect of reporting contact is from a counterintelligence point of view. To the counterintelligence investigator the details of the contact, as well as the method and timing of the contact, may provide insight into a larger campaign to penetrate the agency. It could tie together other contacts with other agency personnel over time and at different locations.

Protecting Conversations

If the theoretical precept that every piece of correspondence and every record produced by the agency holds some intelligence value for the opposition, then this precept can be extended to conversations. Therefore, if personnel discuss sensitive matters in public where others can overhear or carry out conversations on a telephone that is not secured through electronic encryption or have conversations in rooms that are not proofed against technical eavesdropping, then it should be assumed that such conversations are under surveillance.

At first glance this may seem a dramatic conclusion, but the fact is that, unless a technical countermeasures sweep is conducted, or a team of countersurveillance operatives are employed, there is no assurance that these conversations are not being surveilled. Any other view is simply wishful thinking. The point to be made is that personnel need to be cautious in any situation that does not carry the assurance that the area is secure.

Surveillance Detection

Physical surveillance is both an art and a science, and the methods for conducting surveillance could fill several book volumes. Therefore, it is meaningless to try and outline every possible type of method that may be employed against personnel of an agency. Suffice to say that surveillance is the following—or *shadowing*—of a person of interest. The general object of surveillance is to obtain details of the person's movements, the times they shifted location, and places they visited. It also includes the people met (or encountered along the way) and things performed or done while in motion or as an event.

The ability to detect surveillance is, like surveillance itself; art and science. It requires some level of formal study and training given the fact that surveillance is more than merely following a few steps behind someone. It is therefore unlikely that an untrained person could notice surveillance. Nevertheless, there are some circumstances where a person may notice a vehicle or person and take further notice, giving rise to a suspicion that they are being watched. If the staffer suspects, or has evidence of, being the target of surveillance, agency policy should advise that they report this to counterintelligence investigators immediately.

Recognizing Physical Surveillance

Physical surveillance is the observation of people and places. There are many purposes for physical surveillance; some of these include obtaining information that may be difficult or impossible to obtain by any other method, confirming information at hand, developing leads, and establishing links between various people and between people and places. The information gleaned from such observations has inherent value. In addition, this raw information can be used to form the groundwork for more elaborate and extensive plans for information gathering.

All employees should be cognizant of the possibility of physical surveillance of their offices and themselves by opposition personnel. Being aware that something is out of place is an excellent way of recognizing surveillance. It is, however, difficult to define "out of place." Persons loitering in halls, lobbies, or stairways, suspicious visitors, frequent passersby, and so forth should always be noted. If, after consideration, such activity is sufficiently suspicious, the agency's countersurveillance plan for notification should be followed. Employees should also be alert to the possibility of surveillance from the street, adjacent buildings, parked motor vehicles, and areas where employees park their cars.

Agency vehicles themselves should be visually examined occasionally for any signs of "marking" by opposition agents. Identifying marks such as broken taillights, removed lightbulbs, or pieces of reflective tape can permit an agent to distinguish a vehicle in traffic and therefore aid the agent in following the vehicle's movements. Of higher sophistication and much less visible are mobile transmitters. These devices are usually attached to the underside of a car and can be located by *careful* visual inspection (see appendix C for a list of indicative analog electronic surveillance devices).

Rapid Developed Friendships

During normal social interaction, a person may have dozens of personal contacts each day with many people—family members, colleagues, retailers, bus, and taxi drivers, restaurant waitstaff, and people they meet in bars and coffeehouses, to mention just a few examples. From a counterintelligence point of view these contacts are not of interest. There is, however, a class of contacts that are of interest to counterintelligence investigators, and the contact as well as the nature and contact of the conversation are of interest.

The type of contact that is of concern is where the encounter leads to a rapid development of friendship. This is because the person may be trying to position themselves so that they can use their newly formed relationship to obtain classified information. Those who are not schooled in this technique may ridicule it as paranoid, but the literature on espionage penetrations is replete with examples of how this method is used, and with great success.[32] Policy should be to advise counterintelligence investigators if a befriending person has made suggestive or leading statements that could be a prelude to coaxing, coercing, bribing, or blackmailing the staffer into compromising classified data. Recall Mae West's famous advice: "Keep a diary and someday it'll keep you."[33]

Unwitting Agent

It is not an unreasonable proposition to assume that an opposition is continually on the lookout for spies. Agents might be willing to sell secrets; others may be blackmailed in to do so. These people do it knowingly. One of the more insidious forms of spy is the *unwitting agent*; "that is, he is inveigled into loose talk or braggadocio and lets secrets out of the bag."[34] Such people provide either the platform for providing the opposition with a means of dissemination false information (e.g., journalist and online media outlets) or supplying them with information without realizing it.

Technical Countermeasure Sweeps

One response to the reported suspicion of surveillance may be to recommend that a technical countermeasure sweep of the staffer's house, apartment, and/or vehicle be conducted. Security engineers then use both physical inspection of the premises/vehicle and electronic equipment to detect and neutralize listening and tracking devices—or *bugs*.

Husbands, Wives, and Partners

Although staffer's spouses, whether married or in a de facto relationship, are assumed to be close and loyal to that person, they are not employees of the agencies and are not security cleared. Therefore, agency policy should remind staff that they are not to share classified information with these people.

The policy should draw to staff's attention that this is a potential source for leaks—even though inadvertent—but it also places these people at potential personal peril if they hold classified information in their heads. They become potential targets for exploitation, compromise, bribery, and blackmail, just like any security-cleared employee but without the protection that the employee has.

Personal Privacy Plan

Like surveillance and countersurveillance, personal security is somewhat of an art as well as a science. Unlike a building that can be observed, and its vulnerabilities analyzed so that the risks can be treated, people have far more dimensions to them and the lives they lead. Accordingly, to adequately cover the topic of personal security, it may take a sizable manual to address each concern and the different settings. For instance, there are texts that cover dignitary protection (close personal protection).[35]

So, from a general perspective, if there was only one simple staff policy regarding the establishment and maintenance of personal protection, it would be to keep a low personal profile. Having a low profile, by definition, lowers your risk to many hazards—violent individual and groups, and opposition agents seeking you for exploitation. Former CIA official, Patrick Collins, who planned personal protection programs for high-risk personnel working overseas, offered this advice on how to achieve a low profile: "Profile reduction is achieved by avoiding the public limelight. Basically, this means you should do nothing to incite undue interest in your name, personality, or position."[36] Simple advice, but effective.

How this translates into actions is a complex matter because the ways people give away information inadvertently are so numerous. Opt-in and opt-out e-mail lists are just one example. If one does not tick the correct box, or untick it depending on the case, you could grant permission to the service to not only share your e-mail address with others unknown, but also let these services access data on your device or desktop computer. With even provision of some small bit of personal information you provide others is another avenue by which the opposition can gather information about you. Like a ghost, the goal of a personal privacy plan is to become invisible.[37]

Practices to Guard Against

Infiltration

A well-known espionage technique for penetrating an agency is *infiltration*. Basically, there are four infiltration methods—telephone, mail or e-mail, in person, and indirectly.

A *pretext* offers an agent a plausible, common-sense technique for obtaining confidential information. A pretext is any act of deception—ruse, subterfuge, ploy, trick, or disguise—that allows an agent to solicit information by a false reason. This includes entering premises for obtaining information or being in a place (or a country) to which the agent wouldn't otherwise have access or permission. In espionage the term used for this type of infiltration is *cover*—for instance, official cover or non-official cover.

. . . .

The art of using pretexts is a science and should be approached as one.[38]

. . . .

Pretext should not be confused with the term *social engineering*, which has gained popularity in recent years. Social engineering is a slang term that commonly refers to an individual act of manipulation (usually for fraudulent purposes) to gain access to IT systems. This is vastly different from its true meaning, which is large-scale societal planning. The use of the term *social engineering* in this context is incorrect. The technique is nothing more than a ruse, subterfuge, or pretext. In fact, *pretext* is the term most used by private investigators, who rely heavily on this technique as a means of gaining information about their targets.[39]

Telephone

This method is used by operatives, usually on a one-time basis, to obtain general information about an aspect of the agency's affairs. It is the safest and most innocuous type of infiltration to perpetrate. This type of infiltration is carried out by simply telephoning the target agency, using a pretext, and attempting to extract as much information as possible. Several calls could be made over time. On the surface, individual calls would appear to be unrelated, but each is designed to obtain specific pieces of information. Depending on the pretext and the number of pretext calls made, the depth of information an operative could gather might be limited and confined to general details. However, if the target agency has acute security awareness, especially about unknown persons, the information should be limited to general information that one could obtain on a public website. If the agency is suspicious, a staffer may try to identify a telephone caller by requesting the caller's telephone number and then verifying it by using an online telephone directory before calling the operative back (known as *confirmation by callback*).

Mail and E-mail

This is another form of low-grade infiltration. Again, using a pretext, the operative will write to a target agency requesting information. Security-aware targets will look for the warning signs of a mail infiltration, such as the use of post-office boxes, business name "fronts," and out-of-state addresses. As for e-mail, free web-based e-mail accounts can raise the target's suspicions because these are usually non-verifiable accounts.

In Person

Direct personal infiltration of the target may follow pretext contacts by telephone, mail/e-mail infiltration, and physical surveillance. In this way, operatives can gather enough information to establish a credible cover for a direct penetration or acquaint themselves with the information needed to recruit an agent (i.e., a proxy) to carry out the task.[40]

Indirectly

This infiltration method is complex to organize and run but can yield high-grade results. Fundamentally, an operative creates a covert business or organization that is designed to draw in the target agency or a member of the target's staff. The bogus business is controlled by the operative. These covert enterprises can be as simple as a trade newsletter or as elaborate as a fully operational business. Once established, the operative uses this cover to gather the information required in his or her information collection plan. An example of this is the advertising of positions in a new and very attractive-sounding business. The business may offer a salary and fringe benefits package more than those offered in the market to entice the target. Once the target's *curriculum vitae* is received, it is analyzed for the desired information. If it does not disclose the information sought, additional information will be requested from the target applicant and/or a personal interview conducted. The operative, or someone from the bogus organization, would then "pump" the target for information.

Review of Key Words and Phrases

The key words and phrases associated with this chapter are listed below. Demonstrate your understanding of each by writing a short definition or explanation in one or two sentences.

background investigation	net worth analysis
bugs	nondisclosure agreement
confirmation by callback	paper tripping
honey pot	personal history statement
infiltration	pretext
low personal profile	shadowing

Study Questions

1. Explain the central pillar of personnel security.
2. Describe the types of harmful disclosures that might be involved for a staffer who is working in (select one): (a) national security; (b) military intelligence; (c) law enforcement; (d) business; or (e) private security.
3. Explain why the types of information items in a personal history statement are important in checking the trustworthiness of a potential employee.
4. Other than personal, psychological, and financial issues, discuss what types of situations may not be adverse counterintelligence indicators per se, and why.

Learning Activity

Using *yourself* as a case study, apply the four-step formula for determining a person's net worth to your current finances. Was this difficult? What did you find out as a result? What do you think others could find out if they performed this?

Notes

[1] Alissa J. Rubin and Scott Shane, "Assassination in Afghanistan Creates a Void," *New York Times*, July 13, 2011, A1, New York edition. See also news reports of how other inadequate vetting processes allowed insurgents to infiltrate the Afghan National Army. These infiltrators then launched armed attacks against members of the International Security Assistance Force. For example, in late-2011, several Australian soldiers were killed, and others wounded in several of these attacks (Jeremy Kelly, "Rogue Afghan Soldier Sought for Murder," *The Advertiser*, Adelaide, Australia November 28, 2011, 11).

[2] Jennifer K. Elsea, *Intelligence Identities Protect Act* (Washington, DC: Congressional Research Service, 2013).

[3] Mahle, *Denial and Deception*, 134.

[4] Anonymous cited in Martin, *Wilderness of Mirrors*, 197.

[5] Martin, *Wilderness of Mirrors*, 211.

[6] Theodore F. T. Plucknett, *A Concise History of the Common Law*, 5th ed. (Boston: Little, Brown, 1956), 181–83.

[7] Fyodor Dostoevsky with David McDuff, trans., *The Brothers Karamazov: A Novel in Four Parts and an Epilogue* (London: Penguin Classics, 2003).

[8] Barry Reid, *The Paper Trip II: For a New You through New ID*, 1980 ed. (Fountain Valley, CA: Eden Press, 1977). This was formerly entitled *The New Paper Trip*. This book was succeeded by Barry Reid, *The Paper Trip III: A Master Guide to a New Identity* (Fountain Valley, CA: Eden Press, 1998) and *The Paper Trip 4: The Ultimate Guide to New Identity since 9/11* (Fountain Valley, CA: Eden Press, 2014).

[9] For example, in espionage a fake passport, often the basis for establishing one's identity, is known as a "boot" (or a "shoe") and the forger goes by the term "cobbler." These expressions are said to have been derived from secret Soviet operations in Europe in the 1930s. See, William E. Duff, *A Time for Spies: Theodore Stephanovich Mally and the Era of the Great Illegals* (Nashville, TN: Vanderbilt University Press, 1999), 70. These terms are still used today in fiction—see, for example, Martin Roberts, *A Terrorist or Patriot* (Lincoln, NE: Writers Club Press, 2002), 52.

[10] Martin T. Biegelman, *Identity Theft Handbook: Detection, Prevention, and Security* (Hoboken, NJ: Wiley, 2009), 3.

[11] Lester S. Rosen, *The Safe Hiring Manual: The Complete Guide to Keeping Criminals, Imposters and Terrorists Out of the Workplace* (Tempe, AZ: Facts on Demand Press, 2006).

[12] Leigh Edwards Somers, *Economic Crimes: Investigating Principles and Techniques* (New York: Clark Boardman Company, 1984), 99.

[13] David Knoke and James H. Kuklinski, *Network Analysis* (Newbury Park, CA: Sage, 1982).

[14] Judith Kleinfeld, "The Small World Problem," *Society* 39, no. 2 (2002): 61–66. Thomas Blass, *The Man Who Shocked the World: The Life and Legacy of Stanley Milgram* (Cambridge, MA: Basic, 2004).

[15] Jeffrey Travers and Stanley Milgram, "An Experimental Study of the Small World Problem," *Sociometry* 32, no. 4 (December 1969): 425–43.

[16] John Markoff and Somini Sengupta, "Separating You and Me? 4.74 Degrees," *New York Times*, November 22, 2011, B1, New York edition.

[17] Darren Kane, "Aussies Urged to Consider their Cyber CVs as Bosses Head Online," www.telstra.com.au/abouttelstra/media-centre/announcements/aussies-urged-to-consider-their-cybe

r-cvs-as-bosses-head-online.xml#Links (accessed December 1, 2001). Darren Kane is officer of Internet trust and safety and director of corporate security and investigations with Telstra Corporation Ltd, Australia.

18 Lyall, "On Facebook, a Spy Revealed."

19 Nickolus O'Brien and Michael Keelty, "Crime Prevention, Social Networking and Covert Operations," in S. Sim (ed.), *Building Resilient Societies, Forging Global Partnerships* (National Crime Prevention Council: Singapore, 2012), 149–59.

20 Nickolas "Nick" O'Brien and Michael "Mick" Keelty, personal communication, October 18, 2011.

21 John F. Sullivan, *Gatekeeper: Memoirs of a CIA: Polygraph Examiner* (Washington, DC: Potomac Books, 2007).

22 Donald Krapohl and Pamela Shaw, *Fundamentals of Polygraph Practice* (Cambridge, MA: Academic Press, 2015).

23 Richard D. White, Jr., "Ask Me No Questions, Tell Me No Lies: Examining the Uses and Misuses of the Polygraph," *Public Personnel Management* 30, no. 4 (2001): 483–93.

24 Sullivan, *Gatekeeper*, 9.

25 Sullivan, *Gatekeeper*, 9.

26 Sullivan, *Gatekeeper*, 9.

27 As an example, see the CBS News report, dated February 2, 2011, "Specialist Advised Not to Deploy Bradley Manning," www.cbsnews.com/stories/2011/02/02/politics/washington-post/main7309852.shtml (accessed November 24, 2011). See also Fowler, *The Most Dangerous Man in the World*, 130–31.

28 David Wise, *Nightmover*, 87.

29 Rodney Barker, *Dancing with the Devil: Sex, Espionage, and the US Marines: The Clayton Lonetree Story* (New York: Simon & Schuster, 1996).

30 William Hoffman, *The Court-Martial of Clayton Lonetree* (New York: Henry Holt, 1989).

31 In Ian Fleming's book, *From Russia, with Love* (London: Jonathan Cape, 1957), the fictional Soviet counterintelligence agency SMERSH, used Tatiana Romanova as a honeypot to lure James Bond into a death trap.

32 See, for instance, Alex Caine, *Befriend and Betray: Infiltrating the Hells Angels, Banditos and Other Criminal Brotherhoods* (New York: Thomas Dunne Books, 2009).

33 This witticism (circa 1937) seems to have been popularized by West but attributed to the British-American socialite, Emilie "Lillie" Charlotte Langtry (Lady de Bathe) in a 1922 *Boston Globe* (short filler piece), titled, "Keep a Diary," A23, Column 7, September 24, 1925. The article reads in full: "Mrs Langtry—Lady de Bathe—was congratulated at an Anglo-American dinner party in London on the success of her book of memoirs. 'Luckily,' she said, 'I have always kept a very full diary.' And then turned to a pretty Chicago girl and added: 'Keep a diary, my dear, and some day perhaps your diary will keep you.'—*Minneapolis Tribune*."

34 Turner, *Secrecy and Democracy*, 61.

35 These texts are just a sample of what is available: Paul Elhanan, *Keep 'Em Alive: The Bodyguard's Trade* (Boulder CO: Paladin Press, 1985); Kevin Horak, *The New Bodyguard: A Practical Guide to Close Protection Industry* (Shropshire, UK: Clearwater Publishing, 2007); Richard Kobetz, ed., *Providing Executive Protection* (Berryville, VA: Executive Protection Institute, 1991); Benny Mares, *Executive Protection: A Professional's Guide to Bodyguarding* (Boulder CO: Paladin Press, 1994); Burt Rapp, *Bodyguarding: A Complete Manual* (Boulder CO: Paladin Press, 1988); Leroy Thompson, *Dead Client's Don't Pay: The Bodyguard's Manual* (Boulder CO: Paladin Press, 1984).

36 Patrick Collins, *Living in Troubled Lands: The Complete Guide to Personal Protection Abroad* (Boulder, CO: Paladin Press, 1981), 46. The book was later released by the same publisher but under a slightly different title—*Living in Troubled Lands: Beating the Terrorist Threat Overseas*, 1991.

37 J. J. Luna, *How to be Invisible: The Essential Guide to Protecting Your Privacy, Your Assets, and Your Life* (New York: Thomas Dunne Books, 2004).

38 Greg Hauser, *Pretext Manual* (Austin, TX: Thomas Investigative, 1994), 5.

39 M. Harry, *The Muckraker's Manual: How to Do Your Own Investigative Reporting* (Mason, MI: Loompanics Unlimited, 1980), 73–78. Hauser, *Pretext Manual*.

40 See, for example, "cover for action" in Valerie Plame Wilson, *Fair Game*, 160.

Chapter 8

Defensive Counterintelligence: Information Security

In 2014, the Russian political activist and anti-corruption campaigner, Vladimir L. Ashurkov, fled to safety in London. At that time, he was being pursued by Russian authorities for allegedly committing fraud. But, the chargers seem to have been suspiciously concocted given that they related to Ashurkov's management of election campaign funds for an anti-Putin Moscow mayoral candidate.

Although Ashurkov must have felt relieved to be offered political asylum in Britain, he was not safe. As private investigators collect information in civil cases, so too appear operatives of the Russian Federation's intelligence services to have been gathering information about Mr. Ashurkov, his associates, and his thinking; no doubt what he was saying about the political situation in Putin's Russia. Because, six months later, he is reported to have been advised by a friend who had traveled back to Russia that while there, the friend was questioned by security officials about a private conversation Ashurkov had had with the friend in a London café.[1] This case in one of innumerable examples of the need for information security.

Information Security Defined

The term *information security* refers to three pillars that underpin this security approach. These pillars are: *confidentiality*, *integrity*, and *availability*. The term is often used interchangeably in the subject literature with the related term *computer security*. However, this practice of interchangeable terms is not correct. This is because information security focuses on data in all its manifestations: books, journals, reports, photographs, and other images, electronically stored data, and otherwise.[2] Compare this to computer security that focuses on digital systems—mainframes, workstations, servers, notebooks, netbooks, tablets, and handheld devices, whether they are connected to a network or not.

The first pillar, confidentiality, is concerned with the prevention of unauthorized disclosure. The second pillar, integrity, is concerned with being able to detect when information is modified. And, the third pillar, availability, is concerned with ensuring that the data can be accessed by those with a need-to-know when required (which, if you recall, is shared with tenet 5 of defensive counterintelligence in chapter 4). These three pillars are enshrined in legislation in the United States under the *Federal Information Security Management Act of 2002*[3] and are reflected in protocols and standards throughout the security industry generally.

Classifying Information

The first step in protecting information is to assess the impact if it were disclosed to a third party, whether this is the opposition or the public. If the answer is that disclosure could cause harm, then it needs to be *classified*.

Classification is both a process and the outcome of that process. For instance, a staffer can evaluate a piece of information to determine whether it needs protecting under a classification scheme, and the designation assigned the information at the end of the evaluation is the outcome—the information is now classified.

Under tenet 1 of defensive counterintelligence (see chapter 4), the agency head has responsibility for security in all its forms. So, although the agency head would not normally be involved in the activity of classifying information, it is his or her responsibility to ensure that this occurs. In most instances, this responsibility would be assigned to personnel within the agency. In the context of counterintelligence, information refers to data that is recorded in hardcopy documents or on files stored on electronic media (e.g., hard disk drives on a desktop or in portable computers, as well as agency servers). It also refers to knowledge—for instance, *conversations* or *understanding* derived from synthesizing information in a cognitive process.

The reasoning behind the classification of information is to be able to make these data available to personnel who have a need-to-know. Generally, it is in everyone's interest not to hoard information, but to share it. As the saying goes, "information is power." So, it makes sense to use the power of these data to support the agency and its clients in achieving their goals. This is an important issue and is integrally tied to the *need-to-share* principle, as well as the *responsibility-to-provide* principle. Yet, unapproved access to files has been at the center of leaks by the likes of Soviet-era double agents (e.g., Kim Philby[4]), and in more recent times, what could be argued as *unwitting* foreign agents who have leaked classified material.

Finally, under tenet 1 of defensive counterintelligence, it is the agency's chief officer who has responsibility for ensuring that all staff are security trained. This training includes instruction in how the information classification system works as well as the theory that underpins these practices.

. . . .

Sub Rosa

Like romance, intelligence has a long history of secrets, hence the shared symbolism in the rose. "In secret; privately; confidentially.

[Latin, 'under the rose,' from the practice of hanging a rose over a meeting as a symbol of secrecy, from the legend that Cupid once gave Harpocrates, the god of silence, a rose to make him keep secrets of Venus.][5]

* *

Types of Data Requiring Protection

To foil possible attempts by the opposition to penetrate an agency, information about it and its activities should be assigned classifications of sensitivity. This is defensive tenet 13 (delineate and prioritize) of defensive counterintelligence. These classifications are then used to guide access and dissemination. Information in this context means data that requires protection from unauthorized disclosure. By way of example, below is a list of data items from the business sector that require some level of protection through a classification scheme.

* Production plans;
* Production methods;
* Production schedules;
* Product releases and schedule;
* Marketing strategies;
* Advertising campaign details;
* Customer/client lists;
* Trading terms and agreements;
* Details of alliances with other businesses;
* Proposed mergers;
* Policy directives;
* Rationalization plans;
* Sales projections;
* Material costs;
* Supply sources;
* Tenders;
* Research initiatives;
* Research and development funding;
* Technical discoveries;
* Personnel (their numbers, positions, salary packages, and expertise); and
* Employee recruitment, promotions, transfers, and dismissal details.

Equivalents of these and other data items would exist in the areas of national security, the military, and law enforcement. Moreover, parallels exist in private affairs; take the controversial Hillary Clinton e-mails of 2015. Former Secretary of State, Mrs. Clinton used her family's private e-mail server to send and receive for State Department e-mails instead of using the secure State Department server. The e-mails comprised about 100 that were classified when they were transmitted, and over 2,000 that were later classified by the State Department.[6]

Five Basic Classification Levels

Arguably, there are five levels of data classification. The lowest classification of information consists of information of a general and unrestricted nature. The type of information provided in company prospectuses is a good example of this. Such information would be suitable for all general inquiries and posting to a website.

In line with the lowest level of unclassified but not quite making the next classification level is a level that recognizes that there is some degree of sensitivity associated with the data. These pieces of information might be useful to the opposition or its client.

The next highest classification consists of information that should be available to customers only upon request. Information of this type is best described as information and/or material that, if disclosed to an adversary, could reasonably be expected to cause some degree of harm to the agency or its client.

Moving up the scale again is the second highest level of information classification. This information should be available to an agency's most important customers. Information with this designation would be information and/or material that, if disclosed inappropriately, could reasonably be expected to cause "serious harm" to the agency or its client.

. . . .

Sensitive but Unclassified is a security designation used by U.S. federal government agencies. It is used to denote information that does not warrant a classification that restricts access, but nonetheless requires consideration as to how that information is distributed and to whom.

. . . .

Finally, the most sensitive information should be available only to staff with a need-to-know and government departments that have appropriate authority (i.e., a right-to-know). Information of this type, if disclosed to the opposition, would reasonably be expected to cause "exceptionally grave harm" to the agency or its client. (In a business setting, this classification might mean that the company's bottom line could suffer an impact of five percentage points or more.)

The description typology for classified information may vary from country to country as well as between sectors—for instance, the government sector or military may use different descriptors than those used in business or the private sector. There may also be additional classification levels with varying descriptors. As an example, the City of New York uses the following descriptors to identify its data: public, sensitive, private, and confidential,[7] whereas in government and the military the descriptors of unclassified, sensitive but unclassified, restricted, confidential, secret, and top secret are likely to be used (refer to Table 8.1).

In the post-9/11 security environment, a set of universal-sectoral descriptors comprising white, green, amber, and red have been coined. These are information classification descriptors that are based on the easy-to-understand and nontechnical traffic light concept, and hence are referred to simply as the

TABLE 8.1 **Summary of Information Classification Descriptors**

Classification Levels	
Top Secret	Information of this type, if disclosed to the opposition, would reasonably be expected to cause "exceptionally grave harm" to the agency or its client.
Secret	Information and/or material that, if disclosed inappropriately, could reasonably be expected to cause "serious harm" to the agency or its client
Restricted (or Protected or Confidential)	Information and/or material that, if disclosed to an adversary, could reasonably be expected to cause some degree of harm to the agency or its client.
Sensitive but Unclassified	Information that might be useful to the opposition or its client.
Unclassified	Information provided in company prospectuses is a good example. Such information would be suitable for all general inquiries and posting to a website.

traffic light protocol. The protocol was developed by the Group of Eight countries (G8—comprising the world's eight largest economies—Canada, France, Germany, Italy, Japan, Russia, United Kingdom, and the United States) because these nations recognized the need-to-share information between the government and military sectors and the private and business sectors.[8] It is understood that dozens of other countries have since adopted this protocol for the sharing of information. Unlike a national security classification that is based on the notion of damage or harm, the traffic light protocol focuses on the concept of who may receive the information (i.e., in line with the need-to-share doctrine).

TABLE 8.2 **Traffic Light Protocol Descriptors**

Traffic Light Protocol	
Red	Very limited distribution—for example, intended for a person or a group of people named as recipients
Amber	Information for limited distribution for people with a need to know
Green	Information for general distribution to people that have some connected involvement with the topic discussed in the information, but not for posting to the Internet or display on websites
White	For unrestricted distribution to anyone with an interest in the information

Code Names

Classified research projects, as well as secret operations, use code names. The reason for this is because a code name offers a way of referring to the project or operation without referring to the actual details involved. This provides a level of secrecy. For instance, during the Second World War, the code name *Operation Torch* was a more convenient way to refer to the plans for the Anglo-American invasion of French North Africa.[9] But the operation code name did not hint at what it might be. Anyone who may have encountered the code name would have to solve the mystery surrounding the name.

> It soon became apparent that none of the group understood what material deserved which code word or what the rules were for handling documents with different code words. I suspected that the only people who understood the rules were the secretaries who took out the rubber stamps and decided how to mark up the documents—at least, I hope they understood.[10]

Projects and operations are usually given single words to identify them. Compare this to training exercises that are given a code name of two words, or a short phrase (e.g., the biennial Australian-American military exercise that is held in Queensland is *Exercise Talisman Saber*). This is not always the case; for example, *Operation Enduring Freedom* was the code name for the U.S.-led invasion of Afghanistan in 2001. Project code names follow the same rationale, for example, Project Manhattan, the code name for the building of the first atomic bomb.

Code names are also used in business counterintelligence for the same reasons. Take for example the well-known code name used by Microsoft Corporation for its first release of the *Windows 10* operation system—*Threshold*. Some businesses may have a doctrine that prohibits the use of the code name outside the company and might go as far as to require employees and contractors to sign nondisclosure agreements.

> Declassification can be as important as classifying information. Declassification is the removal of the original security restrictions so that the data can be made more widely available. This process can be automatic under legal authority, say, after thirty years; or systematic as a regular practice within the agency; or mandatory under a specific application from an interested party to the information. Declassification can also take place via an application under a freedom of information law. Although, at first glance, declassification seems to be a practice that unnecessarily reveals secrets, it is essential to the maintenance of

democratic principles and the rule of law. And, from a purely practical point, it promotes research and understanding by making more information on the workings of government available to historians, social scientists, and analysts in other academic disciplines.

. . . .

Compartmentalization of Information

Compartmentalization is a simple defense concept applied to partition information and those who access it. Compartmentalization works because data are first classified into security levels (e.g., restricted, secret, etc.) and, once this is done, the need-to-know doctrine is then applied. Using these two defensive security techniques allows the sharing of information that is necessary for staff to understand the issue under investigation and/or the taking of action relating to it without offering open and unrestricted access to all information.

The purpose is simple; the fewer people who know about a secret, the more likely that it will stay a secret. "Under such a system, secrets are divided into discrete segments, or compartments. An individual is allowed to know only those details of a secret operation with which he must deal directly. Others know only their portions. In this way, if there is a leak or defection, the chance of an entire operation being exposed is reduced."[11] Containment of sensitive information in this way complies with defensive counterintelligence tenet 5—if there is a breach of security, the pool of possible suspects needs to be small to help identify the perpetrator.

Usually code words are used to identify sensitive information that has been compartmentalized. For instance, a file containing top secret material may bear a code word that identifies it as belonging to a special project or operation. Note that a code word is different from a code name. An example of a code word–classified project is the well-documented MKULTRA mind control project conducted by the CIA in the 1950s and 1960s. The code word was comprised of the letter-pair MK, which signified the Technical Services Staff branch that ran the project, and the word ULTRA for the project. Until this material was declassified in the 1970s, it would have been only accessible by those with the appropriate security classification *and* a need-to-know denoted by the code word.

. . . .

I'm not totally versed, know what I mean?[12]

. . . .

Personnel who have been cleared to have access to that code word material are the only staff allowed access. This prevents personnel with a secret clearance to access this material and inadvertently discuss its contents with others within the agency, or in liaison with another agency's staff who may also have the same level clearance but are not cleared with the code word.

As "eminently sensible"[13] compartmentalization is, there are potentials for misuse, which must be acknowledged. Take the case in the 1960s and 1970s by the then head of counterintelligence, Jim Angleton. Admiral Stansfield Turner, former director of Central Intelligence put it this way: "I couldn't help wondering, though, if it had been used deliberately to keep people from knowing what they properly needed to know to supervise the ... Angleton's. ... I could see that Angleton had manipulated the system by constructing elaborate barriers within the CIA. ... If anyone challenged him, he could say or imply that there was other information the challenger did not have that justified his actions. He acquired such autonomy that even his superiors sometimes could not find out what he was doing and in many cases were intimidated by him. Angleton's barony was not the only one built in the CIA by controlled access to knowledge, but it was the most harmful."[14]

* *

Herkos Odonton

The legendary writer of spy fiction Ian Fleming used the term *herkos odonton* in his novel *On Her Majesty's Secret Service* several times in dialogue between the book's hero, James Bond, and Marc-Ange Draco, a Corsican crime syndicate boss. Fleming used the term to mean that the conversation between the two men was to be *secret*— not to be discussed with others.[15]

The term is likely to have originated from the ancient Greek as there is a passage in Homer's *The Odyssey* where Zeus admonishes Athena for speaking too freely. He says, in effect: "My child, how could you let words slip through the barrier of your teeth." Although Fleming says *herkos odonton* means "the hedge of the teeth," the word *hedge* may be an English interpretation as there are few hedgerows in Greece. In classic Greek it may have been "fence" or "enclosure," or the like. To support this, Frederick Von Raumer, professor of history at the University of Berlin, used Homer's phrase in a letter to a friend, later published in "Letter X, April 9th, 1835."[16] He too used the word *hedge* in the phrase and in the same way as Homer—something like, "you should keep those thoughts to yourself."

However, Fleming's characters used *herkos odonton* as an idiom for "top secret." Though this has a slightly different emphasis, both meanings are likely to apply—for instance: "herkos" would refer to a hedge, fence, or enclosure, and odonton would refer to teeth, as in peri*odont*ist. It is therefore the context in which it is used that provides meaning.[17]

* *

Handling Sensitive Information

Staff authorized to access secret or top secret documentation should be required to sign a "chain-of-custody record" in order to assure control over its content. The chain-of-custody record also facilitates withdrawal and destruction when the documentation is no longer required (see appendix D). To inform staff members of a document's degree of sensitivity, each document should be identified with a marking indicating its grade (bold letters in red ink).

When marking a document, staff should bear in mind that the entire document need not be classified at a sensitivity level. Take for instance a report compiled on a recent research project. It could be considered ideal for public release in a future counterterrorist awareness campaign in the media (lowest level), but a page (or even several paragraphs) may contain technical data about the research that is best kept reserved. That section can carry a classification stamp, while the remainder of the text displays the general distribution classification of, say, restricted.

By using an information classification system, inappropriate disclosure is less likely to occur, and, as the information contained in various documents becomes dated and less sensitive with the passage of time, reclassifying the information's classification downward can then take place. The extent to which an agency goes to enact a classification system is determined by its size and the overarching authority imposed on it by its mandated creator (i.e., government and military agencies will have standards imposed by law or regulation, whereas private or corporate agencies will be guided by policy). In the case of a sole private practitioner or a small business firm, there will be far less need for formal arrangements when compared to large organizations.

Accounting Practices

Although we have examined classification of information in the broad sense, it is worth discussing the accounting practices of the agency specifically. For, if accounting practices are not taken into consideration when classifying information, such loopholes can create serious weaknesses in a counterintelligence program. This issue is not a concern so much with government agencies that operate in the national security, foreign policy, or military arenas, as their accounting practices are regulated by law. In fact, complex arrangements are in place to shield the unauthorized disclosure of budgets and sensitive expenditures so that the opposition cannot obtain these data. For instance, some intelligence agencies operate front organizations, front groups, and front companies to act as shields. It is this consideration that is the point being made here, but

PHOTO 8.1 Typical Label for Stamping Classified Documents and Files. *Source*: Courtesy of the author.

perhaps it is aimed at those who practice business and private counterintelligence rather than agencies of the government and military.

Accounting is the practice of identifying, measuring, and communicating economic information about a business or private life. Arguably, it is one of the most valuable sources of information for planning and control that a business has. Careful consideration should therefore be given to safeguarding financial data about sensitive matters. Such information should not be recorded openly in journals and the ledger along with supply items and petty cash purchases. Sensitive projects, whatever they may be, should have special accounting practices designed to minimize the risk of exposing their budgets, expenditures, and the like to staff that perform only routine accounting tasks.

- -

If sensitive information has been compromised or just "lost," the following guidelines will assist in minimizing the damage that may result:

* Attempt to regain custody of the documents/material;
* Assess the information that has been compromised (or subjected to compromise) to ascertain the potential damage, and institute action necessary to minimize the effects of such damage;
* Investigate to establish the weakness in the security arrangements that caused or permitted the compromise, and alter these arrangements to prevent any recurrence;
* Take actions appropriate to either educate/counsel/discipline the person(s) responsible.

- -

Advertisements

Advertisements and editorial articles appearing in the print and online media are areas worthy of note. Such information can be very revealing about an agency. All information contained in advertisements for personnel, prestige, product or service development, technical advancements, or marketing should be analyzed as possible intelligence that might be used by the opposition.

Even the size of an advertisement and the frequency at which it appears are in themselves important factors when analyzing an agency's intentions and strategies. Likewise, the type of media a business uses and the positioning of an advertisement in the publication, website, or blog can also provide vital pieces of information. The same applies with editorial information. Customers of the agency are not the only readers of such media articles; the opposition will be privy to them also. To combat unwitting disclosure, a review procedure should be set up to screen information intended for publication or presentation at public meetings.[18]

Meetings, Conferences, and Conversations

If information that is classified as top secret is the subject of a meeting or conference, the date, time, and location of that meeting should only be promulgated to those people who will be attending and others on a need-to-know basis (for instance, the personal assistants or executive officers of those attending). Meeting organizers should be conscious of surveillance through windows and internal glass partitions and select venues accordingly. Agendas and conference notes should not be left behind but destroyed in the manner discussed under the section on document disposal below in this chapter. If the meeting breaks for refreshments, arrangements should be made to secure the room, or have it kept under observation.

Counterintelligence staff training needs to provide employees with an understanding that discussing classified matters over unsecured telephones, in e-mails, in public places, or on public conveyances (including taxis) is prohibited and this needs to be reflected in agency policy.

Reverse Engineering

Reverse engineering is a low-profile form of espionage that has the potential to yield high-impact results. Essentially, reverse engineering is the purchase of an agency's product (or service) and the subsequent disassembling of it into its component parts (or, in the case of a service, a careful analysis of the service's quantity, quality, presentation, follow-up, etc.) to determine how it was constructed and what manufacturing processes were used. Analysis of this type can provide the opposition with important data about the targeted agency.

Such details can be likened to providing the opposition with a guided tour of an agency's facilities or research and development division. There may not be anything an agency can do about this; however, every agency should be cognizant that it will occur as soon as their product or service enters the market.

Once an agency begins its marketing phase, it will need to practice reverse engineering itself to ensure that the opposition is not infringing patent rights (see Trademarks, Patents, and Copyright below). Although reverse engineering is an espionage technique, and agencies need to practice defensive measures to protect their intellectual property, it is also an important *offensive* counterintelligence method, and this will be discussed in chapter 12 regarding detection operations.

Clear Desk Policy

Sometimes termed end-of-day or end-of-shift security checks, a "clear desk" policy dictates that all employees and contractors need to store classified material in accordance with the appropriate classification level—unclassified, restricted/confidential, secret, or top secret or another classification system if used. A system of checking desks, workstations, and meeting rooms, as well as other aspects, needs to be designed to ensure that these data have been secured in the appropriate repositories, and, in turn, these have been secured. A clean desk policy will increase the security of classified documents by

- reducing the frequency of security breaches;
- lessening casual access to official information;
- Providing a quicker lock-up procedure by eliminating the need to sort classified and non-classified material; and
- Allowing for effective cleaning of offices by contract cleaners.

No papers, pens, toys or tape recorders. Or none visible. ... I had the feeling we were being listened to, but in the Office you had that feeling anyway.[19]

When staff finish work each day, they need to remove all folders, documents, and papers (classified only) from their desks, cabinets, cupboards, and so on, and lock them in appropriate containers leaving these surfaces clear. Computer workstations must be shut-down at the end of the work day. Portable computing devices must be locked in a security container that is commensurate to the secrecy level of data the device contains.

Document Storage

Under the tenet of defense-in-depth (tenet 10 of defensive counterintelligence), an agency's first line of defense against penetration by the opposition is its external barriers; that is, its fences, doors, and windows. Its second line of defense is the containers that hold its sensitive documents and data. For example, filing cabinets, hard disk drives, and a range of other devices are all containers in normal agency use.

It is therefore essential that an agency identify all documents and electronic records that may be the target of the opposition and secure these in containers that minimize the risk of their unauthorized acquisition. The concern is with both the theft of the documents themselves and the undetected theft of the information they contain. So, to further reduce the risk of attack on containers designated for sensitive information, an agency should not store valuables such as cash, securities, jewels, precious metals, and drugs in them.

Data backup includes off-site storage of media as well as cloud storage. The same safeguards that apply to an agency's workplace storage apply to these locations too.

When Writing Leaves an Impression

An often-overlooked source of information leakage is the impressions left on writing pads. This issue often arises when staff are traveling and use hotel memo pads or sticky note pads. Hotel rooms are not secure, for example, a pad can reveal the information written on the sheet that was removed. To guard against this a thin piece of aluminum, plastic, or acrylic should be used under the top sheet of all memo pads and writing tablets to prevent the formation of impression marks.

With the ubiquitous availability of laser printers, typewriter and printer ribbons, carbon paper, plates, stencils, and similar items are no longer a problem, but they were. A readable copy could easily be obtained from any of these sources, and in the hands of the opposition that information was as dangerous as the originals.

Dictation recorded on magnetic media should be deleted immediately after being transcribed. There are many commercially available software packages that digitally shred such data, and these should be used to remove the original data once transcribed. Bear in mind that deleting and running a digital shredder to clear or sanitize magnetic media sounds simple and straightforward, but the way modern operating system and software packages work may prevent this. That is, a data file that is accessed by a software program during use may create temporary files of the data, backup copies, or hold data in various forms of memory and swap files on the host computer or on a network server, as well as other possibilities. The point is that sanitizing software needs to be able to locate all associated files and data stored in memory or caches and clean these, or another software utility needs to do this prior to running the sanitizing software. Unfortunately, this cannot be done with data stored in the *cloud*.

Cloud Computing

Cloud computing is an example of "what is old is new again." It is a return to shared computing resources rather than relying on the resources of a single computing device. Once, *dumb terminals* were networked to a mainframe to process and store data. Now, we have data centers and server clusters that are distributed across the globe with users connected to them via the Internet. Although powerful and convenient, this architecture presents a security problem for classified information. Unless the servers are under the direct control of security-cleared personnel, these data are not secure.

The so called Panama Papers affair is an example of a spectacular data breach where data were stored on servers in a foreign country. Some 11.5 million classified private and business documents were stolen from servers of the Panamanian law firm Mossack Fonseca in 2015 and made public. The documents exposed the personal financial information of hundreds of well-known political leaders, politicians, wealth individuals, and public figures worldwide.[20] Although these servers were not technically a cloud, the events are analogous to what can happen when data are stored off-shore, not under an agency's direct control.

E-mail Discretion

There is a saying that there are two types of e-mail users: those that have send a confidential e-mail to the wrong recipient and those that will. It is important that all agency staffers check the recipient's e-mail address before pressing the send button. This is especially important if the e-mail program has an automated address process that provides a suggested recipient.

It is also important to check the e-mail trail when forwarding messages because some of the material contained in trail may not be for the new person's eyes; this information should be deleted before sending. Finally, care need to be exercised when replying to the sender, and not to "reply all." A confidential reply to the sender may otherwise end up on the desks people you do not want to have this information.

If sending a message to several people and their e-mails addresses were supplied to you in confidence, use bcc (i.e., blind carbon copy) rather than placing the recipients' e-mail addresses in the "to" field of the e-mail. This will not expose the others who you included in the distribution list.

Authorized Document Reproduction

The reproductions of classified documents bearing any of the security classifications of restricted, confidential, secret, or top secret should all be marked with that classification on the original material. Only sufficient copies necessary to meet operational requirements should be made, and all reproductions should be destroyed as soon as they have served their purpose. With secret and top secret material, there may be agency policies that require that each copy be numbered and that receipt of the document is acknowledged by signature. Electronic copies are handled in the same manner, but there may be an automatic logging system that generates an e-receipt automatically. Signing and logging fulfills tenet 12 of defensive counterintelligence, as discussed in chapter 4.

Unauthorized Document Reproduction

The surreptitious photocopying of sensitive documents or photographing them using a digital camera are the two most likely ways the opposition could obtain classified information without an agency's knowledge. Another method, although difficult to attempt, is to remove the documents from the agency's secure containers, copy or scan them, and then return them to their repositories undetected.

To guard against the former case, a locking device should be installed on the office photocopier to strengthen this potentially weak security link. And, to counteract both possibilities, the agency should ensure that the containers holding documents or data are fitted with locks and that these locks are used religiously.

Metal containers, such as filing cabinets with padlocks, offer a reasonably high level of security; however, safes and cabinets with combination locks incorporated as part of their physical structure offer a much higher level of protection. These containers are usually constructed to withstand force and their level of resistance is stated by the manufacturer. Secure storage is equally applicable to computer hard disk drives and portable data drives that are used to backup data, as well as magnetic backup tapes.

. . . .

When photocopying or scanning sensitive documents, do not leave the original behind in the automatic feeder or under the document cover.

. . . .

Document Safeguards During Use

When sensitive documents are not held in their secure containers as outlined above, the person using the documents should

* keep the documents under constant visual watch;
* place the documents in a storage container, cover them, or turn them face-down when an unauthorized person is present;
* return the documents to their designated storage container after use;
* not allow classified material to leave the agency's offices unless it is carried in accordance with protective security while in transit at the same level as that when stored in an office environment; and
* in the case of maps, overlays, graphs, wall charts, or other forms of large documents, ensure they are labeled with a code name or code number and not openly bearing a designation that could identify the project to an unauthorized observer.

Document Disposal

An agency's wastepaper basket is an easily accessible source of information for the opposition. Probably two-thirds of the paper generated by an agency contains information that is sensitive to some degree; that is, information that, if acquired by the opposition, could adversely affect the functioning of the agency. This information gathering technique is known as *Dumpster diving*[21] and is carried out simply by collecting the week's paper waste before the disposal truck arrives.

An easily overlooked source of information leakage is the office photocopier. Spoiled and overrun copies should not be indiscriminately dropped into the wastepaper basket. An important piece of equipment for all intelligence units is a document shredder. These devices are so common now that even retail stores carry them as standard items. An alternative for large units is to use a bulk document destruction service. These companies are usually listed in the yellow pages. It is important to ensure that shredding is done with a cross-cut that reduces the document to the size of confetti or smaller. Low-security strip shredders may be cheaper to purchase but, as was found in the aftermath of

PHOTO 8.2 Example of Low-security Strip Shredded Documents. *Source*: Courtesy of the author.

the 1979 seizure of the U.S. Embassy in Tehran, the opposition can reconstruct the documents. Many of the classified American documents that were destroyed using low-security devices were reassembled (though it took some years to complete the task).

Waste Disposal

Obtaining information from discarded office material is a long-standing law enforcement and private investigator technique that is popularly referred to as *Dumpster diving*.[22] Despite any aversion one may have to the thought of rummaging through someone's waste material, it is important to understand that this is a potentially rich and valuable source of information. Sensitive material of all types can be found in Dumpsters—manuals, notes, letters, memos, reports, files, photographs, passwords, identity cards, receipts, schedules, itineraries, telephone numbers, and much more (including computer hard disk drives, USB drives, and a variety of data that have been backed up onto CDs or DVDs). The reason why so much information can be collected from this source is that people believe that, once a piece of paper (or an old computer hard disk drive, etc.) is placed in a waste bin, it has "disappeared." Some people believe that no one would bother getting dirty rummaging through a person's garbage. They are wrong if they hold this belief.

• •

Many computer printers have internal memory that cache data sent to them as a way of facilitating a smooth and uninterrupted printing queue. If this memory is accessible, for instance via theft, the opposition may be able to obtain the data relating to recent documents sent to the printer. In this regard, printers are like workstations and network servers as they store important information in obscure cyber locations not readily understood by the casual user.

Recovery can take place at any point between where the waste leaves the agency's premises to, and including, the landfill site. Information obtained via waste recovery was at one time considered high value and low cost because it yielded more benefit than what it cost to gather it. However, with its popularization in the press and cinema, waste recovery has become more difficult. Government agencies, businesses, and individuals regularly use document shredders and are more conscious of how and what they dispose. Security surrounding waste has improved with commercial-scale confidential document destruction becoming a service that is widely available. The point to be made is that anything that has informational value needs to be destroyed, not just disposed of.

Carriage of Classified Documents

When documents are subject to government security classification, the rules concerning carriage of these documents outside the agency's offices are mandated by policy or other official instruction. It is not possible to outline these here as they are themselves restricted procedures. Nevertheless, the principles of sound document security can be applied to business and private counterintelligence. By studying these examples, the student of counterintelligence theory and practice can understand the gist of these procedures.

The wax seal is a device put across the flap line of an envelope to prevent it from being opened surreptitiously by unauthorized persons. The bar of wax is heated until it becomes a gummy liquid and is applied in that form to suitable spots on the flap line. A metal stamp is then pressed into the molten wax leaving an impression with a distinctive and usually complex pattern. . . . It is almost impossible to duplicate a seal exactly even if the original stamp is available.[23]

When an agency needs to transmit documents of, say, a sensitive but unclassified nature through the public postal system, a service generically known as *registered mail* should be considered. This service is designed to be the most secure method of posting articles of value. Postal services maintain a record of the article's whereabouts from lodgment to delivery, and, for a small additional charge, the agency can receive a receipt, signed by the addressee, confirming the document's delivery.

PHOTO 8.3 Example of the Printed Pattern on the Inside of an Envelope. A pattern helps mask the envelope's contents from unauthorized viewing. *Source*: Courtesy of the author.

To prevent unauthorized viewing of the document's contents while in transit, it should be folded or packed, so the text will not be in direct contact with the envelope or shipping container. Only substantially constructed, opaque envelopes, boxes, and mailing tubes should be used for transmitting classified information. However, another method is to enclose the documents in a shielding envelope, which in turn is placed in the addressed covering envelope. Care should be taken not to call unnecessary attention to the package by labeling it with a description of its contents. The outer envelope should be marked: "Do Not Forward. If Undeliverable to the Addressee, Return to Sender." If the inner shielding envelope method is used, it should be annotated with: "To Be Opened by the Addressee Only."

Trademarks, Patents, and Copyrights

Trademarks, patents, and copyrights are all important elements in an agency's counterintelligence effort. A trademark is any symbol, word, or name or any combination of these that identifies a manufacturer's or merchant's goods or services and distinguishes them from those made or distributed by other businesses. Although there are common law rights granted to the user of a trademark, government registration provides prima facie evidence that an agency holds exclusive rights to its use and permits legal action against others for its unauthorized use.

A trademark must be registered in each country in which an agency trades. If this is not done, a foreign competitor could not only capitalize on an agency's goodwill but wreak havoc by downgrading its product's reputation through less stringent business practices or quality control.

By contrast, a patent is a special right conferred on the designer of a unique process or device, enabling the agency to exercise exclusive privilege in its manufacture, use, or sale for a limited period. A patent, like a trademark, must be applied for and is only enforceable in the country in which the registration is submitted. As with trademarks, if an agency trades overseas, applications for the registration of a patent must be lodged with the appropriate government agency in each country in which trade is carried on. Again, if an agency fails to do so, a foreign adversary may seize its idea through its own intelligence efforts. If this happens, not only will the agency have lost potential markets, it will have paid for all the opposition's research and development expenses.

In contrast to these defensive measures, copyright is a legal right that protects a broad range of intellectual material, from computer programs to works of art. Literature of all descriptions, musical scores, films, photographs, and media broadcasts are also included under the copyright umbrella. Unlike trademarks and patents, copyrights do not require an application to be made to a government instrumentality. Copyright protection is automatic, and copyright owners are protected in foreign countries under international convention. To afford full international protection to all intellectual property that an agency generates, a copyright notice should be placed in the front of these publications. The copyright notice consists of the word *copyright* followed by the symbol © and then the year of first publication followed by the name of the copyright owner—like this: Copyright © 2019 by Hank Prunckun.

Arrow Information Paradox

The Arrow paradox is a conundrum that businesses face when dealing with intellectual property. The paradox is named after its creator, Kenneth Arrow, who devised it in 1971 in connection with his study into risk taking.[24]

The paradox occurs when a company seeks to acquire information or knowledge (i.e., technology) from external suppliers or to promote its intellectual goods or services to customers or the marketplace. Specifically, the paradox is that the potential purchaser of the intellectual property needs to have the technology described or explained in some detail to be able to understand its utility and decide whether to acquire it (or, in the case where a company wants to buy, to sell it). However, once these revelations are made about the technology the intellectual property owner has in effect passed on their intellectual property to the other party without any compensation.

There is a lesson here for counterintelligence. That is, once an employee is given access to classified data to perform his or her job, the agency or its client has in effect transferred these secrets to that person and there is no way of retrieving them. It is only through the practices of counterintelligence that these secrets remain so until deemed appropriate to reveal.

Common Law Protection

Common law affords protection for confidential information and as such does not require parties to sign an agreement. Legal scholars advise that, for someone to exercise their common law right, it is only necessary for the communication between the parties to be confidential—that is, in trust that the other will not divulge the details. Often this is done by the person or business that is asserting confidentiality by simply annotating the e-mail or document with words such as "in-confidence," "personal-in-confidence," or "commercial-in-confidence."

Lawyers advise that four requirements need to be satisfied if confidential information is to be protected under common law. First, the information cannot already be in the public domain or be public knowledge (if so, the proverbial genie is already out of the bottle); second, the information must be clearly identified (hence, adding the words "in-confidence" to the subject line of an e-mail or at the bottom of a document); third, it needs to be clear that the situation in which the information is communicated is an event where trust was assured; and, last, the receiving party cannot indicate a willingness to disclose the information prior to the disclosure being made (again, this would demonstrate a lack of trust).

Legislative Protection

There are numerous pieces of legislation that are designed to protect information. In general terms, these include statutes and government policies. The terms and conditions upon which the information is confidentially held, and the circumstances of disclosure, are specified under each piece of legislation or the individual policy. These authorities also specify the jurisdiction, the enforcing body, and the penalty for breach. The Freedom of Information Act is an example of such legislation.

These laws are designed to allow citizens to obtain information from government agencies through a straightforward application process. Although the title of these laws—*freedom of information*—implies unfettered access, these laws specify information that cannot be obtained by public application. These exemptions are one way governments that protect confidential information. Examples of protected information include law enforcement investigation files, documents that are subject to legal privilege, documents that disclose people's personal affairs, files that contain trade secrets or information that is deemed commercial in confidence, information that if disclosed may cause harm to the economy of the state, and information that was provided under common law principles of confidentiality (see above). They may vary from jurisdiction to jurisdiction, but these categories provide a general picture of the scope of the exemptions.

Review of Key Words and Phrases

The key words and phrases associated with this chapter are listed below. Demonstrate your understanding of each by writing a short definition or explanation in one or two sentences.

classified information   sub rosa
code names   top secret
dumpster diving   traffic light protocol
Herkos odonton   unclassified but sensitive
secret   unclassified

Study Questions

1. Explain how the common law provides protection for information and provide an example.
2. List six data items that might need protection and explain why each data item would require safeguarding and describe what type of defense you would recommend.
3. Explain the reasons for compartmentalizing information and describe how such a system might be devised for your present or past employer.
4. List five levels of security clearance and describe a situation where each level may be used with regard to your current or past employer.

Learning Activity

Inquire as to the format and style of policies used in your current place of employment. Using an existing policy as a template, write a "clear desk" policy. Even if your current employer does not use a system of classification for information, include the categories unclassified, unclassified but sensitive, and commercial in confidence (the latter meaning all business-related documents that should not be public). If your employer uses an information classification system, then use it.

Notes

1. Ellen Barry, "London's Kremlin Spy Nest," *The New York Times*, International Edition, March 14, 2018: 1.
2. For example, see the treatment of information in its widest context relating to the business sector by Henry W. Prunckun, *Information Security: A Practical Handbook on Business Counterintelligence* (Springfield, IL: Charles C. Thomas Publisher, 1989).
3. *Federal Information Security Management Act of 2002*, Chapter 35, *U.S. Code* 44.
4. Kim Philby, *My Silent War* (London: MacGibbon & Kee, 1963), 134–35.
5. William Morris, ed., *The American Heritage Dictionary of the English Language* (Boston: American Heritage Publishing and Houghton Mifflin, 1971), 1, 283.
6. Tom Fitton, *Clean House: Exposing Our Government's Secrets and Lies* (New York: Threshold Editions, 2016).
7. The City of New York, *Data Classification Policy, Version 1.5* (New York: The City of New York, September 9, 2014), 1.

8   Organisation for Economic Co-Operation and Development, Directorate for Science, Technology, Computer and Communication Policy, *Development of Policies for Protection of Critical Information Infrastructure, Ministerial Background Report* (Paris: OECD, June 17–18, 2008).

9   David Khan, *The Code-Breakers: The Story of Secret Writing* (Toronto: Macmillan, 1967), 501.

10 Stanfield Turner, *Secrecy and Democracy, 46: The CIA in Transition* (Boston: Houghton Mifflin Co., 1985), 255.

11 Stanfield Turner, *Secrecy and Democracy*, 46.

12 John le Carré (pseud., David John Moore Cornwell), *Our Game* (London: Hodder & Stoughton, 1995), 60–61.

13 Turner, *Secrecy and Democracy*, 46.

14 Turner, *Secrecy and Democracy*, 46–47.

15 Ian Fleming, *On Her Majesty's Secret Service* (London: Jonathan Cape, 1963).

16 Frederick Von Raumer, "Letter X, April 9th, 1835," in *England in 1835: Being a Series of Letters Written to Friends in Germany During a Residence in London and Excursions into the Provinces* (London: John Murray, 1836), 70.

17 I thank my colleagues of Greek scholarship for their assistance in interpreting the meaning of this phrase—Yiannis Polias, BSc, MA(AppLing), Yerasimos Patitsas, BArch, and Dr. Stamatiki Krita, PhD, personal communications, August 9 and 10, 2011.

18 An example of publishing sensitive information was that of Australia's Department of Foreign Affairs. It was reported that confidential documents outlining details of Australia's embassy in Baghdad, Iraq, had been posted on the Internet as part of a tender process for facilities management. See "Secret Plans on Website," *Adelaide Advertiser*, Adelaide, Australia, September 18, 2010: 41.

19 Carré, *Our Game*, 62–63.

20 Jake Bernstein, *Secrecy World: Inside the Panama Papers Investigation of Illicit Money Networks and the Global Elite* (New York: Henry Holt & Co., 2017).

21 John Hoffman, *The Art and Science of Dumpster Diving* (Boulder, CO: Paladin Press, 1993).

22 John Hoffman, *Dumpster Diving: The Advanced Course: How to Turn Other People's Trash into Money, Publicity, and Power* (Boulder, CO: Paladin Press, 2002).

23 John M. Harrison, ed., *CIA Flaps and Seals Manual* (Boulder, CO: Paladin Press, 1975), 17.

24 Kenneth Joseph Arrow, *Essays in the Theory of Risk-Taking* (Amsterdam: North-Holland Publishing Co., 1971), 152.

Chapter 9

Defensive Counterintelligence: Communications Security

Rummaging through the shelves off a secondhand book shop, a customer saw an interesting spy novel—a paperback with a picture of a middle-aged man's back, hunched sitting at a 1950s style wooden swivel office chair. In front of him on his desk was a reel-to-reel tape recorder to which his headphones were connected. A single bear light bulb burned overhead as it dangled from a cable attached to the basement ceiling. All around him was dark.

At one time this is how it was done. An operative would place a pair of alligator clips on the terminals of the target telephone line, trying to do it as smoothly as possible in fear that the initial contact might make a clicking noise on the line. The cable would be fed into the tape recorder's input socket, then the waiting took place. For hours or days; perhaps even weeks. Shift after shift, sitting in the basement of an apartment building, waiting for that vital piece of information. Yet, as historically romantic such a spy thriller may be, in the real world communications technology has moved on and so has the way operatives intercept information. This means counterintelligence specialists need to know more than the approved technique for attaching alligator clips.

Comsec Fundamentals

Like many terms and phrases used in the intelligence world, the phrase *communications security* has been abbreviated for ease of use by blending the first parts of each of the words into the abbreviation COMSEC.[1] COMSEC entails a number of provinces ranging from the physical security afforded to communication equipment and installations, the security surrounding the transmission of signals, and the emissions given off by cables and equipment, as well as the security of the messages that are transmitted—crypto-security. It also encompasses the frequency, volume, and structure of "stations" communicating with each other—traffic-flow security.

The reason for providing security for these facilities is because the opposition may exploit any of these realms for gathering intelligence—SIGINT, the

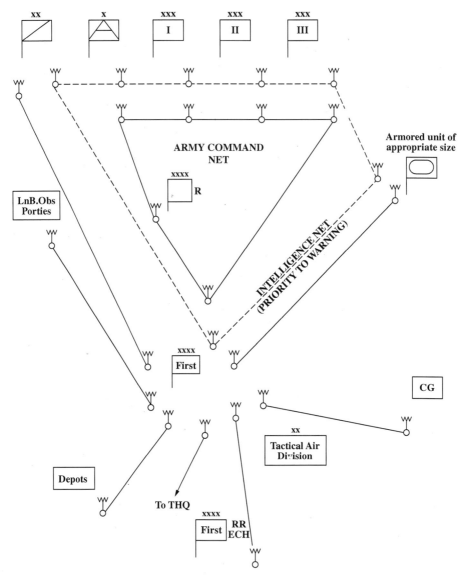

FIGURE 9.1 Notional Example of an Enemy Army Radio Net That Was Constructed from Intercepted Radio Traffic Using Traffic Analysis. *Source*: Courtesy of U.S. Department of the Army and Air Force. U.S. Department of the Army and Air Force, *Fundamentals of Traffic Analysis (Radio Telegraphy)*, 12.

abbreviation for *signals intelligence*.[2] For instance, the simple monitoring of radio transmissions between stations is known as *traffic analysis* and has a long history of producing high-quality and accurate assessments of, for instance, an enemy's order of battle.[3]

To illustrate the COMSEC fundamentals, this chapter describes some of the key areas of concern and some of the basic security precautions. Because installations are highly technical, especially in the military, and communications equipment advances at rapid rates, it is not possible to canvass all. Nevertheless, the principles are presented here and are complemented with examples, as a way of providing a base of knowledge and understanding.

Technical Surveillance Countermeasures

Although it is impossible to determine the extent to which electronic eavesdropping exists in society, media reports indicate that it is widespread and not limited to any one government, industry, or commercial sector. If an agency suspects it is the target of either a wiretap or room bug,[4] an audio countermeasure sweep is the best way of determining if there are any listening devices in operation. The sweep, however, will reveal devices operating at that given time only. Having said that, it must be stressed that no room can be guaranteed to be proofed against all forms of audio surveillance. Experience has demonstrated this to be the case; even the most sensitive rooms in the United States embassy in Moscow were once penetrated. In 1945, Soviet schoolchildren gave a replica of the Great Seal of the United States to the then ambassador, Averell Harriman, as a gesture of goodwill. Seven years later (1952), a technical surveillance countermeasures sweep revealed that the Great Seal contained a listening device—a resonant cavity microphone, dubbed *The Thing*. Accordingly, agency security staff should be aware of the need to examine all gifts for this type of Trojan horse.

Conducting sweeps at irregular intervals is the most effective way of reducing the risk of this hazard. It is arguably the most reliable way to check for, and clear, audio surveillance devices.

There are limitations, however, in conducting sweeps. First, regarding telephones, even if the target agency's telephone *devices* appear to be clear at the time of the sweep, there is no way of determining whether the telephone of another party is under surveillance by inspecting the agency's end of the line. At the time of writing, there was no technology available that can check for listening devices at, or beyond, the central telephone exchange. Second, there are some state-of-the-art devices and techniques used by opposition intelligence agencies, and possibly very well-financed private intelligence contractors and criminal groups, that may be undetectable because of their high level of sophistication. (In contrast, see appendix C for a list of some basic *analog* audio surveillance devices and a brief description of their applications.)

When the analogue telephone exchange was in operation, a court-ordered telephone tap was place on the target line by a technician. Unauthorized taps were placed on the device, the line leading into the target building, or at the first

PHOTO 9.1 A Telecom Cylindrical Distribution Board That Connects Many Hundreds of Pairs of Service Wires from the Central Exchange to Subscribers' Premises. An accessible place to place an illegal wiretap. *Source:* Courtesy of the author.

telecom distribution board that is closest to the device (see Photo 9.1). However, with the conversion to digital, legal taps can be initiated remotely from a computer terminal and data recorded remoting without the need for a technician's assistance. Software-driven taps are hence superior in avoiding detection.

An audio countermeasure sweep can be conducted by specialist counterintelligence firms operated by, say, private investigators and technicians of the government or military. The former is usually contracted by private persons or businesses concerned about eavesdropping, whereas the latter are used to check and clear buildings and meeting rooms for political and government users. Nongovernment services are usually listed in the telephone yellow pages or on business websites.

A professional sweep includes both a thorough physical search, inspecting literally every inch of, and every object in, the suspected area, and the electronic sweep. The electronic sweep may utilize a broadband receiver and/or a specially designed field-strength meter to test for transmitters. Metal detectors can be used to hunt for bugs in nonmetallic objects and planted devices in walls, floors, ceilings, and furniture. There are also a wide range of meters used to test the telephone line voltage for the presence of wiretaps.

Even though cell phones are difficult to intercept, they are electronic sieve in terms of location information. This is because with the advances in wireless data transmissions (e.g., 4G and 5G phones), the cell towers, or base stations, are located closer together, it makes it possible for a surveillant to obtain a high degree of resolution of a cell phone's location, and the direction of travel via the "hand-off" as the signal moves from one base station to the next.

PHOTO 9.2 Excavating a 1,476-foot-long Tunnel into Soviet-controlled East Berlin During 1954–1955 to Install Telephone Taps. *Source*: Courtesy of the Central Intelligence Agency.

Telephone Wiring

Wiretapping is the interception of fixed-line telephone and facsimile communication, as well as computer data that is transmitted via landlines. The interception of these signals can take place anywhere between the sender's offices and those of the receiver. The most vulnerable parts of the telephone system are at the agency's telephones and other data-transmitting equipment such as data routers, switches and modems, and the lines leading out of the building.

Once the targeted lines leave the agency's building, interception is more difficult, but certainly not impossible. Apart from a countermeasure sweep, the chief tactic against wiretapping is to ensure that the telephone wiring closet, terminal box, or data center is equipped with locks so that it can be secured always. In addition, all exposed wiring, or wiring that is easily accessible, should be shielded in metal conduit that is connected to electrical ground or earth. Providing a path to ground for the electric emissions radiated from communications cables and devices is the principal means for preventing the interception of electromagnetic emissions. This is because ground has the theoretical ability to absorb electric currents without changing its electrical potential or charge. The electromagnetic emissions from wiring and cabling are therefore contained by the metal conduit (which, in turn, is electrically grounded). The electrical currents produced by the emissions then flow along the conduit (as it is a conductor of electricity) to ground.

· ·

A sterile telephone is one which cannot be located even by checking with the telephone company; a secure phone is the same, but is safer in that a conversation cannot be intercepted, as it can be on a sterile line.[5]

· ·

Cordless and Cellular Telephones

Although cordless telephones offer many advantages over their wire-bound cousins, their use poses serious security risks. This is because most units operate within the standard radio frequency range of 30MHz to 300MHz (VHF band), 300MHz to 3GHz (UHF band), and 3GHz to 6GHz (the lower end of the SHF band), making it possible for the opposition to intercept the conversation. Furthermore, a cordless telephone may respond to other cordless telephone equipment operating nearby or to radio equipment, including commercial transceivers.

It is unwise to use cordless telephone technology for discussing confidential information of any description, especially using legacy analog devices that operate around 30MHz, because these signals can be intercepted by inexpensive conventional scanners.[6] It is certainly not recommended for any environment that warrants secrecy. Hard-wired telephonic devices are better suited for maintaining communications security.

An added level of security can be obtained by using analog 900MHz, 1.8/1.9GHz, 2.4GHz, or 5.8GHz cordless phones. Even though these devices operate using analog FM signals, they are immune to interception by standard scanners because the upper frequency range of inexpensive scanners is around 500MHz. However, more expensive scanners are capable for eavesdropping on signals much higher in the radio spectrum—around 6GHz (see Photo 9.3). But, the cost of purchasing this type of equipment limits the threat to an OPFOR that is well resourced.

A much better solution is the use of digital cordless phones. Referred to as digital-enhanced cordless telecommunications (DECT) phones, these devices feature encryption, so their signals cannot be intercepted by analog scanners.[7] Although software-defined radio equipment is capable of eavesdropping on

PHOTO 9.3 An Example of One of Many Radio Scanners Capable of Intercepting Signals from 9kHz to 6GHz in Any of the Following Modes: CW, LSB, USB, AM, FM, WFM, FM-stereo, and APCO P25. *Source*: Courtesy of AOR Ltd.

these signals, their cost and the sophistication needed to operate them restrict them to only use against targets that are exceptionally high value. The average private investigator, spy-for-hire, or business competitor is not able to deploy. However, if the secrets being guarded are of interest to a foreign government, these devices are not able to stand-up to the task.

. . . .

Smash cell phones and recycle the destroyed parts. Do not sell or give them away or donate for re-use because data may be able to be recovered even if the device is reformatted or reset to the factory settings.

. . . .

Cellular telephones are ubiquitous.[8] Arguably, the business world and people's personal lives could not function properly without these devices. But, like cordless telephony, they are susceptible to interception because they transmit a radio signal from the handset to a cell tower that connects the signal into what is known as a *trunked network*. The trunked network is the landline telephone network that is connected by computers. Through sophisticated software, this network routes the signals from caller to receiver far beyond the normal transmission/reception distance of the cell handset (in fact, if the receiver has access to a landline telephone or is in range of a cell tower, there can be communication, regardless of where the two are on the globe). Nevertheless, it is the transmitting of the signal from the handset to the cell tower that is the weakest link and it is there that interception is likely to occur.

Granted, the risk of interception is low because it is a more difficult technical task, but it is far from impossible. In fact, commercially manufactured radio receivers (e.g., radio scanners) have the cellular telephone portion of the radio spectrum blocked in some countries to help prevent this from happening. However, these unblocked scanners are available at retail outlets in many countries around the world, and radio engineers can overcome the limitations of these commercially blocked radios on their electronic workbenches in a few hours.

. . . .

Do not use a personal smartphone for business use or vice versa. Carry two phones even if it is inconvenient. If the company recalls its phone (remember, it's theirs), you will not only lose your data, you will also lose the privacy contained in your personal information. If you use your personal phone for business use, you are placing at risk the confidentiality of your employer's data—recall the former-U.S. Secretary of State's embarrassment when she used her private messaging system instead of the State Department's.[9]

. . . .

PHOTO 9.4 General Dynamics' Encrypted 4G LTE Device. *Source*: Courtesy of General Dynamics.

If confidential information is being discussed on a cell phone, agency staff should consider using a device that encrypts the conversation. One such device is General Dynamics' LTE device (Photo 9.4). The manufacturer advises that the device is certified by the National Security Agency (NSA) for communicating information to a level of top secret and, of course, all classifications below. The device can be used in its secure mode as well as an unsecured mode and can be used domestically or while traveling internationally. The device can deliver voice, video, data, text, and chat at high speed with any 4G LTE enabled device, including smartphones, tablets, or via mobile hotspots.

Satellite Telecommunications

Like landline telecommunication, satellite communication is vulnerable to interception. If the opposition is a major foreign power, then it is foolish to think this form of electronic traffic is not being, in some, way monitored. Although an agent sitting at his dimly lit basement desk, leaning over a reel-to-reel tape recorder wouldn't feature on the cover of today's spy thriller, digital interception equipment that can be terrestrially based, or airborne, or positioned in earth orbit do intercept satellite phone signals from every continent, every day.

Systems that intercept voice calls, SMS messages, data traffic, as well as call-related metadata are all possible. In addition, these systems can intercept data that can help establish the location of a targeted satellite phone. Even if the information is encrypted, these data can be deciphered. Everything is possible when it comes to satellite communications interception, but there is a cost.

Large nations' military and intelligence services have these capabilities; smaller nations' services may not, but they may be part of an intelligence alliance that provides for the sharing of these data. If the opposition is a business competitor, it does not eliminate the risk, but it does make it less likely. There is evidence that supports to proposition that with the help of a privately engaged microwave radio engineer and some modified receiving equipment, an intercept station can be constructed.

The coverage area that this type of equipment can intercept would not be worldwide, but likely to be limited to specific area where the target phone user is suspected of operating. This is because the resources need to loft a drone(s) to the heights required to cover a vast area or have a satellite station to do the same are clearly outside the financial realms of private spies. But a more modest attempt with, say, vehicle-borne intercept station could be done.

As an example, if a business competitor of (the fictitious) Eldorado Exploring Expedition Ltd had intelligence that Eldorado was looking for diamonds in a remote location of Australia's outback and wanted to know about the company's chances, intercepting the field crew's satellite communications could be a handy way of gaining this insight. A satellite intercept station fixed in a four-wheel drive vehicle could tail the crew as it deployed to conduct its exploration, and if it was in the footprint of the satellite, it would, in theory, able to intercept the signal.[10] However, identifying the phone call among the hundreds of other calls traversing the satellite link and decrypting the right signal is yet another problem. Nevertheless, with computer software, it is not impossible. Again, it is a matter of costs. The more the information is worth, the more caution should be taken.

Jammers

The state-of-the-art in wireless jamming now applies to cell phones. Once the domain of nations trying to stop the transmission of shortwave broadcasts to their countries, the same concept applies to cell phones. Commercially available jamming units will jam *all* cell phones signals within radius of about 18 m (approximately 60 feet) of the device. Because the device brings down a complete radio frequency "curtain," it presents as a double-edged sword; even the user cannot make or receive calls. Nonetheless, these devices are valuable where not all the parties to a meeting can be trusted to have their smartphones tuned off, or where a phone is suspected of being infected with a spyware application. These jamming devices will prevent eavesdropping. Jammers can also be used where an OPFOR needs to communicate with, say, an field operative, and the conversation needs to be terminated to prevent harm. A jammer will end the conversation as soon as it is switched on. The devices are robust, simply to use, battery operated, and concealable.

There are also white noise generators that work to jam audio. These devices generate random sounds that mask room conversations. The principle is that because the frequency and amplitude vary without a discernible pattern, it is difficult for an eavesdropper to filter the sounds to expose the conversation. Playing background music is a similar technique, but less effective because the music can be filtered. These devises are equally effective in dealing with microphones (e.g., shotgun and hard-wired mics, digital recorder mics, and radio transmitter mics), and microwave and laser-reflected pick-ups. Like cell phone jammers, these devices are easy to use, operated on battery power, but can be installed in a permanent location with an AC power supply.

Pagers

The rule-of-thumb is that if a device transmits a signal, the *signal* can be intercepted, and the device can be located. Even if the signal is encrypted, the signal can be used to identify the user. However, if the device only receives a signal, then there is no such ability. There are such things as numbered stations. These stations broadcast one-way messages to agents in the field. Although the messages can be subject to cryptanalysis, the recipient cannot be located because there is no return signal. In this regard pagers are considered the same—devices that receive a radio signal and convert it into text. So, were one-way communications are useful, these devices offer a level of security.[11] However, the *message* is not secured because anyone with a receiver/demodulator tuned to the pager frequency will be able to eavesdrop. So, the message needs to be in code, like the coded messages broadcast by a numbers station.

Wi-Fi and Bluetooth

Many electronic devices operate with the assistance of Wi-Fi and the commercially patterned wireless technology known as Bluetooth.® Although used

PHOTO 9.5 An Intelligence Officer Prepares Radio Interception Equipment to Eavesdrop on Opposition's Wi-Fi Signals During a Training Exercise. *Source*: Photograph by William Roche. Courtesy of the U.S. Army.

for different purposes, both technologies operate by sending and receiving low-power, shortrange radio signals. Because of this, the rule-of-thumb about intercepting radio signals applies to Wi-Fi as well as Bluetooth devices. Using a device with no encryption or inadequate encryption leaves the device vulnerable to eavesdropping.

Facsimile Machines

During olden days facsimile machines were essential for transmitting documents for business and government agencies alike. Until e-mail and the ability to attach documents electronically, they were very effective in providing high-speed data transmission at very low cost. Their value was and, in some cases, still form an integral part of many communication systems.

However, they pose potential risks. Apart from the risk of the data being intercepted and the way voice communications could be intercepted, the potential for documents to be inadvertently sent to an incorrect destination still exists. Such breaches could occur by misdialing the desired number or entering an incorrect number. Therefore, prior to transmission, it should be confirmed that the number is in fact the correct one for the destination. Following this, the destination number should be entered into the facsimile machine with caution, and then visually checked to make sure that the correct digits have been registered before executing the transmission command.

Two-Way Radio Systems

As with cordless telephone systems, two-way radio networks are highly susceptible to interception, even those employing some form of *voice inversion scrambler*. This is because software and electric kits are available commercially to descramble these signals. These scramblers use simple analog mechanisms to electronically obscure the radio operators' voices. Basically, the method inverts the high tones of the audio with those of the low tones, thus making the scrambled audio sound like Donald Duck speaking gibberish.

Radio silence is an effective countermeasure.

However, if electronic kits are available on the open market and anyone with an interest in monitoring radio transmissions can buy these,[12] then it follows that a radio engineer in the employ of the opposition could construct equipment far more advanced than these commercial descrambling units. Even the more advanced form of scrambling known as *rolling code voice inversion* may be descrambled if the opposition is a foreign power with the technical resources to allocate to the task (these circuits are available commercially and can be modified by radio technicians). Encrypted digital radio signals offer the highest commercial means for privacy, but, again, digital radio scanners are on the open market and decryption, though difficult, is not impossible.

PHOTO 9.6 U.S. Army Signal Corps Operated Several Radio Tractors along the U.S.–Mexico Border During the First World War. These mobile radio intercept stations monitored German diplomatic and agent radio traffic. *Source*: Courtesy of the U.S. Army.

Transmitting an unencrypted signal presents issues regarding interception.[13] By way of example, the operatives who conducted the black bag operation in relation to the June 1972 Watergate break-in used four off-the-shelf Radio Shack TRC100B, five-watt, six-channel, citizens' band (CB) radios that operated on 27MHz. This meant that anyone who had a radio receiver or radio scanner tunable to the 27MHz band could eavesdrop on their conversations. As 27MHz is in the high frequency band (HF), the signal could have travelled well beyond the line of sight and might have been received several hundred kilometers away due to "skip" where the signal bounces-off sun-energized particles in the ionosphere. In fact, the operatives discovered that the frequency they were operating on was shared with a local taxi company. They rationalized not using another frequency or doing what should have been done in accordance with sound counterintelligence practices—use of an encrypted radio system. Instead, they decided that the taxi traffic would provide cover for their transmissions. This tactical decision was consistent with other ill-fated decisions the group made that night, and these decisions demonstrated their lack of understanding of the finer points of counterintelligence.[14]

Therefore, if sensitive information is to be conveyed via two-way radio, a secure radio system designed specifically to thwart interception must be used. Such systems are certified to carry radio traffic up to and including the top secret classification level. These systems are mainly used by the military and diplomatic missions of virtually all nations, but, for any business that relies on two-way communication, such a secure system is also a must. Manufacturers are usually listed in the telephone yellow pages and on their corporate websites.

PHOTO 9.7 The Roof of the Russian Federation's Embassy in Jakarta, Indonesian Bristling with Radio Antennas. *Source*: Courtesy of a confidential source.

PHOTO 9.8 High-frequency Antenna Array of a Foreign Military Intelligence Listen Station on a Pacific Island. *Source*: Courtesy of a confidential source.

One limitation of using a secure radio communication system is that, if it requires encryption and the encryption device or software is classified, it makes interoperability with, say, public safety agencies impossible. This is because the device or software cannot be made available to these agencies if communications in a crisis are crippled. If, however, the radios can be switched between an unencrypted mode and full encryption, it would alleviate this problem.

Encrypted Communications Systems

Agencies that need to send sensitive information of a level that warrants a "secret" classification or above over a telephone network (including SMS— short message service), a radio system, or via interactive whiteboards, or facsimile will need to incorporate encryption to ensure the confidentiality of the information. In military and government agencies, dedicated lines and dedicated communication systems, such as secure Voice over Internet Protocol (VoIP), are permanently in place for this purpose. Agencies in the private or business sectors may not have the resources for such setups but nevertheless should still consider encryption units that can be used on an ad hoc basis. In effect, they can be switched on and off as needed.

It is axiomatic that the more a piece of information is worth, the more it is worth obtaining, and the more the opposition is likely to pay to get it or for the technical expertise to intercept it.

Permanent encrypted communications systems are often located within a strong room or vault and, as such, offer an extremely high degree of security. The security is at a level that meets the requirements of "secret" or above. If the opposition is attempting to intercept a conversation that is using a cipher unit, it would be digital noise.

Encryption units that are less permanent are still able to achieve this remarkably high degree of security by being able to randomly select from encryption codes that can be greater than ten to the thirtieth power. If, for example, the opposition was successful in intercepting and recording an encrypted conference call among, say, a group of counterterrorism policy analysts, it would need the services of a large computer server network and perhaps months, or even years, of around-the-clock computing time to decipher the data. Facilities to do this are realistically only available to intelligence agencies of wealthy nations, and it would be a course of an action not embarked upon unless the benefits outweighed the costs.

Review of Key Words and Phrases

The key words and phrases associated with this chapter are listed below. Demonstrate your understanding of each by writing a short definition or explanation in one or two sentences.

COMSEC
signals intelligence
traffic analysis

trunked (radio) network
voice inversion scrambling

Study Questions

1. List the different provinces, or subject areas, that COMSEC entails.

2. List two limitations of technical surveillance countermeasure sweeps and explain why these limit the effectiveness of debugging operations.

3. Explain why enclosing communications wiring and cabling in grounded metal conduits is an effective countermeasure against eavesdropping.

4. Explain one way the opposition might intercept cell phone communications.

Learning Activity

Imagine that your agency has need for a system of point-to-point two-way communication for several of its field officers. Envisage that the operating distance between the operatives is two miles, or about three-and-a-quarter kilometers. (1) Research what type of handheld radios the agency might select and list these in a column of a table (hint: look for radios that are manufactured for public safety agencies or the military); (2) in an adjacent column, note whether the radios in column one are manufactured with either scramblers or encryption, or have neither; (3) in a third column, note whether the radios could be used for unclassified information (i.e., information that, if intercepted, would have no adverse impact on the work of the operatives or the agency) or could afford some level of privacy (refer to the list of classification of information in chapter 8 to refresh your memory). Based on this information, what is your recommendation for a radio that can provide secure communications at "secret" level?

Notes

1. For example, see Bill Wedertz, *Dictionary of Naval Abbreviations*, 3rd ed. (Annapolis, MD: Naval Institute Press, 1984).
2. U.S. Department of the Navy, *Signals Intelligence, MCWP 2-15.2* (Washington, DC: U.S. Marine Corps, 1999).
3. U.S. Department of the Army and Air Force, *Fundamentals of Traffic Analysis (Radio-Telegraph)* (Washington, DC: U.S. Government Printing Office, 1948), reprinted by Aegean Park Press, Laguna Hills, California, n.d., with an additional glossary and index added.
4. The installation of listening device is termed *plumbing*, as in the question; "Is the plumbing place?" (Phillips, *The Night Watch*, 92). See also, chapter 1 regarding the example of the notorious White House Plumbers—those tasked to stop information "leaks."
5. Phillips, *The Night Watch*, 153.
6. Tom Kneitel, *Tune In On Telephone Calls*, 3rd ed. (Commack NY: CRB Research Books, 1996).
7. There are also cordless telephones that use digital spread spectrum (DSS) technology. Sometimes referred to as *frequency hopping*, these devices spread the conversation's audio across a wide bandwidth (perhaps around 3kHz) using a pseudorandom algorithm. In this way anyone

listening will only hear bursts of noise. This is because the phone's base unit selects a pseudo-random number that is needed to code/decode the signal. These numbers are chosen from a bank of many thousand available. This makes it very difficult to break the code. Eavesdroppers are more likely to attempt to hack your voice mail messages than to attempt to intercept a digital encrypted phone signal.

8 The term *cell phone* may not be used universally in Europe and other parts of the world. There, the terms *mobile phone* (e.g., in Australia and the United Kingdom) and *handy phone* (e.g., in German-speaking countries) are used.

9 Hillary Rodham Clinton, *What Happened* (New York: Simon & Schuster, 2017).

10 "Burst" transmissions are used to help avoid detection. This technique uses ultra-high-speed data transmission to forward compressed information in mere seconds of signal time. Later, the data is uncompressed to read. Turner, *Secrecy and Democracy*, 96.

11 Luna, *How to be Invisible*, 143–45.

12 Interestingly, former CIA operations officer, the late David Atlee Philipps noted that government-licensed amateur radio operators ("hams") have made excellent radio techs for the CIA (Phillips, *The Night Watch*, 228).

13 For instance, history is littered with references to intelligence officers being able to monitor signals sent in the clear, including military units by agents stationed in foreign countries. Phillips, *The Night Watch*, 174.

14 See, Liddy, *Will*, 165.

Chapter 10

Tenets of Offensive Counterintelligence

C arl von Clausewitz once wrote: "The main feature of an offensive battle is the outflanking or by-passing of the defender—that is, taking the initiative."[1] When it comes to taking the initiative in an intelligence war, we talk in terms of offensive counterintelligence—*deception* and *neutralization*. These are the equivalents of Clausewitz's outflanking and bypassing maneuvers.

Like defensive counterintelligence, offensive counterintelligence comprises several tenets and these tenets mirror, to some degree, those of defensive counterintelligence. This is because in defensive engagements counterintelligence practitioners are thwarting the offensive moves of the opposition. Therefore, if we turn the focus around, we can then see how an agency should operate when taking the initiative.

Tenets of Offensive Counterintelligence

Tenet 1—Executive Responsibility

It should not be surprising that the highest order tenet is the same as that of defensive counterintelligence—the responsibility for mounting an offensive campaign against all oppositions rests with the head of the agency. This is because it is a governance issue, and good governance lies with the agency head.[2]

The agency head may never be involved in any of the day-to-day tactical considerations of overseeing an operation, but he or she will be responsible for the program of aggressive secret operations. Functional responsibility therefore needs to be delegated to subordinates (or a committee), and, depending on the size of the agency, there may be several such delegations flowing down the chain of command. Nevertheless, the legal and ethical burdens of orchestration rest with that person, even though individual acts may be conducted by subordinates or agents employed by the agency.

As such, this tenet requires the agency head to put in place policies that convey the importance of following the rule of law and a standard of ethical conduct that projects an atmosphere of principled behavior—and to show through his or her actions that the agency should follow them. Although lower-level managers may ultimately be responsible for poor decisions made, the agency head must be able to stand on the moral high ground and call for them to account, rather than the other way around.

An example of this is Operation MH/CHAOS that the CIA ran from 1967 to 1973.[3] Former director of Central Intelligence, William Colby, pointed out that the operation demonstrated "how the habits and language of clandestinely can intoxicate even its own practitioners and theta internal supervision must be crystal-clear and thorough, especially when secrecy of the operation prohibits external oversight."[4]

. . . .

There is a theory of assumed vulnerability—that is, every target has at least one vulnerability that can be exploited.

. . . .

Tenet 2—Executive Justifiability

To conduct an offensive counterintelligence campaign, the agency head must be able to explain why such a program forms part of the agency's overall counterintelligence posture so that these actions are accepted in the most favorable light. The image of a campaign of unlawful behavior must be avoided, and this is associated with the first tenet. Attitudes must be cultivated to respect offensive counterintelligence's role in providing an active form of security and, consequently, legitimize the program through formal policies and practices that provide transparency for this decision (note, not transparency for the actual operations—they, of course, need by their nature to be managed and conducted in secret). "The test involves both ends and means. The end sought must be in the defense of the security of the state acting, not for aggression or aggrandizement, and the means used must be only those needed to accomplish that end, not excessive ones."[5]

Tenet 3—Ethical Symmetry

People's acceptance of situations is to a large degree based on prevailing social norms that are balanced in proportion. So, if the first two tenets are established within the agency as a norm, ethical behavior will follow and, hence, so will acceptance. A management model that replicates procedural compliance despite staff misgivings, along the lines of, say, "like it or leave," is unlikely to be successful. Acceptance is an important factor for agencies, as, without the support of its staff, any program, let alone one as delicate as an offensive counterintelligence program, will not be successful, or could fail.[6] No longer do people accept the adage that Nathan Hale—one of America's first spies—once argued: "Every kind of service, necessary to the public good, becomes honorable by being necessary."[7] Conducting offensive counterintelligence operations need support by demonstrating that these operations are not nefarious; that they are not being run contrary to law, or in opposition to public values.

Tenet 4—Friendly Access

In defensive counterintelligence the doctrine of *need-to-know* governs the accesses people have to areas where sensitive information is being processed, analyzed, or stored. In offensive counterintelligence operations, agency officers or agents need to be able to either recruit someone who has a need-to-know or be able to gain *friendly access*—meaning gaining access by deception rather than force.

. . . .

When you're catching spies, you have a bad counterintelligence service. When you're not catching spies, you have a bad intelligence service. You can't have it both ways.[8]

. . . .

Tenet 5—Action Against Leaks

If the leak is outside the legal provisions of some form of whistleblower legislation, and is lawful, then it falls to the agency's executive to authorize a counterintelligence investigation into the breach. This includes willful leaks as well as clumsy indiscretions by security-cleared staff. The investigation's results can be used for disciplinary purposes, and possibly, for deceptive operations.

Tenet 6—Deceptive Operations—Counterespionage

Despite all defensive measures to guard sensitive information, the opposition will assume that there will be information that the agency has and/or operations it is conducting that may never be known. Therefore, the opposition will try to discover this information and locate its source.

This tenet deals with deceptive operations—that is, operations that are designed to throw the opposition off track so that the discovery of sensitive data is delayed and consumes a disproportionate amount of the opposition's energy and resources. This is the role of counterspies. A counterspy is different to that of a police officer—where law enforcement will arrest, a counterspy will turn a spy so that he or she can feed the opposition with disinformation, misinformation, and lies.

. . . .

In the history of man's struggle to survive there is no example of victory being won by purely defensive means.[9]

. . . .

It is not enough to catch spies (or accept defectors) because the opposition can replace them with new recruits. It is important to turn them and supply the opposition with false information to negate and discredit authentic information they may have. The goal of counterespionage is "to discover hostile intelligence plans in their earliest stages rather than after they have begun to do their damage. To do this, [counterespionage] tries to penetrate the inner circle of hostile

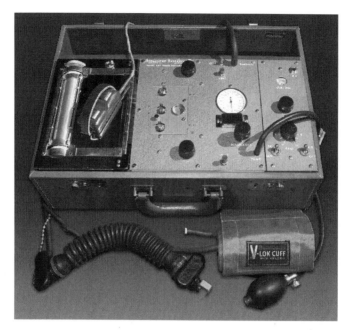

PHOTO 10.1 Polygraph Used to Question Jack Ruby to Test whether He Was Part of a Conspiracy. *Source*: Photograph courtesy of the Federal Bureau of Investigation.

services at its highest possible level where the plans are made, and the agents selected and trained, and, if the job can be managed, to bring over to its side 'insiders' from the other camp."[10]

Tenet 7—Counterreconnaissance and Decoys

History shows that opposition forces conduct reconnaissance missions to gather data about the agency's programs and operations, as well as data that exists under the wider protective umbrella of its mandate (e.g., regarding national security and military intelligence).[11] Therefore, this tenet addresses an agency's need to practice counterreconnaissance to be better able to place decoys to redirect the opposition to other areas that will yield nothing (though the opposition will be led to believe these data are meaningful). A simple example is to set up a sting-like operation to see if the agency can attract the opposition and, once attracted, feed it with misleading and deceptive data. Another is for the agency to simply actively scan the environment for signs of probing—for instance, on the Internet there are facilities that allow individuals to monitor the World Wide Web of new content. Though these commercial facilities have their own security shortcomings, an agency could establish a secure version for its own monitoring to "watch the watchers"—in this case, the opposition.

Tenet 8—Red Team Testing of Defenses

Agency personnel should be probing its own countermeasures through *red team*[12] exercises to determine if there are any systems or procedures in place that are so

PHOTO 10.2 Tenet 7—Probing Defenses and a Missed Opportunity. Here an impressively uniformed, but inattentive, security guard protects a landmark building in Hyderabad from criminals and insurgents. As part of a police "red team" counterintelligence exercise, the author was able to gather data unchallenged regarding the building and its occupants, including the taking of this target acquisition photograph. This was a missed opportunity for the target's intelligence program as it failed to notice an offensive counterintelligence operation being conducted. *Source*: Photograph courtesy of the author.

inflexible that they allow exploitation by the opposition. Rigid defensive tactics are predictable and, given time, the opposition is likely to find a way around them. For instance, agency staff may be tempted to bypass security procedures if they are overly complicated or time-consuming. Red team exercises should result in recommendations for fluid, random, changing, and unpredictable tactics to present a more difficult situation to penetrate. Surprise is one of the underlying assumptions of the overall theory of counterintelligence and this element underscores this tenet.

Tenet 9—Synergy with Defensive Counterintelligence

As offensive counterintelligence is active, especially those aspects that deal with neutralization (e.g., counterespionage operations), each operation needs to dovetail with components of the defensive program that might otherwise interfere with the success of these operations. For instance, if a double agent under the control of the agency is meant to have access to classified data of a particular type, then the defensive arrangements need to be structured in order to allow these data to be accessed and handed over to the opposition (perhaps as part of a more elaborate plan of flushing out a mole or to sow disinformation, etc.).

Tenet 10—Synergy with Positive Intelligence

An opposition may move aggressively toward acquiring agency information or information under the agency's protection umbrella. The agency's defensive security program will frustrate these moves. But the fact that the opposition is moving to probe or penetrate the security defenses is, in fact, valuable data for both intelligence analysts (i.e., researchers) and counterintelligence analysts (i.e., spy catchers). An opposition's desire to seek certain data types is an important factor in developing and/or enhancing security. It is also important information for strategic intelligence analysts (i.e., positive intelligence) who are examining issues relating to the opposition or its interests. In this regard, this tenet requires that counterintelligence works closely with the intelligence side of the agency (e.g., positive collection).

You can often predict what is going to happen, but it is devilishly hard to forecast when.[13]

Tenet 11—Synergy with All-Source and All-Discipline Collection

Data collection needs to incorporate strategies that seek information from domestic and overseas sources. This approach will lay a wide foundation for analysis as the world is arguably borderless; in practical terms, the universal convenience of air travel and information and communications technology have dissolved almost all international borders. This means the opposition can operate in multiple regions of the world simultaneously. Moreover, data sources need to include technical collection methods[14] as well as human sources.[15] No source of information should be discounted.

Review of Key Words and Phrases

The key words and phrases associated with this chapter are listed below. Demonstrate your understanding of each by writing a short definition or explanation in one or two sentences.

backup security support
complicity
early detection
neutralization

quality defensive system
red team
time-delay system

Study Questions

1. List the eleven tenets of offensive counterintelligence and provide a brief explanation of each.
2. Tenet 6 deals with deceptive counterintelligence operations. Describe a deceptive ploy that a counterintelligence officer could use in one of these intelligence settings: military intelligence, law enforcement intelligence, or business intelligence. Describe the situation and the information

that needs to be protected. Then describe the ploy that you have designed to throw the opposition off track. Explain how this strategy is designed to delay the discovery of the sensitive data, and/or consumes the opposition's energy and resources.

3. Describe in summary form the purpose of tenet 7, counterreconnaissance. Give an example of how this tenet could be applied in practice to one of the following contexts: national security intelligence or business intelligence.

4. Tenet 9 discusses offensive counterintelligence in relation to neutralization. Envisage a national security situation where a counterespionage operation is underway—for the purposes of this question, let's use the 1994 Aldrich Ames case. Explain why the counterespionage operation would benefit by dovetailing with components of the agency's defensive counterintelligence program.

Learning Activity

Consider the offensive tenet of red teaming—tenet 8. Using an everyday situation, practice red teaming. For instance, select a building near your current workplace or where you live that you know no details of other than it is in the neighborhood. With this building identified, assume that your agency has been tasked to prepare a penetration plan for a business that resides in this building. Assume that the business is your notional opposition force (perhaps it might be fictionalized as a front for foreign intelligence operations).

. . . .

WARNING! If you decide to conduct this learning activity, you do so at your own risk. And, if you decide to accept that responsibility by carrying out the exercise, it is important that you do not breach any law or local ordinance or place yourself or anyone else in danger while doing so. Remember, if you cause any harm to others in carrying out this learning activity, you have not only failed the assessment by being indiscreet, but, also, you risk being arrested, fined, or reported. Ensure you operate within the law always and that you act safely and have regard for the privacy of others.

. . . .

To write your plan, you will have to conduct reconnaissance and/ or surveillance to gather data. You would normally do this by reconnoitering the building and making observations and taking photographs. But, in a security conscious world, a person conducting surveillance of buildings or people may be reported to the police (or may even be assaulted by people who feel threatened by such behavior). If this is a possibility, then an alternative is to conduct a simulated physical reconnaissance by conducting a (somewhat limited) surveillance via open-source data and images via the Internet and by using information held in public libraries.

What did you find out about the building's physical attributes that might assist analysts? What did you discover about the business and what it does? Were there any conclusions (firm, tentative, or otherwise) that you could draw from your observations of the people entering or exiting the building? Now that these data have been collated, would you say that any form of counterintelligence was practiced? Are there vectors that could be exploited for penetrating the notional opposition target? If so, which ones and how would offensive measures be deployed?

Notes

[1] His words regarding fighting forces are analogous to offensive counterintelligence operations. Clausewitz, *On War*, 200.

[2] Godson, *Dirty Tricks or Trump Cards*, 185–87.

[3] Frank J. Rafalko, *MH/CHAOS: The CIAs Campaign Against the Radical New Left and the Black Panthers* (Annapolis, MD: Naval Institute Press, 2011).

[4] William Colby with Peter Forbath, *Honourable Men: My Life in the CIA* (London: Hutchinson, 1978), 317.

[5] William Colby with Forbath, *Honourable Men*, 114.

[6] The memoirs of former CIA case officers (i.e., operations officers) Robert Baer and Melissa Boyle Mahle illustrate this point. Their stories of how management mishandled various situations underscore the importance of this tenet. Robert Baer, *See No Evil: The True Story of a Ground Soldier in the CIA's War on Terrorism* (New York: Crown Publishers, 2002), and Mahle, *Denial and Deception*.

[7] William Colby with Forbath, *Honourable Men*, 21.

[8] Judge William H. Webster, former director of Central Intelligence, 1987 to 1991, as cited in Wettering, "Counterintelligence: The Broken Triad," 294.

[9] Peter Hamilton, *Espionage, Terrorism and Subversion in an Industrial Society* (Leather-head, UK: Peter A. Heims Ltd., 1979), 131.

[10] Allen W. Dulles, *The Craft of Intelligence* (Lanham, MD: The Lyons Press, 2006), 119.

[11] Philby, *My Silent War*, 103.

[12] The concept of a red team has existed throughout history in various forms. Exercises using red teams are used worldwide by governments and the private sector alike. Red teaming sees the problem through the eyes, and mind-set, of the opposition. It then emphasizes attack vectors based on vulnerability analysis. (Gregory Fontenot, "Seeing Red: Creating a Red-Team Capability for the Blue Force," *Military Review*, September–October 2005). Warrick describes how the CIA had implemented red teams to test the security of bases around the world in the aftermath of the Khost, Afghanistan, suicide bomber attack in 2009 (Joby Warrick, *The Triple Agent*, 199). For more on red teams, see also, Michael K. Meehan, "Red Teaming for Law Enforcement," *The Police Chief* 74, no. 2 (February 2007): 22–28, and Stephen Sloan and Robert J. Bunker, *Red Team and Counterterrorism Training* (Norman, OK: University of Oklahoma Press, 2011).

[13] Alexander Downer, Australia's former minister for foreign affairs from 1996 to 2007, writing in an op-ed editorial in *The Advertiser*, Adelaide, Australia (August 8, 2011).

[14] For an examination of technical intelligence, see Robert M. Clark, *The Technical Collection of Intelligence* (Washington, DC: CQ Press, 2010).

[15] Human intelligence can include the interrogation of nonofficial cover operatives, defectors, immigrants, liaisons, agents, double agents, defectors, and variations of these.

Chapter 11

Offensive Counterintelligence Planning

*D*enial and *deception* go together. Denial equates to defensive measures, whereas deception to offensive stratagems. "It is almost impossible to imagine a deception effort that does not involve denial,"[1] unless the operation is to project the illusion that something is going on, when it is not. An example is the Potemkin[2] village that North Korean created on the Demilitarized Zone to entice South Koreans to defect. However, the operation to promote the village of Kijŏng-dong was so poorly executed that since its creation in the 1950s, it has been referred to as "Propaganda Village."

Offensive counterintelligence is about plotting, trickery, and intrigue; and intrigue is a concept that has been described as the following: "To strategize, coordinate, and sustain a concerted effort to remove someone from power, to secretly move against an enemy, to do what Machiavelli would say was one of the hardest things to do in the world: to overthrow an existing order and do something new."[3] Arguably, since the Kennedy assassination, even the mention of *conspiracy* has been demoted to the realms of UFO spotters, monitoring alien space signals, and survivalists seeking a route to the center of the earth to escape the coming of the New World Order that will be controlled by the likes of the Illuminati.

Even though such conspiracy theories attract the skepticism and ridicule they deserve, there are people who *do* plot conspiratorially to change the world, or at least some aspects of the world. These people are intelligence officers. Their job is to remove power and influence from the opposition. Using detection and deception, they craft schemes to neutralize the opposition. If we view their work in crafting these plans as storytelling, it will hopefully remove the mystique and make sense as to how the task is approached.

Humans are susceptible to cognitive bias. Psychologists describe this as errors made in cognitive process such as reasoning, decision-making, evaluating, and remembering. This occurs when a person holds fast to beliefs without weighing-up evidence to the contrary. Exploiting cognitive bias is important for

PHOTO 11.1 North Korea's Poorly Executed Deception Operation on the Demilitarized Zone; the Potemkin Village of Kijong-dong. *Source*: Photograph by Don Sutherland. Courtesy of the U.S. Air Force.

planning deception operations. Pranks are an example of deception. But, what offensive counterintelligence seeks is more than this. Diversions provide cover, masking the true intent—take the deception perpetrated during the Operation Neptune Spear, the killing of bin Laden, where a team maintained a patrol of perimeter for anyone trying to escape the compound. Soon, civilian on-lookers appeared, but the group's translator told them that "there is a security operation under way."[4] They believe the ruse and went home.

Deception uses "the literary theory known as the *paradox of fiction*. Essentially, this theory states that for a story (fiction) to achieve believability, it must convince the reader that it is real. Although the reader knows the story is fiction, the writer can, to a large degree, convince (i.e., deceive) the reader into believing the story through the use of various literary tropes, techniques, and imagery. This is evident when a reader says, "the book was a page turner," "I couldn't put it down," "the writing made my heart race," and so on."[5] In planning an offensive counterintelligence operation, this theory is relied on to produce a story that become a live "stage production" (i.e., theatrical fiction).

Stories comprise three parts—beginning, middle, and end.[6] The art of storytelling is centuries old; Aristotle's theorized about the structure of a good story in what is now termed *Aristotle's Incline*. This is a graphical depiction of the rising action of a story through three acts of the narrative. Figure 11.1 is one such representation that shows the transition points between the three acts, which delineate the set-up, the main events, and the culmination of, in our case, the deception.

There are other variations of Aristotle's Incline that writers can use to help develop their story, as well as changes that can be introduced into the raising

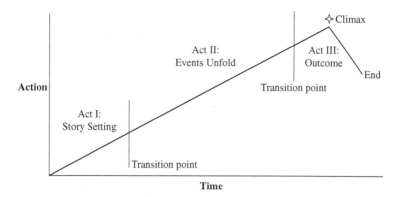

FIGURE 11.1 Aristotle's Incline.

storyline, such as plateauing action, oscillations action, and minor rises or falls. Reminiscing and revising past events and many other literary techniques can be used to make the story interesting or show artistic flair. But, in crafting an offensive intelligence operation, the writers are the planners, and what might be an interesting story or one with flair to a novelist is translated into an operation that is believable; one that will "make the enemy quite certain, very decisive, *and wrong.*"[7] This approach is consistent with many psychological operations.[8]

Planning Sequence

State the Outcome

What is the end state of the operation? This can be expressed as a summary statement, a premise, or the story's overall idea. The statement acts to guide the writing of the plan. The summary needs to outline the following: What the situation is? Who is the protagonist? and what the protagonist's object is? It also needs to state the opposition's role in the situation and how it will react to the deception. This summary statement follows the raising action of Aristotle's Incline, and can be condensed into two sentences. Take as an example, Operation Copperhead (see chapter 13):

> A key commander of the D-Day invasion (situation), General Bernard Montgomery (protagonist), needs to be close to his troops to oversee the imminent invasion of Europe (objective). But, he is seen just days before the real invasion visiting Gibraltar and Algiers, places where the Allies know German intelligence agents will observe him (deception) and draw the conclusion that the invasion is still some time away (end state).

Sketch the Scenes

The story's overall idea lets planners brainstorm various scenes that need to take place to create the story. The ideas can then be listed in the order that will make a believable narrative. The result should record the various ideas so that the details can be added to each scene.

- Details that General Montgomery will visit British troops are sent via radio knowing that German intelligence will intercept the transmission.
- Montgomery uses the Prime Minter's aircraft to fly to Gibraltar.
- The General inspects troops in view of areas where the public can observe him, and hopefully German intelligence agents.
- Montgomery flies to Algiers and the Gibraltar performance is repeated.
- After his staged appearances, Montgomery flies to safe house in Cairo and remains there until Normandy invasion.

Develop the Characters

Details are added at this stage of the plan. In our example, we need a body-double to take the place of General Montgomery so that the real General can remain in Britain overseeing the last-minute details of the invasion, while the decoy general is presenting the illusion that he is far from home base.

The body-double needs to be costumed and made up to appear like the general and he needs to study the leader's manners and physical movements, and speech patterns. Details about the generals' life, likes, and dislikes also need to be studied so he can answer questions asked to him. If the characters are concocted, then a new cover story needs to be developed, as was the case with the *Man Who Never Was* (see chapter 14).

Develop the Final Story

This is the completed story. Using the scene sketches, planners consolidate their ideas into a smoothly worded story that is well-structured. For a covert operation, the amount of detail will not be the same as, say, a novel, but perhaps resembling more of a playscript.

The amount of detail that goes into this writing will depend on how much the intelligence officers are able to control the situation. If it is under compete control of the agency's operative, then more detail is possible. If the operation is not under complete control, then to some degree there needs to be some room for the key actors to exercise "artistic judgment" (i.e., to "wing it"), if awkward or unpredicted issues arise. This is the reason why a character impersonating another needs to understand the other's personality, so that they react in-character.

Final Edit and Proof-of-Concept

Once the final story has been written, planners can read the story to a group of critics to identify any issues in the deception. The story is then edited to eliminate extraneous material or to include details omitted. Once this proof-of-concept has passed review, it is ready for implementation.

Show Time!

Support staff need to be briefed and counterintelligence officers need to implement procedures that will prevent disclosure of the operation. Props (e.g., the prime minister's aircraft), costumes (e.g., uniforms), equipment, travel, and other logistical arrangements (e.g., radio messages) need to be made and coordinated. If time and resources allow, a dress rehearsal would be beneficial. Or, in some operations, some aspects of the "performance" can be rehearsed. In the case of General Montgomery, practice walking and greeting simulated troops; eating, joking, and carrying-on conversation can be done to perfect the show.

Canadian Caper

Protests against the Shah of Iran began to form in October 1977 and continued with demonstration, general strikes and civil resistance until he left for exile in January 1979. The radical religious leader, Ayatollah Khomeini, returned from his long exile overseas, and the Shah's regime collapsed a month later. Iran voted to become an Islamic Republic in April 1979 and the so-called Iranian Revolution was complete.

Except that anti-America sentiment still lingered. When the Shah was diagnosed with cancer he sought treatment in the United States. In a controversial move, the then president Jimmy Carter admitted him in November of 1979. Militant Iranian students protested and sized the American Embassy in Tehran, taking over sixty hostages. Some Americans were released in the days that followed but 53 remained captive for 444 days. However, six Americas were outside the Embassy and were able to evade capture by finding a haven in the Canada Ambassador's private residence.

CIA officer Antonio Mendez began a plan to rescue the six Americans. Mendez was no James Bond; he was a technical operations officer who supported clandestine and covert operations. He received a bachelor's degree in Arts and trained as a graphic artist. His skills augmented "chemists, physicists, mechanical and electrical engineers, and an assortment of PhD scientists who specialized in extremely narrow fields, such as batteries, hot air balloons, special inks. . . . These were the folks who designed and built [CIA's] gadgetry."[9] His work title was "chief of disguise," but was in the process of being promoted to the position of "chief, authentication branch," which would put him "in charge of CIA's worldwide disguise operations, as well as any cases involving false documentation and the forensic monitoring of these documents for counterterrorism purposes."[10]

The stratagem was to create a fictitious Hollywood film company that was scouting a location to shoot a scene for a science-fiction film, titled *Argo*. With this outcome agreed, the scenes were sketched, the characters developed, and the final story laid out. Refinements and changes were made as the process was being created. Developing the back story for those involved and "backstopping" the other operational details began. Of course, all of this took place under the protective umbrella of defensive counterintelligence.

When show time came, Mendez and an undercover operative traveled to Iran and enacted the ruse. On January 27, 1980, the subterfuge was ready to be executed. At Tehran's Mehrabad Airport the six Americans boarded a commercial Swissair flight to Europe and escaped.

PHOTO 11.2 President Carter Thanking Mendez for his Role in the Canadian Caper. *Source:* Courtesy of the CIA.

Mendez was like a magician, projecting an illusion that deceived the Irian's cognitive processes—and that is what offensive ops are about, deception. What the mind sees is a projection of the brain because the brain collects data from the five senses. So, technical services officers try to fool the senses (and memory) to perceive what they want the viewer to see. It is not possible to catalog all possible schemes or combination of tricks, illusions, and deceptive plots because counterespionage is an art. It responds to need, circumstance, and what you think the opposition will believe at the time.

Review of Key Words and Phrases

The key words and phrases associated with this chapter are listed below. Demonstrate your understanding of each by writing a short definition or explanation in one or two sentences.

Aristotle's Incline   paradox of fiction
cognitive bias   storytelling

Study Questions

1. Explain how cognitive bias is used to fool the subject of a ruse.

2. Describe the steps in creating a deceptive plan.

Learning Activity

Assume that you are working as a creative writer for an intelligence agency. You have been approached to create a story to allow an office in nonofficial cover to enter a foreign country that is openly hostile to your nation, but movement of each's citizens is still allowed. The objective of the officer's mission is to confirm the identity and location of a person-of-interest.

Using the story sequence planning guide, create a simply plan that will allow the office to enter the country, find the person-of-interest, and exfiltrate. You can use a real country and city or create a notional country. The purpose of the activity is to demonstrate your understanding of the basics of creating a cover and backstopping it with disguises, props, and logistics to make the story believable. Assume that you have a modest budget for the operation, which will help keep you thinking within the realms of pragmatism.

Notes

1 Shulsky, "Elements of Strategic Denial and Deception," 18.
2 Potemkin villages are Hollywood-like urban areas created to look real—like a movie cowboy town. The building facades that comprise such a village are named after its inventor, Prince Grigory Aleksandrovich Potemkin-Tavricheski, who tried to project the illusion of prospering urban development when the war with the Ottoman Empire ended so he could curry favor with Catherine the Great.
3 Ryan Holiday, *Conspiracy* (New York: Portfolio/Penguin, 2018), 5.
4 Mark Owen with Kevin Maurer, *No Easy Day* (New York: Dutton, 2012), 250.
5 Prunckun, "The Paradox of Fiction and Terrorism's Overshadowing of Organised Crime as a Law Enforcement Concern," 65–66.
6 Jokes (i.e., a form of short story) have just two—the setup and the punchline.
7 Barton Whaley, *Stratagem: Deception and Surprise in War* (Cambridge, MA: MIT Center for International Studies, 1969), 135.
8 U.S. Department of Defense, *Psychological Operations Leaders Planning Guide*, GTA 33-01-001 (Washington, DC: Department of the Army, 2005), 13.
9 Antonio Mendez and Matt Baglio, *Argo* (New York: Viking, 2012), 29.
10 Antonio Mendez and Matt Baglio, *Argo*, 29–30.

Chapter 12

Offensive Counterintelligence: Detection

Television detective series abound. Some based on old themes made modern, some in period settings. Author Conan Doyle's *Sherlock Holmes* stories, Agatha Christies's *Murder on the Orient Express*, Edgar Allan's *Poe's Dupin* stories, and Robert Louis Stevenson's *The Strange Case of Dr. Jekyll and Mr. Hyde* immediately present themselves as some of the genre's classics that have been adapted for cinema and the television screen.

Detection is an act of discovery. Detectives try to use their wits (the *art* of the craft) and science to determine the facts of a matter. In the case of counterintelligence, it is an event that is associated with a breach or potential breach (including an attempted breach) of confidential information. The practice of detection follows five premises:

1. Identifying an event of concern;
2. Identifying the person(s) who were involved in the event;
3. Identifying the organizational association of the person(s) of interest;
4. Identifying the current location of the person(s) of interest; and
5. Gathering the facts that indicate that the person(s) committed the event.

Each of these premises is examined in this chapter starting with an *event of concern*, but in the context of defensive tenets 9, 10, 11, 12, 16, and 17. This examination will be in a general sense to avoid limiting the application of detection to any class of event, or to limit it to any practice (i.e., national security, military, law enforcement, business, or private). Nevertheless, the event of concern must be the center of a hostile information collection operation and is the beginning point for what can be considered the pre-investigation stage of an offensive counterintelligence operation.

Pre-Investigation

If, for example, an employee temporarily removes classified documents from the office and copies them, then there must be mechanisms in place that allow counterintelligence officers to recognize that this event has occurred (or to *identify* or signal/flag the event as requiring attention). The chapters on physical, personnel, information, and communications security discuss the practice of setting-up systems to do this. Such systems are sometimes referred to as *trip wires*. Trip wires can be human assets (e.g., guards) or technical systems—alarms or digital image recording equipment, as well as others.

If the opposition is skilled in tradecraft, even trip wires may not be enough; it may take an operational mishap. Experience demonstrates that it is sometimes the observant person who has exposed a spy ring by alerting authorities, who place the suspect under surveillance. Take the case of Mihail Gorin, a Soviet Union intelligence agent, and Hafis Salich, a civilian employee in U.S. Naval Intelligence. Salich sold Gorin information about Japanese activities in the United States. The spy ring was only discovered in 1938 when Gorin left secret documents and cash in his pants pocket when he dropped them off at the dry cleaners. The cleaner contacted the authorities. The FBI prosecuted the case, obtaining convictions for both men. Gorin "was eventually returned to the Soviet Union, where he surely must have been shot for his sloppiness."[1]

Once counterintelligence investigators are alerted to an event of concern, the person or people involved need to be identified. Without a positive identification of the perpetrator(s), the ability to assess the damage caused by the breach is greatly reduced. That is, a counterintelligence officer could not conclude with confidence who may have been interested in the data and how that information was to be used and, from that, the implications the compromised data could have for the agency or its client. Although counterintelligence investigators could estimate the potential damage and those who sought the information, as well as how they could possibly use it, this method would be based on inductive reasoning and hence not as reliable as knowing the identity of the person and the exact details involved in the breach.

* *

Spies are operatives who go forward to obtain sensitive information. Their methods are many, but the point is that their task is usually focused on a single purpose—to collect restricted information. In contrast, a *counterspy* is a colloquial term for counterintelligence officers, security personnel, and investigators. Their job is to protect sensitive information, investigate breaches of security, or run offensive counter-intelligence operations against the opposition. "If the spy is the sword, the counterspy is the shield."[2]

* *

The next step is to link perpetrators to the organization (opposition or otherwise) who would have been (or is) the ultimate recipient of the information. Although it is possible for a person to act alone without opposition support—a lone-wolf situation—in reality, this is not a likely situation. Why would an individual act on his or her own without any association with anyone else or with any other organization? Even "leakers" work with others who receive the information. Take as an example, the Snowden case. Edward Snowden claimed to have leaked tens of thousands of secret National Security Agency (NSA) files for moral reasons; however, investigations into the matter show another side to his duplicity—one of a deeply resentful person, driven by personal revenge.[3]

Logically, an agency's spies collect data to pass on to intelligence analysts who process the information to produce intelligence reports. Unless the event of concern involves an individual who has unilaterally embarked on a personal mission to uncover sinister happenings, it is hard to conceive a situation where no one else is involved. Even the "man-on-a-mission" person would surely give the information that is at the core of his or her distress to some legal authority for action or to the news media to expose. Accordingly, the perpetrator's association with others needs to be identified. This allows for an assessment of damage and will aid evidence gathering—motivation is key to many a successful counterintelligence investigation. It also means that counterintelligence investigators can locate and interrogate the person as part of the investigation in chief.

Investigation

Once the event of concern has triggered an alert, and the person(s) involved as well as their organizational affiliation have been identified the pre-investigation stage moves to the next stage—the evidence-gathering phase. This phase sets out to establish the facts of the event. These facts help the counterintelligence investigator draw a picture of the event—what, where, when, who, how, and why. This approached is based on scientifically based techniques to locate, collect, and preserve evidence of the event. These are known as *criminalistics* or *forensics*. Whereas a criminal investigation seeks to collect evidence to prosecute the matter in a court of law, a counterintelligence investigation may not[4]—such an investigation may purposefully end in a counteroperation that obscures, confuses, or deceives the opposition (see chapter 11—Offensive Counterintelligence Planning). Nonetheless, a counterintelligence investigation has the same purpose in mind—to discover the truth of an allegation or a suspected breach of security policy or law.

Although there are many approaches to how to investigate, and equally many techniques for conducting investigations, this section canvasses some of the more prominent methods. This is not to suggest that these are the only methods—they are presented as a way of exposing new counterintelligence officers to the practice.

Walk Back the Cat

This is a term that has gained popularity in spy fiction and journalism. The phrase is a metaphor for the corkscrew path a cat takes as it makes its way through the day—wandering here, meandering there; taking a detour when it likes, but rarely following a straight path.

In the case of a leak—the unauthorized disclosure of information—a counterintelligence investigator will have a few facts, but unlikely a clear picture of what happened, when, and by who. Walking back the cat means retracing the events to discovery the perpetrator and the reasons for the deceit.

Walking back the cat is analogous to reverse engineering a device. Some have suggested that the process is like putting the proverbial genie back in a bottle, or putting toothpaste back into its tube; but this is not an apt analogy. Such metaphors are about not being able to *undo* something. Walking back the cat is about trying to *find out* about an event and people behind the event; it is not about trying to undo the event.

The New York Times political columnist, the late William Safire wrote an opinion piece titled "Walk Back the Cat."[5] In it he explains the technique in relation to an alleged split in Saudi Arabia's policy on Israel. Safire alludes to the method as one used by intelligence analysts. However, what he described in his article is not walking back the cat, but a method of positing several hypotheses (based on inductive logic), the way a detective would do at the start of an investigation. Developing a hypothesis simply acts as a springboard for investigation. "The hypothesis is based on a survey of the crime scene. It is simply a set of reasoned assumptions of how the crime was committed and the general sequence of acts that were involved."[6]

Walking back the cat involves more. It involves the same methods as reverse engineering—looking at what is front of you and asking the Five Ws and H questions:

1. Who was involved and why these people?
2. What happened?
3. What was the target?
4. Why this target?
5. When did it take place?
6. Where did it take place?
7. Why did that happen (motive)?
8. How did it happen (means)? and
9. Why was it able to happen (opportunity)?[7]

Then, it requires the counterintelligence investigator to not just make assumptions, but to verify the facts and leads via old fashion, gumshoe detective work. The result is an understanding of how the situation developed and who was responsible. This can lead to an exposing weak or ineffective security methods, and to establish what damage has been done.

Crime Scene

Every person leaves a trail as they go through life. From the time one rises in the morning to the time when they retire for the evening, every person touches or comes in contact with objects during the day. They are seen by others doing what they do, and perhaps they leave physical and/or electronic "footprints" in the places where they have traveled. It is in these contacts that the concept of the crime scene arises. A crime scene can be a place in the kinetic world or in the cyberspace. It is an area where activities of interest are thought to have taken place—in the context of counterintelligence an activity of interest could be, for instance, the suspected theft of classified material or a person's unauthorized access to a restricted area.

The crime scene is more than the immediate area where the activity of interest took place—for example, the filing cabinet where a file was taken. It includes the surrounding area within a reasonable distance, perhaps the entire room as well as doors, windows, and other access points to the room. The rationale is that these adjacent areas may hold clues to what took place and when it took place. More important, they may yield facts about who was involved. It is the counterintelligence investigator's knowledge of crime scene searches and his or her experience in collecting physical evidence at crime scenes that may prove the most important aspect of the investigation. A small but vital clue could make or break the investigation.

The first step in a successful crime scene search is for the area to be isolated and secured from those not tasked with the investigation. This is to ensure that the area is not contaminated by others moving in and out of the area. It also ensures that any evidence remains where it was when the perpetrator(s) came in contact with it and ensures chain of custody (see appendix D).

Recording the Scene

Once the crime scene has been secured, counterintelligence investigators need to record the area to help recall its details later. It is particularly important to do this if the matter will be prosecuted in a court of law.

The three ways of recording the crime scene include sketches, photographs, which also include digital video recordings, and notes. Ideally, all three methods should be used but, as with any busy, pressured job, not all three can be employed in every case. Such considerations as higher priority cases, limited resources, and agency policy may be factors that dictate a compromised approach to using all these methods of recordings.

Nevertheless, in making that determination it is important that the investigators project their thinking to a point in the future where they need to act on this information. The question to be asked is, "If shortcuts are taken now, how might they affect the outcome of the investigation?" At the very least, some handwritten notes in a field notebook can be made along with a rough sketch of the area. Smartphones have high-quality cameras built-in (and digital video as well), so it would be a simple matter of taking a few photographs before departing the crime scene.

Sketches of the crime scene can be as simple as a drawing or as elaborate as a computer-aided diagram using a software package. When drawing a crime scene, it is important to record the positions of each piece of evidence in relation to other objects in the area. If the crime scene is inside a building, it might be distance (even an estimate) to doors, windows, desks, computer workstations, and other room features. If the area is outside, say a dead drop used by the suspect, then distances to trees, utility poles, pedestrian crosswalks, shops, and the like, depending on the situation, should be recorded.

Photographs do not have to be limited to the scene, though one effective approach is to photograph the crime scene starting from the general and moving to the specific, and the specific can be several areas within the overall area. Take for instance the outside crime scene of a discovered dead drop. The counterintelligence investigator may start with several photographs of the area looking from what might be the center out in the four directions—north, east, south, and west. He or she may then walk north, east, south, and west of the crime scene center and photograph the area looking back at it.

The investigator may also locate these area photographs in a larger photograph that has been organized from the air, looking down on the area and its surrounds. If this latter point is beyond the budget of an agency, recall that there are satellite maps available from commercial providers on the Internet and remote controlled aerial drones that can be used.

Then moving to the specific, the investigator may take several midrange photographs as a way of drawing the viewer's attention toward an object within the crime scene. These would be photographs that are not at the distance of the wide-area images but at a distance that is closer, but not close enough to cause the viewer to wonder where in the scene the photos were taken. Finally, close-up photographs should be taken of specific items or areas that show clues of value. In the case of the dead drop, it might be the hollow where the container holding the classified data was placed, the mark left to signal the dead drop needed "servicing," and so forth.

It is possible for a counterintelligence investigator with some degree of experience to take several purposeful photographs and then, using these, sketch the area (rather than rely on memory). Notes can also be deduced from photographs—for instance, descriptions of objects within the photographs, distances between objects, and where evidence was found. As the camera will record what the investigator sees it may be an efficient way of accomplishing the overall objective—accurately recording the crime scene. Having said that, this is a compromise method and one not recommended unless under pressure and where the alternative is not to record the crime scene. As with all compromises there may be practical drawbacks that may only come to light after the investigator leaves the crime scene.

If the photographs are to be used in a criminal prosecution, then the way the details are recorded and how the digital photographic media are handled (i.e., so that the images are not inadvertently altered) need to comply with the rules for evidence in the legal jurisdiction in which the matter will be heard. These requirements will vary from country to country and by state, province, and tribunal (say, a military tribunal).

Notes should be made of any important aspect of the crime scene that the investigator may need to further his or her inquiries, or that may prove to be a lead for a further line of inquiry sometime in the future (recalling that the future may be years hence). If note taking is not possible while the investigator is on scene, perhaps because they are in "hot pursuit" in an unfolding event, then digital recordings can be made, and, here again, cellular telephones have this facility. The investigator then transcribes his or her notes to paper or to an electronic document/database once back in the office, or via a communications link from a portable electronic device.

Search for Physical Evidence

The search for evidence can be approached several different ways and no one way is correct. It depends on the activity being investigated, area to be searched, and the objects within the crime scene. As a general proposition, the search needs to be based on some system. A systematic approach will help ensure that nothing is overlooked. There is nothing wrong with an investigator attending the crime scene and looking first for, and focusing on, obvious clues. But, the counterintelligence investigator should then conduct a systematic search of the area to ensure that all possible evidence is collected and that the perpetrators have not placed decoy pieces of evidence in the area in the hopes of throwing investigators off track.

Regardless of thoroughness of any search, evidence may not be at the crime scene. Take the case of Russian double agent Kim Philby. As soon as he realized that investigators might be closing in on him, he disposed of his incriminating covert photographic equipment by burying it in a wooded area far from his residence.[8] Police files contain innumerable cases where criminals have disposed of weapons, and paraphernalia used in the commission of crimes from bridges into muddy waterways; from boats into deep seas; or have been dissembled/crushed/burned/melted and the unidentifiable pieces then discarded into landfill sites. In some instances, even the victims of crimes have never been located, for example, Jimmy Hoffa.[9]

There are four common search patterns, and these are shown in Figure 12.1—the line search (upper left), the grid search (upper right), the spiral search (lower left), and the sectorial search (lower right). Even though these patterns are shown as separate approaches, there is nothing preventing the counter-intelligence investigator from combining two or more patterns if the objects within the crime scene prevent or obstruct the use of a one of these patterns. For instance, returning to the dead drop example, if the dead drop is in a public park that features garden walls, ornamental ponds, and so on, a sectorial search might be appropriate, but within one sector a grid search could be conducted and, in the others, spiral searches.

Barium Meal Test

Leaks come in many forms that are as different as the people who break confidence. It may be able to only trace a leak so far because the trail ends with several people. Surveillance and other covert means may not be of any assistance, so another option is to feed the leaker a *barium meal*.[10] The term refers to ingestion of a barium containing liquid that makes the digestive system visible under X-ray examination.

The meal is served by distributing a classified document to the suspected group. For all intents and purposes the document is the same copy except that in, say, the executive summary or conclusion or dotted throughout the document, certain words, or phrases have been changed making each document unique. In a sense giving each a fingerprint. Tom Clancy's fictional character, Jack Ryan, describes the procedure in *Patriot Games*,[11] which Clancy refers to as a *Canary Trap*:

> Each summary paragraph has six different versions, and the mixture of those paragraphs is unique to each numbered copy of the paper. There are over a thousand possible permutations, but only ninety-six numbered copies of the actual document. The reason the summary paragraphs are so lurid is to entice a reporter to quote them verbatim in the public media. If he quotes something from two or three of those paragraphs, we know which copy he saw and, therefore, who leaked it.[12]

The investigative technique is not only used in national security settings but also in industrial espionage. In 2007, it was reported that Steve Jobs concocted a fictitious product called "Asteroid" that he is said to have feed different aspects of the project to various people in the organization. Then, he watched to see if it was leaked to the media, and if so, which version.[13]

Physical Evidence

Evidence of a counterintelligence breach or an attempted breach can be either physical or digital. Here we summarize the physical aspects of evidence but will touch on evidence in the realm of computers and cybernetworks later in this section. As it is not possible to outline every possible event in which a security breach might take place, an overview will be provided to paint a picture of the depth and breadth of the type of objects that could be included.

Physical evidence can be large or even very large objects. They can also be small to microscopic particles. Those that are large enough for the investigator to see are logically those that can be detected in a crime scene search as being, say, out of place or, if common to the setting, somehow different or ones that might have been handled by the perpetrator, thus yielding clues.

There are two types of evidence, and these are termed *trace evidence* and *link evidence*. Trace evidence is created when two objects meet each other and, in the contact process, material from one object is exchanged with the other, or both. For instance, when a person sits in the seat of a car with fabric seat covers, fibers from the person's clothes are left on the seat cover and fibers from the seat cover are picked up by the person's clothes. This is known as *Locard's exchange principle*. Dr. Edmond Locard was a forensic scientist who in 1910 established what many consider to be the world's first crime laboratory in Lyon, France.

If one was to compile a list of the types of evidence that exist, the list would be very long indeed. However, the more common types of evidence include fingerprints, DNA, hairs and fibers, documents, glass, impressions, paints, residues, soil, tool marks, and vegetative matter. In this section a few of the principal types will be discussed—fingerprinting, DNA, hair and fibers, and documents.

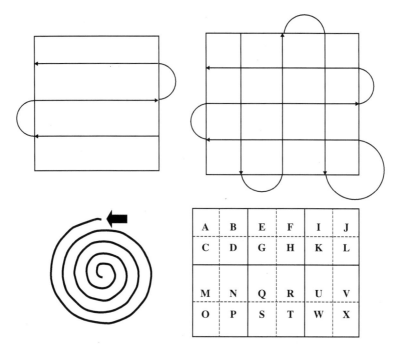

FIGURE 12.1 Search Patterns—Clockwise from Upper Left—Strip Search, Grid Search, Spiral Search, and Sectorial Search. Line search pattern—An investigator walks across the area in a line, then walks back across the area from the opposite direction, and so on. Grid search is the same as a line search, however the area is canvassed again; this time in a direction that is at a right angle to the first pattern. Spiral search pattern—Starting at the outside of the crime scene and working in, or vice versa. Sectorial search pattern—Each sector is divided into smaller zones and labeled so that each can be recorded as completed before moving to the next, and the next, and so forth, as illustrated in this example. *Source*: Courtesy of the author.

Fingerprints

The first type of physical evidence that comes to mind is a person's fingerprints. Fingerprinting has been used as a reliable source of identification for almost 200 years. The first attempt at formally classifying people's fingerprints was made by the Czech physiologist Professor Jan Evangelista Purkinje in 1823. Since that time a series of scholarly developments and operational procedural refinements have increased the reliability and validity of the fingerprint system. Suffice to say that fingerprinting is a well-established science and is accepted in courts of law worldwide.

Counterintelligence investigators should therefore consider the collection of fingerprints as a potential source of evidence. The likelihood of a false positive (i.e., a Type I error) is enormously small and it is in this aspect that the power of this evidence lays. Fingerprint pioneer Francis Galton put this question forward when in 1892 he stated: "Given two finger prints, which are alike in their minutiae, what is the chance that they were made by different persons?"[14] Galton calculated that the chance of a Type I error was in the order of one in

| Arch | Loop | Whorl |

PHOTO 12.1 The Three Basic Fingerprint Patterns—Arch, Loop, and Whorl. *Source*: Courtesy of the U.S. Department of Commerce.

sixty-four billion. The chief drawback of fingerprinting is that there needs to be a sufficient print left on an object. A large enough print area is required so that the examiners can view the print to establish several points of similarity. Tied with this limitation is that the examiner needs a reference fingerprint to conduct his or her analysis. Without a reference print, no comparison can be done.

· ·

The absence of fingerprints is itself a fingerprint. It tells the investigator something about the incident.

· ·

The arch pattern is characterized by ridges that pass from one side of the fingerprint to the other, forming a raised formation in the center that resembles

PHOTO 12.2 Over Several Decades, the FBI Has Converted Millions of its Fingerprint Cards, Criminal History Folders, and Civil Identity Files into Searchable Digital Records. *Source*: Courtesy of the Federal Bureau of Investigation.

an arch. The loop pattern features a series of ridges that do not pass from one side to the other but rather "loop" in the center and terminate at the same starting point. The whorl is formed by a set of ridges that make a circular pattern in the center of the fingerprint. These three patterns are shown in Photo 12.1.

DNA

DNA is shorthand for deoxyribonucleic acid, the material that is present in every cell in the human body. As such, collecting material at the crime scene that contains human DNA is another way to help identify a perpetrator as no two humans have the same DNA. Sources of DNA are many and include the following: blood, skin, sweat hair, dandruff, mucus, ear wax, and saliva. As with fingerprints, the power of being able to say that the sample collected does not match anyone other than the suspect is very strong. Unlike fingerprints where a partial print may not contain enough of the pattern to be able to make a comparison, the amount of DNA needed to conduct a laboratory analysis to read the DNA "markers" is around one billionth of a gram.

Hairs and Fibers

Hairs and fibers can provide clues in two directions—linking the suspect to the crime scene and linking the crime scene to the suspect. That is, if the suspect has left hairs or fibers that he or she brought to the crime scene in the process of breaching security, these clues link the suspect to the scene. Moreover, if the suspect inadvertently collected hairs or fibers that were part of the area now determined as the crime scene and took these away, they link the scene to the suspect.

In the case of the latter, the suspect may have touched curtains or drapes in the office area that left fibers on his or her clothing. In the case of the former, the suspect may have had hairs of his or her pet dog on his clothing and these fell off in the crime scene area while they were there. In either case, these pieces of physical evidence can be analyzed in a laboratory and a probability assigned to the likelihood that these appearances of the hairs or fibers occurred by chance. Hairs can be either human or animal (fur), and fibers can be from plants, minerals, or synthetic sources.

As an example, in 2017 a Texas woman was arrested by the FBI for allegedly sending two improvised explosive devices in 2016 to then president Obama and the then Texas governor.[15] Crucial among the various pieces of evidence collected by the FBI were hairs from the accused's cats; these proved to be microscopically consistent with hairs found on the homemade explosive.

Documents

Document examination covers a wide range of forensic analyses that look to verify the source and authenticity of a document. It includes examining the words printed on the page as well as examining the document itself. Issues that might present for the counterintelligence investigator could include alterations to change the content or meaning of the words that appear on the printed page or alter the appearance of the physical form of the document. A person's handwriting may also be the subject of examination.

By way of example, an applicant for a security clearance may submit several documents in support of the application and one or more of these may be questioned. These *questioned documents* will have to be checked by an examiner with skills in detecting erasures and words that have been overwritten or crossed-out using techniques of infrared and ultraviolet photography and microscopy. The actual paper stock and printing techniques may also be examined if the document is considered falsified—say, in the case of a passport.

When examining the printing techniques, the document examiner may need to examine documents produced by laser and other computer-associated printers, older facsimile machines, and photocopiers. With the steady increase in the quality of computer-based printing, forged documents are relatively easy to create using software packages. Although these documents may present as having no "alterations," their authenticity is what is questioned—that is, were they issued by the authority that is asserted on the document?

Interviews and Interrogations

The terms *interview* and *interrogation* are sometimes used interchangeably though in practice the two are different. An interview is an event where the investigator talks to a person who he or she considers having information relevant to the issue under investigation. An interrogation is to determine the innocence or guilt of a person. Although the two are integrally related, they are nonetheless distinct and different.

One way to look at interviews is that they are intended to collect information about the alleged breach, its background, events surrounding its occurrence, and what might have taken place after. It is information from those who observed it in its entirety or those who observed only aspects of it or observed related events. Interviews can be informal—a brief, unstructured discussion lasting a few minutes—or formal, where the investigator systematically takes the interviewee through a sequence of events and then records the person's recollection in a written statement. The statement is then signed by the interviewee, the investigator, and perhaps a third party who witnesses their signatures. Alternatively, the interview may be recorded using audiovisual recording equipment and the discussion transcribed into text afterward.

The outcome of the interview process is to help build the case. Information from interviews can be used to discover new evidence and/or to obtain clarification about already discovered evidence.

If the purpose of an interrogation is to ascertain whether the suspect is innocent or guilty, then this is done by inducing the suspect to reveal

- facts and circumstances pertinent to the breach under investigation, which might include the location of evidence that remains undiscovered (or even unknown), or alibis that support an assertion of innocence;
- an admission of guilt (e.g., a confession);

- accomplices to the security breach; and
- other security breaches by the suspect or his or her accomplices.

It is important to weigh all facts in the matter and follow up on all leads generated in the interrogation process, because selecting only the facts that support the hypothesis that the suspect is guilty is not only ethically wrong, it is wrong in law (i.e., colloquially known as *framing* a person). It also means the true perpetrator has not been identified and risk of future damage remains.

Surveillance

Physical Surveillance

"Intelligence work is not all fun and games but more often plodding perseverance in collecting what might appear to be trivia."[16] And, surveillance is one of those tasks—the observation of people, places, and objects. Surveillance is not something that is performed openly where the intent of the observer is declared. Surveillance is conducted covertly, or secretly, even though the *surveillant* (or *operator*) may be observed. So, surveillance is a secret activity not because the surveillants cannot be seen, but because their purpose would be considered by anyone observing them to be other than that of collecting information.

Surveillance can be used in several applications, but a common use is to supplement information obtained from interviews or from evidence already collected. However, it can also be used to develop new leads in a case that is lacking direction or to corroborate existing information.

Surveillance is arguably both art and science. It uses time-tested techniques for carrying out observations of fixed locations (i.e., places and objects, and sometimes referred to as *static surveillance* or, more informally, as a *stakeout*) and for moving surveillance (referred to as *tailing* or *shadowing*). The techniques used to do such surveillances are voluminous and have been developed through a process of science and skillful interpretation of human behavior—this is where the art comes in.

As the craft of surveillance has developed, practitioners have developed their own terminology. A few examples suffice to demonstrate these terms: the subject of a surveillance operation is termed the *target* and the group tasked to conduct the surveillance is termed the *surveillance team*. The surveillant who has visual observation of the target is termed to have *command* (in the case where the surveillant changes throughout the operation). There are many others, but it is worth noting that, when discussing the use of surveillance in an investigation, those who are tasked to carry out the job may lapse into their own jargon.

Although surveillance can yield high-grade results, it is time-consuming and has drawbacks. One limitation is that, if a surveillance team is tasked to do a job, there is no guarantee that the operators will be at the right place at the right time. Large amounts of time and financial resources can be spent on surveillance with no results. For instance, a surveillance team may miss observing the anticipated event by minutes without even knowing it—the target may have departed

PHOTO 12.3 Covert Photography is an Integral Part of Surveillance Operations. *Source*: Photograph by Sgt. Micah Merrill. Courtesy of the U.S. Army.

just before the surveillance team arrives to take up their observation post, or the operators may depart at the end of their shift only to have the target then arrive. And, the opposition's tradecraft comes into play also—the use of dead drops, brush pasts, and hand-offs are hard to observe. To a large degree, there is the element of chance involved with being successful with surveillance, unless operational resources and funds are available for twenty-four-hour operations.

The biggest weakness is that all the advantages gained by carrying out a surveillance could vanish if an operator or the surveillance team is discovered (termed *burned*). As soon as the target is aware that he or she is being watched, they are likely to implement countersurveillance tactics and/or avoid the activity that the surveillance was designed to capture.

Information captured by surveillants may include a log of their stakeout or shadowing activities as well as pertinent events under their gaze. A log might record such details as start and finish times/dates, locations, field of view, people observed and what they were doing, the times these people were observed, and physical descriptions of them and the things they were doing. In short, anything that may help the investigation should be collected and recorded. In recording people and events during a surveillance, still and motion photography are almost always used. These images combined with logs and information provided by operators during their debriefing can be invaluable to the investigation.

Electronic Surveillance

Electronic surveillance covers a wide range of techniques for collecting evidence but is most likely to be in the form of audio surveillance (i.e., room listening devices or *bugs*) and telephonic intercepts. There are other forms of electronic surveillance, such as radio frequency intercepts (i.e., the interception of various forms of wireless transmissions) and data interception relating to the Internet, but the most commonly used intercepts are likely to be audio methods.

The fundamental principle of any audio surveillance operation is to be able to plant a quality microphone as near as possible to the target and, in doing so, avoid background noise that may render the intercept unintelligible. There are hundreds of devices and as many methods for installing these devices, enough to fill many technical manuals. But, all these aspects relate to two simple principles. Because the farther a person is from the surveillance microphone, the less chance there is for collecting an intelligible voice message. And, the more background noise, the less likely it is that the target's voice and the message it carries can be deciphered. Though there are several software packages that can filter background noise, it means a further step in digital processing that may degrade the fidelity of the original recording.

The telephone is arguably the most useful medium for electronic surveillance as its use is ubiquitous, even in the most remote places on the planet. Obtaining information using the telephone involves two methods: the first uses devices that intercept conversation directly from landlines and requires no entry into the target's property, and the second is intercepting the voice message as it passes over landlines to the telephone exchange. This applies to both landline telephones and cellular telephones as the latter share part of the landline system via what is termed a *trunked network*. That is, although the sender and receiver may be using radio signals to transmit to the nearest cell tower (i.e., a full-duplex repeater), the voice message is then conveyed to the next cell tower via landlines.[17]

Undercover Investigation

Operatives who go undercover during an investigation can get close to individuals or inside organizations to make firsthand observations. Such information can be valuable to an investigation because it is an opportunity to get a glimpse of the target's intentions, thereby providing an insight into the target's thinking, rationale, and behaviors that could not be obtained by other means.

The use of operatives is risky for the operative, both physically and psychologically, and it is risky for the agency in many ways, too. The operative risks physical harm in the form of bodily injury and death as well as a range of psychological injuries spanning from mild anxiety to severe psychiatric disorders. The physical risks are more apparent as one can easily visualize the ramifications of having to penetrate an illegal enterprise. The psychological injuries arise from the stresses associated with working in isolation, working in a dangerous environment, and perhaps engaging in activity that is illegal (including the need to consume illicit drugs and alcohol in binge quantities to maintain cover).

However, given the risks and the monetary costs of conducting an undercover operation, it is a method that is not often used in the first instance. It is usually reserved as a means of last resort or for counterintelligence cases that pose a danger to society or national security.

Because the operative will be in direct contact with the target, there are a few issues that must be kept in mind. The most important is that the operative's identity must be guarded with utmost secrecy. If knowledge of the operative leaks to the target, the operative's cover will not only be "blown," but also the operative is likely to suffer injury.

The goal of an undercover operative in a counterintelligence investigation is to infiltrate "as deep as possible and [gather information and evidence] on the opposition or enemy."[18]

Part of the operative's brief is to obtain evidence of wrongdoing (or innocence), as well as information generally related to the investigation. Evidence may be in the form of admissions, but intelligence data may also be in the form of indicators of intent. To capture these data the operative can either commit the details to memory and then record them later for transmission back to the agency or use some electronic device that transmits the data live for recording and transcription. The latter is the most reliable and the best solution as it does not rely on the operative's ability to remember the details, which, from an intelligence point of view, can be critical. Data can be qualitative (e.g., discussions with the target) and quantitative (e.g., numbers of items, times, routes, colors, preferences, and others).

Computer Forensics

Investigating the recording, storage, retrieval, and transmission of electronic data, as well as the means for transmission of these data packets over networks, falls to the investigator who is skilled in computer forensics. Although this may be a specialized field within counterintelligence investigation, all counterintelligence investigators should have at least an advanced working knowledge of the issues involved in probing the digitally based events. Such inquiries are known as *computer forensic examinations*.

The days where data were predominately contained in paper files started to disappear in the 1980s when the microcomputer (later known as the *personal computer* or, simply, *PC*) became affordable to businesses and individuals. Now, governments, businesses, and peoples' personal lives could not function without digital computing. It follows that security breaches are most likely to first occur in a computer system and then lead to the kinetic world. So, given this scenario, digital evidence should be a prime consideration in investigating security breaches and other counterintelligence issues. The forensic processes and investigative techniques parallel the physical world and similar steps are taken to secure the crime scene and prevent people from destroying or removing potential evidence by the electronic equivalent of cordoning-off the equipment and network access and well as restricting physical entry into the area.[19]

Depending on the situation, equipment may need to be removed from the crime scene or it may be able to be examined in place. Like with a physical crime scene, procedures are sequential to ensure preservation of data vital to the investigation. This information may lead investigators to other sources or the potential identity of the perpetrator(s). There are growing numbers of analytic software programs that allow the computer forensic investigator to explore the digital crime scene looking for clues.

Review of Key Words and Phrases

The key words and phrases associated with this chapter are listed below. Demonstrate your understanding of each by writing a short definition or explanation in one or two sentences.

barium meal

burned

computer forensic examinations

criminalistics

forensics

interrogation

interview

investigation

Locard's exchange principle

shadowing

stakeout

surveillance team

surveillant

tailing

target

trip wires

walk back the cat

Study Questions

1. In order, list the five premises of detection.
2. Describe three ways a counterintelligence investigator can record a crime scene and then discuss the pros and cons of each method.
3. List the four generally accepted search methods and explain the theory that underpins systematic searching.
4. What is the fundamental principle of any audio surveillance operation? In a hypothetical situation, explain how this might be accomplished.

Learning Activity

For this learning activity you will need (1) a black ink pad; (2) a sheet of paper; and (3) a magnifying glass. Starting with your index finger, gently roll the finger on the ink pad and then roll the finger on the sheet of paper leaving room for the other fingers. Follow this with a print of each of the remaining fingers and thumb. Once the ink dries, use the magnifying glass to observe the patterns. Although there are many different fingerprint patterns, there are three that form the basis for all others—the arch, loop, and whorl. These three patterns are shown in Photo 12.1. Using these indicative patterns as an initial guide, determine the basic pattern of your fingerprints. Are all the fingerprints of the same pattern? Compare your fingerprints to those of, say, another family member, a friend, or work colleague. What have your observations revealed? Explain.

Notes

1 Dulles, *The Craft of Intelligence*, 202.
2 Bob Burton, *Top Secret: A Clandestine Operator's Glossary of Terms* (Boulder, CO: Paladin Press, 1986), 30.
3 Edward J. Epstein, *How American Lost Its Secrets: Edward Snowden, the Man and the Theft* (New York: Vintage, 2017), 34, 229, and 259–60.
4 Although a deception or neutralization operation may be the prime focus of such an investigation, a criminal prosecution cannot be discounted; take for instance the cases involving Aldrich Ames (Wise, *Nightmover*) and Robert Hanssen (David Wise, *Spy: The Inside Story of How the FBI's Robert Hanson Betrayed America* [New York: Random House, 2002]).
5 William Safire, "Walk Back the Cat," Opinion, *The New York Times*, April 29, 2002.
6 U.S. Army, *Law Enforcement Investigations, FM 3-19.13* (Washington, DC: Department of Defense, 2005), 1–15 and 1–16.
7 Of course, these are not the only questions that an investigator could be asked; they simply demonstrate the type of facts that are needed to walk back the cat.
8 Philby, *My Silent War*.
9 James (Jimmy) Riddle Hoffa was President of the International Brotherhood of Teamsters from 1958 until 1971. When he was a union leader, he was linked to organized crime and convicted of several fraud and bribery offenses. After his release from prison, he vanished— last seen at a restaurant parking lot in a Detroit suburb on July 30, 1975. He body has never been found.
10 Peter Wright, *Spy Catcher* (Richmond, Victoria: William Heinemann, 1987).
11 Clancy also described his *canary trap* in the novel, *Without Remorse* (London: HarperCollins, 1993), and a barium meal was also severed by Robert Little in his book *The Company* (Woodstock, NY: The Overlook Press, 2002).
12 Tom Clancy, *Patriot Games* (New York: Putnam, 1987).
13 Leander Kahney, "Steve Jobs, Spymaster," *Wired*, March 6, 2007, https://www.wired.com/2007/03/steve-jobs-spymaster/?currentPage=all (accessed April 6, 2018).
14 Francis Galton, *Finger Prints* (New York: Macmillan, 1892), 110.
15 Keri Blakinger, "Houston-Area Woman Accused of Mailing Bombs to Abbot, Obama, Benefits Agency," *Houston Chronicle*, https://www.houstonchronicle.com/news/houston-texas/houston/article/Waller-County-woman-accused-of-mailing-bombs-to-12380370.php (accessed March 9, 2018).
16 Phillips, *The Night Watch*, 115.
17 This is a simplified explanation of what happens—for instance, the transmission from the two parties could also include satellite links if the people are in different countries. Or, it could include microwave links and other combinations if in different regions of the same continent. Nevertheless, interception can be by accessing a node that handles the transmissions from the cellular handset.
18 J. Kirk Barefoot, *Undercover Investigation* (Springfield, IL: Charles C. Thomas, 1975), 4.
19 Bear in mind that people can access information stored on workstations and data servers remotely—physical presence at a terminal in the restricted area may not always be required.

Chapter 13

Offensive Counterintelligence: Deception

Deception can be used to overpower the cognitive processes of opposition agents, operatives, officers, and analysts to induce errors in their thinking. These errant perceptions can, in turn, be exploited. The historical record is replete with examples: one of the finest collections is Allen Dulles's *Great True Spy Stories*[1].

Not surprisingly, deception finds its theoretical roots in cognitive psychology. This is a subbranch of the discipline of psychology that examines a person's mental process relating to perception, memory, reasoning, and decision-making. Because it recognizes internal mental states, such as mental imagery, belief, motivation, and desire, the reverse application of cognitive psychological principles can be used to deceive. This is done by presenting a situation that resembles what one might expect to exist in a particular setting, but in fact is a pure fiction. Magic is an act of deception that comes to mind and this was used by the CIA (and no doubt other intelligence services) to its advantage. These exploits are discussed in the now declassified manual, *The Official CIA Manual of Trickery and Deception*.[2]

. . . .

A mirage is something that appears real but is not.

. . . .

Pretexts and ruses are used regularly by private investigators and can be exploited in counterintelligence operations in the same way. In espionage, pretext is synonymous with *cover* (e.g., a cover story, a cover identity, etc.). Camouflage is a trick technique that makes objects disappear. And decoys achieve deception by presenting the opposition with what appear to be viable targets but are nothing more than illusions.

The military uses ruses to mask the true intentions on the battlespace to mislead the enemy. A commander might, for example, use false designations for her units, or announce that leave is being granted the day before an attack, or shifting reconnaissance units to reconnoiter an area not associated with the attack. Intelligence agencies use the pretext of being a journalist as a ruse to gain access to denied areas or to obtain information that couldn't be obtained in other ways.

A *pretext* is used in espionage as a method for obtaining confidential information. A pretext is any act of deception—ruse, subterfuge, ploy, trick, or a cover story—that allows an operative to solicit information by a false reason.[3] This includes entering premises or countries for obtaining information or being in a place that an operative wouldn't otherwise have access to or permission for or simply to be inconspicuous. In a counterintelligence context, the pretext can be used for the same purpose; however, the intent is not to obtain intelligence to supply analysts with data for synthesizing into an intelligence product. Instead, it is a deceptive technique that allows access to information to provide operational security.

Decoys

Anyone familiar with duck hunting will be aware of the use of decoys. These are usually wooden or plastic replicas placed in, say, a pond to tempt ducks passing overhead to stop and join them. Once the real ducks are sitting next to the decoys, the hunter has his target. The same intent and psychology are employed in offensive counterintelligence operations. Counterintelligence personnel conducting an offensive operation can use decoys to confuse the opposition. There are several contexts in which decoys can be used and the chief uses—political decoys (or body doubles), voice decoys, ghost armies, and computer decoys—will be discussed here.

A political decoy is someone who stands in for a high-profile political leader, usually in times of peril, to deceive the opposition. The political decoy is selected for his or her physical resemblance to the leader being protected. Acting lessons and instructions as to how the decoy should impersonate the protected person are part of the operation, as is dress, deportment, and elocution.

The use of a political decoy has great offensive advantage as it not only offers an alternative target (in the literal sense) to the leader; the planned activities and places visited by the decoy can mislead and/or confuse the opposition. This has the effect of expending surveillance resources and analysis time and energy on tasks that are barren and fruitless.

· ·

Deception—Those actions taken to create the false image of our activities and operations.[4]

· ·

To deceive the Nazis about the time and place of the June 6, 1944, Normandy landings Operation Bodyguard was conceived. The deception plan comprised several sub-plans, one of which was Operation Copperhead.[5]

The objective was to mislead German intelligence about the location of General Bernard Montgomery who the German high command expected to be directly involved in the anticipated European invasion. Allied intelligence reasoned that if the general was seen some distance from the English demarcation areas, the Nazis would conclude the invasion was still some time away.

The plan called for Montgomery to make several high-profile appearances in North Africa. This was done by use of a decoy in the form of a body-double. M.E. Clifton James,[6] an Australian actor serving in the British Army was found to have a likeness to the general, so he was tasked to study the general and became familiar with his stances, movements, and gestures.[7]

The operation began on May 26, 1944, when James, as General Montgomery, visited Gibraltar and then Algiers, places where the Allies knew German intelligence agents would observe him. After his staged appearances, James was flown to safe house in Cairo until the real general appeared at Normandy after the D-Day invasion.

A voice-only decoy performs the same role and function as a political decoy but is limited to oral impersonation of the protected person. This may include providing telephone interviews or radio and other media appearances. Terrorists and leaders of outlawed and underground groups, as well as a range of criminals, have been known to use this method. These are usually voice recordings sent to authorities to make demands, taunt, or simply waste their time and energy and, in the process, project the appearance that they are somewhere where they are not, or in a place at a time when they were not, or both.

A *ghost army* is the term soldiers used during the Second World War for a unit of the U.S. Army—the 23rd Headquarters Special Troops. Its mission was to present a false picture of the Allied military's strength, location, and intent to the Nazi military leaders. This unit used many creative deceptive methods to achieve this, including visual, sonic, and radio deceptions. Inflatable rubberized

PHOTO 13.1 General Montgomery (Left) and His Body-double, M. E. Clifton James (Right). *Source*: Courtesy of the Government of the United Kingdom.

PHOTO 13.2 Decoys Come in Many Forms—Here an American AH-64D Apache Helicopter Firing Flares as Heat Decoys During a Mission over Iraq on April 29, 2011. *Source*: Photograph by Chief Warrant Officer Daniel McClinton. Courtesy of the U.S. Army.

tanks, field artillery, jeeps, and even inflatable aircraft were used so that enemy reconnaissance aircraft would spot them and report these decoy sightings.

Using troops with an abundance of imagination, creative skills, and artistry, it is now known that the once-classified project could erect airfields, bivouacs, and tank formations with a very short period. It is estimated that some twenty battlefield operations were staged by the ghost army during the Second World War.[8] The 23rd Headquarters Special Troops also used fictitious radio signals and wireless traffic, special effects ("atmosphere"[9]), and noises (e.g., the grinding and clanking of tanks) to deceive Nazis forces.

In 1954, the stratagem was used to help defeat the communist government of Jacobo Árbenz in Guatemala. With the help of a shortwave radio station— Voice of Liberation—about 150 CIA-backed insurgents set up camp only a few miles inside Guatemala, giving the impression that an army of –5,000 liberators had "invaded." But, in fact it was a ghost army in the jungle generating deceptions such as fabricated battles to start rumors and undermine the confidence of the communist government. After a series of deceptions and other tactics:

> The radio announcement of two imaginary columns of soldiers was broadcast on Sunday morning. . . . Arbenz resigned in a nationwide radio speech that night. He drove to the Mexican embassy to seek asylum, and six hundred of his supporters followed him and to other embassies. The revolution was over.[10]

It is understood that, during the Vietnam War, U.S. forces used dummy paratroops made of ice to simulate an airborne assault to flush out hidden Viet Cong units. The Viet Cong troops would see the paratroopers land nearby and would come out of hiding to move to the landing zone to engage these enemy troops. When the Viet Cong arrived the ice (i.e., the paratroop decoys, or PDs) would have melted in the heat of the steamy jungle. It was reasoned that the Viet Cong would then be duped into believing that the decoy troops were, perhaps, in a defensive position nearby. In the meantime, an air strike would be called in to destroy the Viet Cong at the PD landing zone. Because of their effectiveness, it is understood that paratroop decoys are still being used from time to time in various conflicts around the world.

Decoys can be in either two-dimensional or three-dimensional models. Two-dimensional decoys can be configured in a vertical or a horizontal profile. Vertically constructed decoys are used for presenting a view from the front or sides (e.g., a battlefield decoy presented to the opposing forces), whereas horizontal decoys are used for presenting a profile to over-flying surveillance aircraft and satellites. Three-dimensional decoys can be used for either application—ground surveillance from the front or sides, as well as aerial reconnaissance.

. . . .

You can fool all the people all the time if the advertising is right and the budget is big enough.[11]

. . . .

A red herring is a type of decoy. It's usually thought as false clues that throw the pursuer of the track. It's a means of causing confusion. Fiction writers are known for using this literary device to add suspense to a story. Intelligence operations use the fallacy to deceptive the opposition by presenting evidence that diverts them from discovering the truth, until it is too late.

Another decoy variant is the stalking horse. In espionage, a stalking horse can be either a person or thing that allows an officer to get close to a target without attracting undue attention or frightening-off the quarry. The term is borrowed from the technique used by hunters who used a figure of a horse as cover when stalking game. An officer who wants to contact someone who is too weary to be approached directly may feel more comfortable being approached by someone they know (i.e., the stalking horse), but behind that person is the officer who will announce his presence once the quarry is "within range."

Decoys can even be created for the ether. Coded radio broadcasts have been used in most conflicts and in secret duels between intelligence forces. During the Bay of Pigs invasion, CIA operatives used the medium-wave AM broadcasts from Swan Island to transmit supposedly coded messages to non-existent sabotage teams, like was done on D-Day. "I hurriedly composed cables for Swan Island to begin broadcasting cryptic messages of the type beamed to resistance fighters by the BBC in World War II: 'Look well into the rainbow. The fish will rise very soon. Chico is in the house....'"[12] The objective was to give the impression that the exile forces landing on the beach were being supported by irregulates in the Cuban countryside. But, as history shows, although this part of the plan was well-conceived, the overall operation was not.

PHOTO 13.3 A Hunter Uses a Stalking Horse to Cover His Approach. Henry Robert Robertson, *Life on the Upper Thames* (London: Virtue, Spalding & Co., 1875), 196.

In cyberspace physical decoys have no value. However, the concept can still be applied to these digital zones on the Internet. Termed *honeypots*, these are decoys that attract the opposition like duck decoys do for the small-game hunters. This honeypot method is not to be confused with the method of recruiting an agent through sexual seduction, though the principle of luring the opposition into the trap is analogous and hence the use of the term. A computer honeypot can be used to simply detect interest in an agency or its client's activities or to deflect the opposition away from the real activity.

A honeypot as its name implies is considered a piece of bait or a lure that attracts the opposition to it. The honeypot might be a computer, stored data, or a network. Although it appears to be part of a larger network, the honeypot is usually an isolated facility that allows counterintelligence personnel to monitor those accessing the honeypot. Computer honeypots can also be used to sow disinformation in another type of offensive counterintelligence operation—neutralization (see the section on "traps" in chapter 14).

Camouflage

If the purpose of a decoy is to present the illusion that something that does not exist is present, then the purpose of camouflage is the reverse—to make something that is present disappear. Camouflage is therefore the polar opposite of decoys. It is a time-tested and proved method of deception.[13]

Although the prominent image of camouflage is a military vehicle hidden under a net of natural or manmade material so that it blends in with its surrounds, the principles of camouflage extend well beyond such a narrow application. For instance, the opposition may use camouflage to cloak their espionage activities. If the opposition is a terrorist group, then camouflage can be used to screen their subversive doings. One of the first forms of screening that comes to mind when thinking about such a group is the use of a *front organization*. For all intents and purposes, a front organization appears to be a legitimate organization with visible business-like activity. However, behind the organization's movie-set image will lay a clandestine operation that has an entirely different purpose.

Camouflage can also be used in an urban setting. Although mainly thought of as a means of disguising personnel and materiel deployed about the countryside, the same techniques can apply to city and suburban settings to make people and things blend in.

Sometimes an agency might need to run an operation that needs to operate in the open—perhaps as a business or company trading in goods or services. Ostensibly, this company operates as any other business in the commercial marketplace, but behind the management structure exists a clandestine purpose; one that is designed to support an intelligence operation.

An example of a front company for intelligence operations is Air America.[14] It supported covert action in Southeast Asia, Central America, and Africa. The bona fide airline was needed to maintain cover for the paramilitary operations that included, "supplying guerrilla forces in Laos, moving Cuban émigrés to their training bases or ferrying arms to Angola."[15] Many other dummy companies have existed from time to time in both Western and the former Soviet-Bloc countries. These were used for a variety of tasks ranging from procurement to storage to transport. Also, they have been used to maintain facilities and staff to conduct specialized training, or to conduct propaganda operations. Take for instance the use of clandestine broadcasting stations as a form of front company. These stations transmit politically based messages and programs, or information that has an underlying political tone. They use call signs like other broadcasters and have scheduled programs and news, but the backers of these stations are intelligence services.[16]

The purposes of clandestine front organizations can be as varied as the secret groups operating. However, in the context of an offensive counterintelligence operation using deception, a front organization may be one that is established by the agency to mask its undercover operatives—for instance, a warehouse-type operation where operatives come and go camouflaged as tradesmen (say, as electricians) or a B&B-style accommodation that is a safe house for agents and operatives. In this sense, camouflage can be used to screen personnel, organizations, installations or buildings, and other objects.

Returning to the traditional application of the term—the use of natural or manmade materials to make an object or person blend in with the surrounds—several methods have been used to make objects disappear. These methods can use live or cut vegetation, or artificial materials arranged as drapes, flat tops, and screens. Or, they can be used to simply disrupt the true outline or pattern formed by the person or object. An example of the latter can be seen in the

PHOTO 13.4 USS Cony (DD-508) (Background) Laying Down a Smoke Screen off Leyte, Philippine Islands, October 24, 1944. The smoke screen was to hide the Colorado-class battleship, USS West Virginia (BB-48, foreground) from Japanese torpedo bombers. Also note USS Cony's wartime camouflage pattern. *Source:* Courtesy of the U.S. National Archives.

archival photograph of the Fletcher-class destroyer USS *Cony* during the Second World War (Photo 13.4). In these photographs the ship's hull is painted a disruptive pattern to distort the ship's outline, thus causing confusion about its size and distance.

A drape is a hiding device that is erected vertically, whereas a flat top is erected a meter or so above an object (but can drape down at the edges). This can be used to camouflage small, fixed positions, or mobile units that are at rest (e.g., a parked vehicle). An example of a screen is the use of smoke. A smoke screen is a thick "cloud" of smoke that is laid between the object at the center of the deception and those trying to view the same (see Photo 13.4).

Review of Key Words and Phrases

The key words and phrases associated with this chapter are listed below. Demonstrate your understanding of each by writing a short definition or explanation in one or two sentences.

camouflage   ghost army
computer honeypot   pretext
decoy

Study Questions

1. Explain the role cognition plays in counterintelligence deception operations.

2. Describe two hypothetical situations where the use of camouflage could be employed in counterintelligence—one in a military context and the other in a private counterintelligence setting.

3. Describe two hypothetical situations where a pretext could be employed in counterintelligence—one in a law enforcement context and the other in a corporate counterintelligence setting.

4. Argue the case why Operation Mincemeat was so successful.

Learning Activity

Using the concept of a front organization in the context of a law enforcement and operation of your choice, describe how such a deception could be created and employed. What type of information could be protected using your example? What type of information, if any, could be collected this way? What are the key considerations for the deception to succeed? Explain.

Notes

[1] Allen W. Dulles, editor, *Great True Spy Stories* (Secaucus, NJ: Castle, 1968).

[2] H. Keith Melton and Robert Wallace, *The Official CIA Manual of Trickery and Deception* (New York: William Morrow, 2009).

[3] See, for example, Hauser, *Pretext Manual*, 2nd Rev ed.

[4] School of the Americas, *Study Manual: Counterintelligence, LN324-91* (U.S. Department of Defense), 14.

[5] Operation Copperhead was conceived by British Army Brigadier Dudley Clarke. Clarke adapted the idea from the plot of the film, *Five Graves to Cairo*.

[6] After the war, Meyrick Edward Clifton James (April 1898–May 8, 1963) wrote a book detailing the operation—*I Was Monty's Double* (London: Rider & Co., 1954). The book was subsequently adapted for screen with James playing himself.

[7] Costumes and make-up are also part of the art of creating a believable deception.

[8] Jack M. Kneece, *Ghost Army of World War II* (Gretna, LA: Pelican Publishing Company, 2001), 280.

[9] The term *atmosphere* includes the wearing of uniform shoulder patches, vehicle bumper markings, the display of signage, and the production of traffic that would be associated with the activity trying to be created. Kneece, *Ghost Army of World War II*, 154.

[10] Philips, *The Night Watch*, 48.

[11] Attributed to the late American film producer Joseph E. Levine (September 9, 1905–July 31, 1987).

[12] David Atlee Philips, *The Night Watch*, 109.

[13] For an insightful discussion about the artists and designers who contributed to giving invisibility its place in modern defenses using camouflage, see Ann Elias, *Camouflage Australia: Art, Nature, Science, and War* (Sydney: University Press, 2011).

14 William Colby with Forbath, *Honorable Men*, 170.
15 Harry Rositzke, *The CIA's Secret Operations: Espionage, Counterespionage and Covert Action* (New York: Reader's Digest Press, 1977), 183.
16 Hank Prunckun, "The Secret Spectrum—Clandestine Broadcasting," *Amateur Radio*, September 2006, 10–11.

Chapter 14

Offensive Counterintelligence: Neutralization

The use of neutralization as a method for dealing with the opposition is clearly an offensive stance and is termed *counterespionage*. At face value, counterespionage can present as simple spying, but it is a specific counterintelligence function. It is a precise function that is the most subtle and sophisticated of all the counterintelligence functions. It calls for the engineering of complex strategies that deliberately put one's operatives and/or agents in direct contact with the opposition's intelligence personnel. This is done so that the opposition can be fed disinformation, which should lead to confusion, thus disrupting the opposition's plans and allowing the agency and its client to prosper.

In his landmark study of subversion, Professor Edward Luttwak described counterespionage as "the most subtle and sophisticated of all the functions. . . . [As such,] it is unlikely that more than one agency carries out this work because it requires an extremely precise control over operations . . . especially over counterintelligence, which relates to counterespionage as a butcher does to a surgeon."[1]

Although Luttwak's description sums up the function's complexities, it unfortunately separates counterespionage from counterintelligence, which is not the view taken by this writer. Counterespionage is in fact integrally tied to counterintelligence but forms the offensive arm—to neutralize the opposition. Counterespionage has been described as "the clandestine warfare waged between rival intelligence agencies, [and] usually referred to more delicately in the spy business as counterintelligence."[2] The key stratagems that comprise neutralization involve "cunning entrapments, agents provocateurs, spies and counterspies, double and triple crosses. It is the stuff spy novels are made of, with limitless possibilities for deception and turns of plot."[3,4]

> Counterespionage is often touted as the aristocratic sector of secret operations. In the romantic image the counterespionage man is pitted against his fellow professionals on the other side who are trying to get his nation's secrets. His job

is to foil them. It is a true adversary relationship unlike the espionage situation, in which two men work together to purloin secrets. Most spy stories are not about spying but about counterspying.[5]

As a case study, let us examine the situation between 1942 and 1943 when the Allies were preparing to invade Italy. A seaborne invasion relies on several factors to be successful and the ability to establish a beachhead is just one. If reinforcements and resupply, as well as the ability to advance off the beachhead in a reasonably short period of time, were not possible, these issues could factor against the operation's success.

The Axis forces were highly aware that the Allies were anticipating such an invasion, having fought them throughout North Africa and monitoring their advance in the region. The Nazi's Supreme High Command had focused its many intelligence assets on the production of intelligence assessments that would inform them where such an invasion might take place to anticipate this and to have the potential beachhead fortified to destroy the Allies' forces.[6]

Trying to destroy the opposition by overt means alone shows a lack of understanding of what counterespionage could achieve.[7]

The British mounted an offensive counterintelligence operation using deception to safeguard the location of the invasion—Operation Mincemeat. The plan was to convince the Supreme High Command that the invasion was to take place in Greece and Sardinia instead of the actual location of the island of Sicily.

To deceive the Nazis, British Naval Intelligence devised the scheme to plant several falsified documents so that the Germans would find them and believe them to be true, and act on their content. The documents were secret plans of the invasion of Italy as well as supporting documents. The documents were planted in an official British government briefcase carried by the corpse of Welsh civilian Glyndwr Michael (Photo 14.1). Mr. Michael was presented as the fictitious Captain (Acting Major) William Martin of the Royal Marines and fitted with battledress—hence the description, "the man who never was."[8]

Major Martin's death was concocted to appear that he died at sea after an aircraft crash (hypothermia and drowning) while couriering the secret documents. His body was placed overboard from the British submarine HMS *Seraph* off the coast of Huelva, Spain, at a place where the tide would take the corpse ashore. Huelva was selected as the spot of the deception as it was consistent with Allied air traffic to North Africa and British intelligence understood that there was a Nazi *Abwehr* agent who maintained contact with the local Spanish officials. As such, the secret documents would subsequently become known to German intelligence. Major Martin also carried several personal effects and personal papers that, when inspected by the German intelligence, would draw them to conclude the scenario was true.[9]

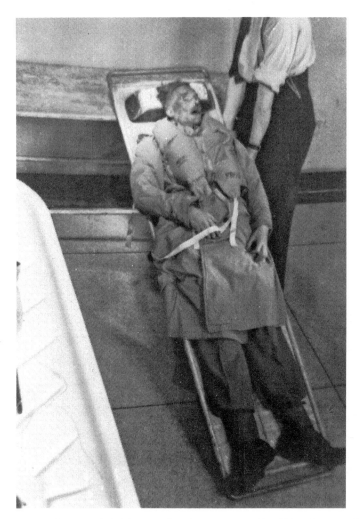

PHOTO 14.1 The Corpse of Welshman, Glyndwr Michael, Who Was "Recruited" into the Royal Marines After His Death to Become, Captain (Acting Major) William Martin in the 1943 Offensive Counterintelligence Deception Code Named Operation Mincemeat. *Source:* Courtesy of the Public Records Office, United Kingdom.

The British then perpetuated the ruse by placing a death notice in *The Times* and transmitting messages that gave the impression that British military commanders were desperate to retrieve the briefcase and its documents. This appeared to work as German intelligence put pressure on Spanish secret police to locate the papers. Once German intelligence finally examined the secret documents, they considered them authentic and the deception was complete.

History shows that on July 10, 1943, the Allies successfully invaded Sicily, and there is little doubt that the effectiveness of this military operation was due in large part to this counterespionage operation. As a case study, the "man who never was" combines all the theoretical elements of defensive and offensive counterintelligence, and, in keeping with Tenets 6, 7, 9, and 10, demonstrates the power that is at the heart of offensive counterintelligence.

Traps

In a law enforcement sense, entrapment is where an officer of the law, or an agent of the government, coaxes a person or group to commit (or omit) an act that is illegal. It is where the commission (or omission) was not in the mind of the person or group before the law enforcement officer or the government agent put it forward. In effect, there was no criminal intent before the notion was advanced and encouraged by the officer/agent. While entrapment is not legal, it is, however, permissible in law to "dangle bait" for those who have already formulated intent to see if the bait taken. In this sense, offensive counterintelligence officers may do the same thing. That is, they may set up a *trap* to entice an opposition spy or place one of their own operatives purposefully in front of the opposition as bait for them to attempt to recruit. It is this sense of the terms that is used here—not the illegal setting up of innocent (criminal) victims.

Many variations of traps are possible including *sting operations*.[10] For instance, say there is a newly assigned officer to a foreign post who is given cover that makes her look attractive as a potential recruit. She may be in an area of operations that allows her access to sensitive information or have access to people who have that access. She may present at, say, social engagements in any number of personas that project the image that she may be approachable as a recruit. All along, she is a counterintelligence officer waiting for the "offer" and, once recruited by the opposition, she is viewed as their double agent. But, the opposition has been caught in a sting operation. Some indicative examples from law enforcement include

- positioning an attractive motor vehicle to catch automobile thieves;
- arranging for a person under the legal drinking age to ask an adult to purchase them alcoholic beverages;
- placing an officer/agent in the street where illicit drugs or contrabands are sold to catch traffickers;
- passing small arms or (deactivated) explosives to a would-be terrorist; and
- setting up a honeypot computer to lure criminal hackers or to gain information about hackers' activities.

Of course, the opposition will be anticipating the possibility and before making their approach to her, they will have tried to establish whether there is any chance of her being a plant. They will continue to watch and observe her induction into their scheme; interrogation and polygraph examination may feature as part of this process. The opposition may request that their newly recruited agent obtain certain information as a way of testing her: first, to determine whether she has access to the types of information claimed; second, to confirm she is willing to follow through with her commitment; and, third, to establish a hook that the opposition can use as blackmail to help ensure continued pressure.

One method of setting up potential traps is to present defectors (including new immigrants and other such categories of displaced people) to the opposition. Then, in the interview/interrogation process, the opposition realizes the intelligence potential in the person and tries to "turn" them into a double agent. In fact, if they were placed in this position (as in the example just given), they become a triple agent.

Or, it could involve setting up a situation made legion in espionage fiction—the *honeypot*. Honeypot is a term that loosely refers to a situation where the opposition uses a person who can engage the agency's officer in a romantic or sexual relationship, and then use either the emotional dependency thus established or the dependent need of the sexual contact as blackmail to exploit for intelligence gathering.

In the computer realm, honeypots are situations that are "as sweet as" the promise of sexual contact and attract cyberspies. The computer honeypot appears for all intents and purposes as the real thing (whatever that may be) but is in effect false (a deception)—like a decoy discussed in the previous chapter. Once lured into the trap, the counterintelligence officer can then exploit the trapped spy as deemed necessary.

The core of a counterespionage trap is the theory of *assumed vulnerability*. That is, everyone is deemed to have at least one vulnerability. If this vulnerability is discovered, say, through poor physical, communications, or personnel counterintelligence practices, then this weakness can be exploited. There is little sense in sending a physically attractive male to entice a potential woman agent if the woman is not heterosexual. Likewise, there is no sense offering money to someone who is financially well-off or otherwise not attracted to the idea of material wealth. The vulnerability must be targeted.

Agents Provocateurs

In the previous section we discussed the setting of traps to catch those who are intent on committing treason and, depending on the operation, turn the agent (a double agent operation) or exploit the information they have (defector). We differentiated between the legal interpretation of entrapment and trapping. However, in some situations where an agency can engage in entrapment, the concept of *agents provocateurs* is used. This method of offensive counterintelligence is where an operative somehow induces others to engage in an activity that, once committed, leads them into disrepute, unlawfulness, or other forms of infamy. This can be seen in the following theoretical sequence:

- A counterintelligence operative works for Agency A.
- Opposition B is antagonistic, belligerent, and/or in competition with Agency A or Agency A's client.
- Opposition B (or its client) has a friendly relationship with Group C.
- Operative A contacts Opposition B using the ruse that he is with Group C.
- Operative A using various methods gains the confidence of Opposition B and induces its personnel to do certain acts.
- These acts are then exposed by Agency A and public opinion/legal authorities condemn Opposition B, or take legal action against it.

By way of example, take the following as a possible situation. There exists a large and growing group of prodemocratic protesters in an authoritarian country. To discredit the hitherto peaceful protests in the eyes of the world, the authoritarian regime sends a unit of counterintelligence officers—the agents provocateurs—into the large group of protesters to cause the group to become agitated and unruly and either commit or see the agents provocateurs commit violence. Anticipating this outcome, the authoritarian regime has provided for the world's media to be present to record and televise the violence. The authoritarian regime then denounces the protesters as violent criminals and uses this provocation as the reason to crack down on the protesters.

A case that demonstrates this in 1963 was the *Northwoods* scenario to engineer a provocation (i.e., "frame") Cuba for violence on the streets of America. The now declassified Joint Chiefs of Staff plan stated: "We could develop a Communist Cuban terror campaign in Miami area, and other Florida cities, and even Washington. . . The terror campaign could be pointed at Cuban refugees seeking haven in the United States. We could sink a boatload of Cubans en route to Florida (real or simulated)."[11]

Many and varied scenarios can be crafted around the theoretical underpinning of provocation. These can be either against an opposition or in support of a friendly ally. The latter point—in support of a friendly ally—should not be overlooked. Counterintelligence work can often be in support of allies.

Double Agents

Double agents are likely to be both a scourge and a blessing for counterintelligence officers. They are a scourge in the sense that identifying one that may be operating in an agency will be a task of sizable proportions. However, if the double agent is under the control of the agency, an operations office, then the tables are turned on the opposition.

A double agent, usually, starts off working for, say, the opposition. He is, at some stage of his career, with the opposition recruited (or self-recruited in the form of a secret defection). The defecting opposition operative is debriefed by the agency on all important aspects of the defector, his life, and career, and details of the opposition and/or its client are obtained, recorded, and analyzed. If the defector stays in the employ of the opposition and continues to provide sensitive information to the agency, he is known as an *agent doubled in place*.

Although this may be a common route into the doubling of agents, another method is also known—that is, the recruiting of an opposition-leaning officer who, once employed with the agency, defects. A case in point is that of the former British intelligence officer Harold Adrian Russell "Kim" Philby. Philby was one of several Cambridge University students who, in the 1930s, became absorbed by the romantic notions offered by communism. This philosophical position later led him (as well as others) to side with Soviet intelligence and to be a double agent. His espionage activities naturalized many British, and perhaps other allied intelligence services, operations and, in some instances, ended in the deaths of agents. Philby also fooled the head of U.S. Counterintelligence,

James Angleton, who unwittingly shared intelligence secrets with over many years.[12]

A triple agent is an extension of the double agent. Using the above example of an agent doubled in place, he would become a triple agent if he then had second thoughts about his defection and confessed to his opposition service what he had done and what he told the agency. If the opposition considered it worthwhile, they could then turn him again, thus becoming a triple agent. This, however, would be a very difficult case to manage. Although there is no empirical evidence to support this, it would be reasonable to conclude that such cases would be rare because of the inherent difficulty in dealing with such a disloyal and intensely narcissistic person. For instance, what would stop him from becoming a quadruple agent? Nevertheless, Joby Warwick documents a case where an al-Qaeda mole infiltrated the CIA in a triple-agent operation.[13]

In this regard, there is little doubt that agent controllers have a perennial problem in continually assessing the accuracy of the information being provided by a double agent. Even if the double agent is reliable and provides what he considers to be quality information, it is possible that the opposition may suspect his treachery and place in his way what is akin to a "barium meal"—that is, a piece of information that can be traced back to him through, say, an opposition double agent in the agency. This could flush out the defector and make him ripe for turning again. Or, as the British did during the Second World War under what has become known as the *double-cross system*, the agent could be eliminated (one way or another) and replaced with one of their own to feed disinformation to the opposition.[14]

Double Crosses

Although the exploits of British intelligence under the Twenty Committee during the Second World War are legendary, another example from history will serve to underscore how this method can be used to neutralize the operations of the opposition. During the tail end of the Russian Civil War (which followed the October 1917 Bolshevik Revolution and ultimately resulted in the collapse of the Russian Empire), the secret police ran a decoy underground organization that held itself out as anti-Bolshevik. This counterintelligence operation was known as the *Operation Trust* and ran from 1921 to 1926. History documents many of the trust's operations, but one of the most well-known is the double-cross operation that captured British secret agent Sidney Reilly.

Reilly, whose "real name was Rosenblum . . . [having] taken his name from his father-in-law, an Irishman named Callahen,"[15] was born in Odessa under what was then the Russian Empire. He was involved in counterrevolutionary stratagems against the Bolsheviks and was, among several roles he played in espionage, an operative for the British Secret Intelligence Service (MI6).

His secret operations ended in 1925 when he was caught in a double-cross operation orchestrated by the trust. Lured into Russia by counterintelligence operatives posing as anti-Bolsheviks, he was reported to have been shot by Russian border guards while trying to cross at the Finnish frontier, but was likely taken to a dacha near Moscow and interrogated.[16] Reports state that he was executed shortly thereafter.[17] British secret agent R. H. Bruce Lockhart, writing in his memoirs, stated that "such evidence as is available would seem to prove that he walked into a Bolshevik trap, and that his [anti-Bolshevik White] Guards officers, whom he met abroad, were really Cheka agents,"[18] who betrayed the faith and alliance he gave them in a double-cross operation.

Case managers for double agents need access to agency files across many compartmentalized groups so they don't, for instance, "buy" the same agent twice, or run an agent against himself. This practice aligns with tenet nine of Offensive Counterintelligence (synergy with defensive counterintelligence).

Yet, double crosses are not only the purview of national security or military operations. The world of commerce and industry is also a topical area for double crosses. For many decades the area of industrial spying has been in the subject literature but mainly to document intelligence-gathering methods and some security issues. However, there are a few books that specifically examine the use of the double-cross system. Stephen Barlay in his book *Double Cross: Encounters with Industrial Spies*[19] tells of numerous cases of betrayal in business, with serious financial and security consequences.

In a contemporary assessment of economic espionage, Colonel Kevin J. Degnan of the U.S. Army explores the impact of the unauthorized acquisition of sensitive information and technology, as well as the countermeasures needed to guard against this subversive activity, in his strategy research report titled *America's Soft Underbelly: Economic Espionage.*[20] There are many other treatments of the topic, all of which indicate how the double-cross system extends beyond what might be regarded as national security and military operations.

A *false flag* operation is a specific type of double cross. Recruitment takes place by contriving circumstances for a recruiter to approach a person with access to targeted information. The recruiter pretends to represent a government or organization that is not his. "A Russian-speaking officer from a Western service, for instance, might cultivate a Marxist anywhere in the world, to ask him to report on his government as a favor to the Kremlin."[21] False flag ops are ingenious schemes designed to lure unsuspecting extremists who are then "managed and paid as spies; they sell their countries secrets believing all the while they are helping 'the good guys.'"[22]

Disruption

Neutralization is not just by destruction, but also by paralysis—disruption. Although not as dramatic as destruction, it is an effective method nonetheless.

Disruption operations play a key part in this counterintelligence strategy. The operational goal of disruption is to inflicting paralysis (usually temporary in nature) on some aspect of the opposition's operation or the entire operation itself. The intent is to cause the opposition to abandon its undertaking in this area and dismantle any ongoing espionage operation—perhaps an active sleeper cell—to avoid detection. Paralysis can be initiated by the agency as a preemptive measure to, say, flush out an opposition operative.

Disruption is also classified as actions to frustrate hostile intelligence operations. This includes identifying who the perpetrators are (via record keeping, logs, etc.), expelling operatives and agents, trailing and jailing them for espionage or related crimes, or denying them entry or access to sensitive information or people who hold or access that type of information. Other methods include controlling their movements or observing their activities (e.g., via fixed and mobile surveillance, as well as electronically).[23]

An example of an offensive counterintelligence that entailed disruption was the case of the ten Russian sleepers in the United States in 2010. Such operatives are termed *illegals* because they took civilian jobs within the community in which they lived and not under official cover at, say, the Russian embassy. The mission of these sleepers was to establish quiet lives in middle-class neighborhoods and work ordinary jobs as a way of burrowing into American society (i.e., develop a *legend*). Under this cover, they were to cultivate contacts within and among academic circles, business enterprises, and government policy- and decision-makers who had links to a range of Russian strategic interests—computer and communications technology, defense developments, economic matters, and the list goes on.

One of the issues pointed out in the subsection titled "Social Networking" under "Background Investigations" of chapter 7—Defensive Counterintelligence: Personnel Security—was the matter of not being able to effectively hide a covert operative's background if parts of that background have been exposed on a social networking website. Well, here the opposite is true if an operative is trying to develop a legend. That is, an operative may find it difficult to develop a credible legend if the identity they are using for cover is not a member of a social networking website.

Sleeper agents can be left in place for very long periods of time before being activated. One extreme case, although not strictly a sleeper agent, was that of the Japanese intelligence officer Lieutenant Onoda Hiroo who was inserted on Lubang Island in the Philippines during the Second World War. His instructions were to carry out a guerrilla-style campaign to hinder the Allied invasion and not to surrender. He was advised that, no matter what happened, someone would come back for him. Dutifully he carried out his irregular war on the island and waited. But once Imperial Japan was defeated he was advised by various messages to stand down; however, as he had been advised before his deployment that there might be attempts like these to deceive him into believing he should surrender, he remained hiding and resisted all attempts to flush him out. He waited thirty years in the mountain jungles before the Japanese government, in 1974, located his former commanding officer and flew him to the island to order the intelligence officer to stand down. Lieutenant Onoda's case demonstrates the will some sleeper agents can exercise in their mission.[24]

As part of Operation Ghost Stories, the Federal Bureau of Investigation conducted a ten-year counterintelligence operation involving these operatives that employed a variety of surveillance methods that gathered data about the spies, their motives, their topics of interest, and their operational methods (as well as other aspects that remain classified). In the end, the FBI exposed the operatives by arresting them before any sensitive information was obtained and provided to Moscow. The FBI then arranged for these sleepers to be swapped for four Russians who were imprisoned for spying for the West.

Arguably, the offensive counterintelligence operation netted a vast amount of data on Russian espionage methods and intents and in the process wasted vast amounts of Russian time and money for an operation that yielded nothing. The Americans then ridded themselves of this nuisance by expelling them, and in the process gained the freedom of four of their agents whose service was valuable to the West.

Neutralization also involves physical sabotage and subversion. Take the example of Britain's SOE during the Second World War. Special Operations Executive was successful in performing many disruptive operations involving physical destruction.[25] One of the most celebrated was the destruction of the wireless listening post that operated on the Italian ocean liner *Duchessa d'Aosta* from the neutral Spanish port of Fernando Po. The *Duchessa d'Aosta* was providing the Nazis with information on the Allies' shipping movements and hence needed to be neutralized. Operation Postmaster was an elaborate plan that used commandos to commandeer the ship, and two other German ships, as they lay at anchor and destroy them at sea.[26]

Subversion can be imagined as political neutralization. Termed many things—black propaganda, underground propaganda, or subversive propaganda[27]—the stratagem is designed to persuade people to do something that they would not originally do. In the military, these operations are known as *psyops* (psychological operations, pronounced, *cy-ops*). Take the case of the propaganda campaign conducted in Guatemala in 1952. In the lead-up to the Bay of Pigs invasion, the CIA established a medium-wave radio station on Swan Island, which is situated between Cuba and the Central American coast. It broadcasted ostensible commercial programs but operated under cover to establish a psychological climate receptive for the hoped political regime change. As history has shown, the military invasion by the Cuban exiles was a failure; nevertheless, the subversive propaganda program had all the hallmarks of being a successful component of the larger, yet unsuccessful, operation.[28]

"An example of a psyop success comes from the Korean War. A North Korean pilot was paid a $100,000 bounty for flying his Soviet MiG-15 to the south, after the bounty was offered by leaflet and radio. The benefits were enormous. The Communists grounded all MiG flights for eight days; and getting the MiG turned out to be a TECHINT windfall."[29]

. . . .

If a Lie be believ'd only for an Hour, it has done its Work, and there is no farther occasion for it. Falsehood flies, and the Truth comes limping after it; so that when Men come to be undeceiv'd, it is too late; the Jest is over, and the Tale has had its Effect.[30]

. . . .

Subversion applies to other forms of political persuasion. In February 1956, Nikita Khrushchev gave a speech to the twentieth Congress of the Communist Party of the Soviet Union. The speech was secret because it criticized the late Joseph Stalin. It was one thing for the Western media to do this, but for the now head of the Party to do this was another matter. The CIA wanted a copy of the document.

By some quick thinking and slight-of-hand maneuvering, a Polish journalist and his girlfriend obtained a copy from the offices of the Central Committee of the Polish Communist Party. Passing the document onto the Israeli Embassy, which forwarded it onto Tele Aviv, and with the consent of the prime minister, Ben-Gurion, forwarded it to James Angleton at CIA. Angleton edited the document to include derogatory remarks about the Indians and Chinese. He released the edited version to create a stir among the Indian and Chinese political leadership.[31] The operation delighted President Eisenhower, and in his memories, Allen Dulles, the director of Central Intelligence at the time, wrote that this was "one of the major intelligence coups of my tour of duty in intelligence."[32]

. . . .

Get your facts first and then you can distort them as you please.[33]

. . . .

In March 2018 *The New York Times* and *The Observer of London* reported how UK-based consulting firm, Cambridge Analytica, "harvested the data from more than 50 million *Facebook* profiles in its bid to develop techniques for predicting the behavior of American voters."[34] The purpose? To apply the company's psychographic modeling software to the data "to target voters on behalf of the Trump campaign during the 2016 presidential election."[35] By doing so, the targeted audience(s) was presented with a psychological climate that was intended to make them receptive pro-Trump messages.

Review of Key Words and Phrases

The key words and phrases associated with this chapter are listed below. Demonstrate your understanding of each by writing a short definition or explanation in one or two sentences.

agents provocateurs	double agents
counterespionage	double cross

honey pots
illegals
psyops
sleepers

sting operations
theory of assumed vulnerability
traps

Study Questions

1. Explain how a sting operation works and cite two examples in any counterintelligence context where these have been used.
2. Explain the theory of assumed vulnerability and how this is used in a counterespionage trap.
3. Explain some of the difficulties that might be encountered in doubling an agent. Provide an example to illustrate your points.
4. Using a hypothetical example, describe how a sleeper agent could be employed in the following two contexts: law enforcement and national security.

Learning Activity

Research the use of agents provocateurs. List three examples of their use in history and describe the counterintelligence context (e.g., law enforcement, national security, military, corporate, private, or a combination) in which they were used. What was the outcome of these operations? Were they successful? Why or why not? In hindsight would you suggest another variation to the use of an agent provocateur in these cases? Explain.

Notes

[1] Edward Luttwak, *Coup d'etat: A Practical Handbook* (Great Britain: Allan Lane, The Penguin Press, 1968), 101.
[2] Victor Marchetti and John D. Marks, *The CIA and the Cult of Intelligence* (New York: Knopf, 1974), 211.
[3] Marchetti and Marks, *The CIA and the Cult of Intelligence*, 211.
[4] David Atlee Phillips asserted that the scenarios are "so complex they would be poor material for fiction writers; the stories would not be believed." Phillips, *The Night Watch*, 207.
[5] Rositzke, *CIA's Secret Operations*, 119.
[6] J. C. Masterman, *The Double-Cross System in the War of 1939 to 1945* (Canberra: Australian National University Press, 1972), 133–38.
[7] Anonymous.
[8] Ewen Montagu, "The Man Who Never Was," in Allen Dulles (ed.), *Great True Spy Stories* (Secaucus, NJ: Castle, 1968), 256–62.
[9] This is termed *pocket litter*. These bits of paper (e.g., a theater ticket stub, a wallet photograph, clothing labels, etc.) produce "footprints" that help to establish evidence in support of the false story being presented. H. H. A. Cooper and Lawrence J. Redlinger, *Catching Spies: Principles and Practices of Counterespionage* (Boulder, CO: Paladin Press, 1988), 261–62.
[10] See, for example, Henry Prunckun, "It's Your Money They're After: Sting Operations in Consumer Fraud Investigation," *Police Studies* 11, no. 4 (Winter 1988): 190–94; Henry Prunckun,

"Sting Operations in Consumer Fraud Investigation," *Journal of California Law Enforcement* 23, no. 1 (1989): 27–32. In the national security context, see Joby Warwick, *The Triple Agent*, 81.

11 Jefferson Morley, *The Ghost: The Secret Life of CIA Spymaster James Jesus Angleton* (New York: St. Martin's Press, 2017), 129 and 298.

12 Morley, *The Ghost.*

13 Warwick, *The Triple Agent.*

14 Masterman, *The Double-Cross System in the War of 1939 to 1945.*

15 R. H. Bruce Lockhart, *Memoirs of a British Agent* (London: Putnam, 1932), 323.

16 Christopher Andrew and Oleg Gordievsky, *KGB: The Inside Story of its Foreign Operations from Lenin to Gorbachev* (London: Hodder and Stoughton, 1990), 74.

17 Andrew and Gordievsky, *KGB*, 72–77.

18 Lockhart, *Memoirs of a British Agent*, 324.

19 Stephen Barlay, *Double Cross: Encounters with Industrial Spies* (London: Hamish Hamilton, 1973).

20 Kevin J. Degnan, *America's Soft Underbelly: Economic Espionage* (Carlisle Barracks, PA: U.S. Army War College, 2009).

21 Phillips, *The Night Watch*, 206.

22 Phillips, *The Night Watch*, 207.

23 Frederick L. Wettering, "Counterintelligence: The Broken Triad," in Christopher Andrew, Richard J. Aldrich and Wesley K. Wark (ed.), *Secret Intelligence: A Reader* (London: Routledge, 2009), 291–294.

24 See details in Hiroo Onoda, *No Surrender: My Thirty-Year War,* trans. Charles S. Terry (Tokyo: Kodansha International Ltd., 1974).

25 E. H. Cookridge, *Inside SOE* (London: Arthur Barker Ltd, 1966).

26 Marcus Binney, *Secret War Heroes* (London: Hodder and Stoughton, 2005).

27 Philby, *My Silent War*, 14.

28 Phillips, *The Night Watch*, 88–91.

29 U.S. Department of the Army, *Technical Intelligence* (FM 34-54) (Washington, DC: U.S. Department of the Army, 1998), 5–10.

30 Jonathan Swift, *The Examiner*, Number 15 (near Stationers-Hall, London: John Morphew, November 2 to November 9, 1710), page 2, column 1.

31 Morley, *The Ghost*, 76–78.

32 Allen Dulles, *The Craft of Intelligence* (Lanham, MD: Rowman & Littlefield, 2006), 84.

33 This quotation has been attributed to Samuel Langhorne Clemens (November 30, 1835–April 21, 1910), the American author and humorist who wrote under the pseudonym of Mark Twain.

34 Matthew Rosenberg, "Offering to Entrap Politicians," *The New York Times*, International Edition, March 21, 2018: 10.

35 Kevin Roose, "Sharing Data Backfired for Facebook," *The New York Times*, International Edition, March 21, 2018: 9.

Chapter 15

Ethics of Counterintelligence

Topics such as morality, politicization, principles, codes of conduct, and values are not that common when it comes to textbooks on the practice of counterintelligence. Concepts like these might be more common in a course of study relating to theology rather than intelligence tradecraft. Indeed, such a collection of ethics-based issues is an unlikely feature for the intelligence profession, which, arguably, focuses on analysis that is based on fact and reason.

Nevertheless, counterintelligence practitioners are likely to face many dilemmas if they remain in the profession for any length of time. These dilemmas will probably come without warning and arise over routine matters. However, the event, when it does present, will not only test the individual's moral fabric but will also test the individual's sense of what is needed to be done to safeguard the agency and its client, which may be the nation and its people. At the center of many of these ethical dilemmas is the fact that counterintelligence officers are required to act ethically but at the same time engage in what some may portray as an unethical business—counterspying—with its Orwellian overtones of a secret police state.

. . . .

Experience is something you don't get until just after you need it.[1]

. . . .

Decision-making is not an easy task at the best of times but being faced with a choice that will cause a clash between the counterintelligence officer's personal moral views and his or her professional duties and obligations needs to be anticipated. Given the nature of counterintelligence work, it is likely that such a situation will occur at some time in a person's career. Given this likelihood, one view is that liberal democracies are founded on high ideals, so its counterintelligence service should be staffed with officers who hold equally high ideals.

Ethics is a term that is often used interchangeably with *moral philosophy*. *Philosophy* is the study of many concepts including knowledge, existence, reality, values, and others, and how these concepts can be interpreted, understood, and applied to everyday life. *Moral philosophy* is a subfield of the academic study of philosophy that examines questions pertaining to morality.

Morality in this sense includes the examination of such concepts as what is right and what is wrong, what is good and what is bad, what is virtuous and what is sinful, and, of course, what is legal and what constitutes a crime. Certainly, there are other examples, but for examining counterintelligence practice, a simple examination of right and wrong may be sufficient to illustrate that there is not going to be a clear or decisive answer to any dilemma a counterintelligence officer may face during his or her career; it may be a matter of exercising balance and maturity in the context of the circumstances that prevail at the time and, above all, what feels like the best thing to do.

* *

While laws are always formal, ethics may be either codified or informal, undocumented principles. [And the interpretation of] . . . ethical standards is likely to be left to the individual.[2]

* *

It must be said that there are no definitive answers as to what "doing the right thing" means in any given situation. So, if this is the case, then how does a counterintelligence officer consider all the issues that will be running through his or her thoughts when such an event presents itself? One source of advice can be found in a *code of conduct*. A code of conduct is a broad set of guidelines that outline what personnel entrusted to do, what counterintelligence officers do and, in doing so, what would be considered by the "reasonable person"[3] as proper practice or what is fair and reasonable.

In this regard many places of employment outside the intelligence community—both public and private—have implemented codes of conduct for their employees. Many organizations that represent professionals have also instituted codes of conduct for their members. In some cases, holding membership of a professional body is required for government licensing, and therefore this means adhering to the code of conduct is a mandatory requirement for continued registration and practice.

As intelligence analysts face many ethics dilemmas in carrying out their duties as secret researchers, so do counterintelligence officers. Whether operating in defensive counterintelligence or offensive counterintelligence, officers and their agents will find that every situation will potentially pose some form of ethical dilemma for them. Here are a selected few of what could be an endless stream of such situations that could conceivably arise. The common ethical impasse is whether to give priority to one's conscience or one's career.

* Being approached by a new co-worker who is waiting for his security clearance to come through and asks a "favor" to access classified data

in the meantime—do you allow him to use your computer log-in ID and password?

* Being asked by a work colleague to cover-up a security breach that she committed "inadvertently."
* Being told by a close associate about that person's new friend who you know to be a person of interest as you have read the friend's name on a classified report—do you breach security to tell your associate?
* Does keeping quiet about something one considers illegal make that person an accomplice?
* If a person "blows the whistle" on illegal activity within the agency (or its client) how does that person deal with the fear of being accused of being unpatriotic (or, worse, being accused of aiding the opposition)?

. . . .

Unethical conduct can also include managers providing inadequate training or underequipping staff, or knowingly under resourcing operations, as well as underpaying and overworking personnel. All of these factors can lead to mission failure and risk the safety of officers.

. . . .

As with defensive counterintelligence, an officer operating within the field of offensive counterintelligence faces a set of equally perplexing ethical dilemmas. To demonstrate this point, here are a couple of illustrative examples of situations in which agency personnel may find themselves:

* A private psychologist is asked to work with a counterintelligence interrogation team to question a suspect. The psychologist, who holds a government license to practice, is asked to assess the suspect and based on that assessment provide advice as to how to reduce the person's mental health to the point that the suspect will reveal the information required by the interrogators. Should the private psychologist participate? If so, what might the agency do to help overcome the dilemma?
* Countries A and B have long-standing friendly political and economic ties. Country A makes inquiries of country B about an agent it is dealing with. The agent is controlled by B, but does country B expose its agent to country A, even though it is considered an "ally"?
* A counterintelligence officer becomes aware that one of the agency's case officers is "skimming" money from payments destined for the contract agents being handled by the case officer. When confronted, the case officer thrusts cash into the pocket of the counterintelligence agent to "forget" about it and move on to other issues. Does the counterintelligence officer accept the "gratuity"?
* The agency head is called before a Congressional Committee to answer questions about past intelligence operations, including counterintelligence related activities that were suspected of being illegal. Should he appear

before the committee or "stonewall"? If he does appear, should he answer truthfully all questions put to him?[4]

Although these examples only scratch the surface, these dilemmas stand as illustrations of what career counterintelligence personnel may face. Although some of the examples outlined may seem clear, the ethical dilemma seems insignificant when confronting the reality of being in a foreign place, perhaps operating on the edge of legality within that country, and being faced with an aggressive and potentially hostile situation, placed under time and resource pressures. However, back in the office and reflecting on what went on, such reflections may shine a different light on the magnitude of what was decided. The point that needs to be underscored is that sitting in a classroom and discussing ethics is a different world when compared to the pressures imposed by the reality of working in a dangerous and uncertain environment.

If the counterintelligence officer is an employee of a government (e.g., military or national security, as well as law enforcement and regulatory or compliance), then it could be said that the agency that employs the officer has a social contract between it (or, more precisely, between the government client the agency represents) and the people it governs. This social contract is usually translated and embodied in a constitution (and/or statutory and common law). It is therefore an undertaking that the officer gives to that social contract, through other legal instruments, such as secrecy agreements, which must be honored. So, it is more than just being clear about what a person opposes, but also what that person stands for. Counterintelligence officers should not only be concerned with dealing with "bad guys," but also dealing with "bad systems."

If the counterintelligence officer is in the employ of a business or is a private individual, then it could be argued that that officer is not discharged from the social contractual arrangements that exist between governments and their populaces. Businesses and private persons also have an obligation to act not only within the law but within the framework of what is fair and reasonable.

Having discussed some of the issues involving the ethics of counterintelligence, it is obligatory to address the equally perplexing dilemma of dealing with issues that purport to be in the public interest yet go beyond what could be considered a responsible limit to criticism. Former CIA officer Philip Agee, who exposed classified information, arguably undermined the intelligence service of the United States (and consequently the Five Eyes allies) under the guise of exposing injustices.[5] A strongly put view is that without a robust intelligence service, detractors of the craft of intelligence, like Agee, would not have been able to criticize the system because the system made it possible for such freedoms.

Another thought is that of perspective. For instance, it could be said that the most unethical position in which to place yourself, your agency, or your nation is in the position where you/they lose. This may sound trite but righteous positions that are blind to the reality of intelligence operations, particularly counterintelligence operations, deny the fact that these operations will always remain a feature of the world of realpolitik. To consider otherwise is to show the same naïveté U.S. secretary of state Henry L. Stimson displayed in 1929 when he advanced the now often-cited dictum that "gentlemen do not read each other's mail."[6] That is, when Stimson learned of the existence of Herbert O. Yardley's "Black Chamber," he rejected the argument that the ends justified covert code-breaking ops. Stimson disapproved of Yardley's clandestine activity, regarding it as a low dirty business that violated the principle of mutual trust upon which, in Stimson's view, foreign policy should be based. Stimson then shutdown Yardley's Black Chamber. Since then, history has shown the fate America suffered in the years leading up to the Second World War because of Stimson's morally based but politically ill-conceived decision. It could be said Stimson lost perspective.

It has been said that "idealism and realism are at opposite ends of the scale when defining ethical intelligence,"[7] but shouldn't practitioners seek to arrive at an ethical way of "doing intelligence" that is not only seen as striving for the ideal, yet is realistic and achieves operational goals? If it is morally justifiable to take another's life in war (Just War Theory), it can be argued that it is morally justifiable to "subvert, sabotage and destroy our enemies"[8] under what could be termed a *Just Intelligence Doctrine*.

The post–Cold War global community faces threats different from those of the past. There are nontraditional challenges for which the state-centric paradigm no longer applies (e.g., organized crime and terrorism). Free societies face threats from weak and corrupt governments, rogue states, substate and transstate actors, as well as criminal, radical ethnic, racial, and religious groups, and ultra-right-wing political groups—all openly defying international control.

Threats involving these actors materialized in series of terrorist attacks that followed September 11, 2001; hence the question that presented itself repeatedly is, "Do secret operations corrupt secretly?" As cogent as this proposition is, a balanced reply might be: "Can free societies tolerate groups that, if they came to power, would destroy the freedoms that tolerated them?"

Moira Rayner stated that "public faith in the ideals of 'justice' is perhaps the most fundamental sign that a society is truly civilized."[9] However, hero of the American Revolutionary War, and one of the nation's first spies, Nathan Hale said: "Any kind of service necessary to the public good becomes honorable by being necessary."[10] Regardless, the issue lies in deciding what is necessary for the public good, especially when that decision falls to an officer or agent at the operational end of the decision-making chain where the interpretation of "any kind of service" may be seen as permissible for the public good, when it may not be.

Former British intelligence officer David Cornwell wrote, "Intelligence work has one moral law—it is justifiable by results."[11] This view was expressed by James Angleton under questioning by the Select Committee to Study Government Operations with Respect to Intelligence Activities.[12] When asked why the CIA had ignored a presidential order to destroy a small stock of biological weapons, Angleton responded, "It is inconceivable that a secret intelligence arm of government has to comply with all the overt orders of government."[13] His reason was simple, "When I look at the map today and the weakness of this country, that is what shocks me."[14] This situation is reminiscent of Henry

Stimson's direction to dissolve America's Black Chamber. In the same position as Yardley, would Angleton have disregarded the order thus saving the U.S. from defeat at Pearl Harbor? Looking at the aggression exhibited by the Russian Federation in the poisoning of former spy Sergei Skripal and his daughter Yulia in England in 2018, and China's numerous links to industrial espionage in the West, as well as North Korea's covert cyber hostilities, Angleton's words have an understanding resonance to them.

What appears to the observer as an agency acting outside the law and the Constitution is viewed as doing the right thing by those within. It is not necessarily a case of viewing an agency as having a few "bad apples" in the barrel—of being deceitful and untruthful. There are many cases in which "the golden apples" among an agency's staff do the wrong thing—as in the case of Angleton. This is known as *noble cause corruption*—where people do the wrong thing but for the right reason and where the ends are believed to justify the means. This could be regarded as a person becoming what they oppose.

Perhaps what is needed is training not only in counterintelligence tradecraft, but also in how to deal with some of the ethical issues that are likely to arise for officers engaged in counterintelligence work. This approach may empower officers by providing them with moral signposts that can guide them to make quick decisions that will withstand public scrutiny should the event come to light. Likewise,

Just Intelligence Doctrine would also benefit the media and consequently the public to understanding why intelligence operations are run and what is at stake if these secret missions are not conducted. As "collateral damage" has occupied public debate in counterterrorism and counterinsurgency campaigns, "Is it unreasonable to expect that we may similarly use 'collateral intrusion' resulting from unintentional collection of privileged material rather than reaching for the nearest copy of Orwell?"[15] The same could be said for understanding "the difference between murder and lawful killing in war [according to Just War Doctrine], can we not expect just intelligence to help frame the difference between the forbidden (torture) and the essential (interrogation)?"[16]

If one needs an example to illustrate this, take the Nazis bombing of industrial city of Coventry during the Second World War. German radio and teletype intercepts deciphered at the Government Code and Cypher School, Bletchley Park, revealed that Luftwaffe planned to raze the city using over 500 Heinkel bombers. If the British intervened to either prevent the air raid or evacuate the civilian population, it would have alerted the Nazis command that their ciphers had been broken. The Germans would have changed its encryption and the Allies would not have been able to decrypt future messages.[17] Churchill's decision was not to intervene and protect Allied signals intelligence (code named Ultra).

> It was the only way to protect Ultra. Ultra had already proved a weapon of decisive importance in the Battle of Britain, and Churchill could not risk losing what he hoped would become—what, indeed, did become—one of the principle weapons of victory in the war. Britain had the means to protect Coventry, it its defenses were left as they were, and all reaction to the raid would follow a normal course.[18]

Guidelines may best originate from public opinion that exists at the time because what may be viewed as "wrong" changes with time. Take, for instance, the firebombing of Japan in the Second World War. The public view at the time was largely accepting of this tactic. Yet, at the time of this writing, the idea of mass destruction of highly populated cities is far less accepted, if tolerated at all (in fact, even minor collateral damage is met with public outrage).[19]

Even so, there is a balance to be struck, and this needs maturity and wisdom to know what is required for any given situation, and to never be placed in a situation where you lose sight of the "big picture" for the narrower questions. This too would equally be unethical. So, it is worth repeating—the most unethical position in which to place yourself, your agency, or your nation is the position where losing would be judged by history as being as unethical as if you had acted unethically. This is not an easy decision, and one with no clear answer. Decisions teeter on an uneasy equilibrium between moral philosophy, legislation, government policy, and community expectations. But above all, this is what Angleton alluded to as the national good—the survival of the nation even if means ignoring a direct order. Given these dynamic, it is likely that no one will know what to do until they face the question in a field situation "under fire."

Until a practitioner experiences the gravity of such a situation and the weight such decision-making has (i.e., the consequences of acting on those factors, or not acting on them), this thinking is merely an academic exercise. Regardless, there is surety in the knowledge that those who practice counterintelligence will one day face such a dilemma. When confronted, their preparation for such decision-making will then be as important as the preparation they undertook for the more technical side of the profession.

Review of Key Words and Phrases

The key words and phrases associated with this chapter are listed below. Demonstrate your understanding of each by writing a short definition or explanation in one or two sentences.

code of conduct

ethical dilemma

ethics

Just Intelligence Doctrine

moral philosophy

philosophy

Study Questions

1. Explain what your understanding is of a "reasonable person."
2. Explain what the concept of being "fair and reasonable" means.
3. Explain the term *realpolitik*.
4. Describe *noble cause corruption*.

Learning Activity

Suppose that you are a police officer tasked with a group of other officers to execute an arrest warrant for an alleged narcotics dealer. The raid takes place in an urban area of your state or in your provincial capital. You and your team execute the warrant by bursting into the specified house, and, as you do, shots are fired from the alleged drug dealer. One of your fellow officers is hit by the spray of bullets and is killed. The drug dealer instantly surrenders and is taken into custody. However, in the immediate aftermath of the shooting, you hear some of your fellow officers in the raid whispering that the information that formed the basis of the warrant was based on false information from a fictitious informant. You know that, if this information is made known, there is an almost certainty that the courts will dismiss all charges against the accused, including the murder charge for the dead officer.

Explain what you would do if you found yourself in this situation. For instance, would you withhold this information from investigators? Why, or why not? If you revealed this information, what would this mean for your career? How do you think other officers would view you if you spoke up? How would the thoughts and opinions of the dead officer's family weigh on your mind? If you withheld this information, are you not guilty of a felony for covering up a serious crime? How could you continue to work with officers who you know have committed such a crime and, in doing so, caused a fellow officer to die?

Notes

[1] Anonymous.
[2] Hans Born and Aidan Wills, "Beyond the Oxymoron: Exploring Ethics through the Intelligence Cycle," in Jan Goldman (ed.), *Ethics of Spying: A Reader for the Intelligence Professional*, vol. 2 (Lanham, MD: Scarecrow Press, 2010), 38.
[3] The term *reasonable person* is one used in common law countries as a standard against which an individual's actions can be judged.
[4] For a discussion of how an agency head grappled with this dilemma see William Colby with Forbath, *Honorable Men*, 7–21. Colby's reasoning was to assist the Congressional inquiry as he saw his duty to uphold and defend the U.S. Constitution, which Congress was exercising its right and duty in conducting the inquiry. Others have argued that his loyalty should have been to the U.S. president (at the time it was Gerald Ford) and that he should not have cooperated. Colby was subsequently criticized for taking the position he did and President Ford terminated him as the director of Central Intelligence. Clearly, Colby put his conscience before his career and willingly accepted the price this levied—an end to his thirty-year intelligence career. However, vindication came from President Ford's secretary of state, Dr. Henry Kissinger. It was reported that Kissinger told Colby before he left office that Colby had done the right thing (19).
[5] Chapman Pincher, *Traitors: The Labyrinths of Treason* (London: Sedgwick and Jackson, 1987), 47, 167, 174.
[6] Cited in Colby and Forbath, *Honorable Men*, 33. As Michael Herman points out, "Note, however, that the actual words were [Stimson's] rationalization seventeen years later: see correspondence in *Intelligence and National Security* 2, no. 4 (October 1987)." See Michael

Herman, "Ethics and Intelligence after September 2001," in Jan Goldman (ed.), *Ethics of Spying: A Reader for the Intelligence Professional*, vol. 2 (Lanham, MD: Scarecrow Press, 2006) 119.

7 Jenifer Morgan Jones, "Is Ethical Intelligence a Contradiction in Terms?" in Jan Goldman (ed.), *Ethics of Spying: A Reader for the Intelligence Professional*, vol. 2 (Lanham, MD: Scarecrow Press, 2006), 25.

8 James H. Doolittle; William B. Franke; and William D. Pawley, *Report on the Covert Activities of the Central Intelligence Agency* (Washington, DC: Special Study Group, September 30, 1954).

9 Moira Rayner, with assistance from Jenny Lee, *Rooting Democracy: Growing the Society We Want* (St. Leonards, NSW: Allen and Unwin, 1997), 63.

10 James M. Olson, *Fair Play: The Moral Dilemmas of Spying* (Washington, DC: Potomac Books, 2007), 34.

11 David John Moore Cornwell writing as John le Carré, *The Spy Who Came in From the Cold* (London: The Reprint Society, 1964), 13. Cornwell is the author of numerous espionage novels. He worked for the British Security Service (MI5) and the Secret Intelligence Service (MI6) during the 1950s and 1960s.

12 *Hearings Before the Select Committee to Study Governmental Operations with Respect to Intelligence Activities of the United States Senate*, 94th Congress, 1st Session, vol. 2, September 1975.

13 James Angleton cited in Morley, *The Ghost*, 255.

14 James Angleton cited in Morley, *The Ghost*, 255.

15 Major John Jeffcoat, British Army, "Regaining the Moral High Ground: Time to Think About 'Just Intelligence Doctrine'," *Foreign Policy*, December 14, 2014, http://foreignpolicy.com/2014/12/18/regaining-the-moral-high-ground-time-to-think-about-just-intelligence-doctrine/ (accessed April 8, 2018).

16 Jeffcoat, "Regaining the Moral High Ground."

17 According to British historian Sir Harry Hinsley, Ultra "shortened the war by not less than two years and probably by four years—that is the war in the Atlantic, the Mediterranean and Europe." Harry Hinsley, *The Influence of Ultra in the Second World War* (Babbage Lecture Theatre: University of Cambridge, October 19, 1993).

18 Anthony Cave Brown, *Bodyguard of Lies* (London: W. H. Allen, 1976), 42.

19 Paul Ham, *Hiroshima Nagasaki* (Sydney: HarperCollins, 2011).

Sample Personal History Statement

This is an example of what a personal history statement might look like. It shows the types of information that employers should consider asking of a job applicant. The purpose of asking these questions is to obtain background information about the person and their life in relation to the skills, abilities, and knowledge that the job calls for. The applicant's *curriculum vitae* usually contains evidence of the latter while the personal history statement contains information regarding the former.

The personal history statement shows the types of requests that can provide information that a counterintelligence investigator can use to test the honesty and integrity of the applicant. The personal history statement does this by providing a basis for checking gaps and contradictions as well as embellishments of the truth.

This sample personal history statement is provided as an exemplar only. Your jurisdiction may be governed by federal and/or state/provincial laws that regulate the types of questions an employment application can ask of applicants. Anyone contemplating using such an instrument to collect data should first seek legal advice. The information presented here is for illustrative purposes only and is not to be construed as legal advice.

Application Regarding Possible Employment

[Insert the agency's name]

[Insert the agency's address]

Position applied for: _____

Personal Details

1) Name:_____

                First   Middle   Last

    a) Previous name(s) used and dates: _____

2) Residential address:_____

    _____

    _____

3) Home telephone: (   ) _____

4) Date of birth: _____

5) Place of birth: _____

6) Marital status: _____

7) Drivers licence: Yes/No

    a) State of issue: _____

    b) Licence number: _____

    c) Licence type/class: _____

8) If successful with this application, on what date would you be available to commence work:

    _____

9) List the names, addresses, and telephone numbers of two referees who are not related to you.

    _____

    _____

    _____

    _____

You may attach copies of your curriculum vitae, academic credentials, or any other supporting documents that you feel may be helpful in considering your application. Use additional pages if there is insufficient space to answer any of the following questions.

Employment History

10) Are you currently employed? List employer: _____

Who can we contact at this business for a work report?

Telephone: (   ) _____

11) List your employment history, starting with current or last job and work backwards. Do not omit any period and include volunteer activities if applicable. A break-in employment is to be explained. Please include the following details:

a)   Occupation

b)   Employer

c)   Employer's address

d)   Starting date

e)   Name of your supervisor at the time

f)   Termination date

g)   Reason for leaving

_____

_____

_____

_____

_____

_____

_____

_____

_____

_____

_____

_____

_____

_____

12) In the last five years have you ever been fired from a job? Yes/No

13) In the last five years have you ever resigned from a job after being notified that you would be fired? Yes/No

If you answered yes to either 12 or 13, please explain:

_____

_____

_____

_____

14) Have you ever been convicted of a felony? Yes/No

15) Have you ever been convicted of an offence involving violence? Yes/No

16) Have you ever been convicted of an offence involving dishonesty? Yes / No

17) Are you currently on probation or parole? Yes / No

If yes to 14, 15, 16, or 17, please explain:

_____

_____

_____

_____

Education

18) List your educational history, including the following details:

a)   Name of school/college/university

b)   Years completed

c)   Highest Certificate/Diploma/Degree awarded

d)   Description of course of study

e)   Specialized training, apprenticeship, skills, or other courses if applicable.

_____

_____

_____

_____

_____

_____

Military Service

19) Have you ever served on active duty in a branch of the armed forces? Yes / No

   If yes, please state:

   a) which nation _____

   b) branch of service _____

   c) dates of active duty _____

   d) highest rank held _____

   e) type of discharge _____

   f) date of discharge _____

Special Skills and Qualifications

20) Summarize any special skills and/or qualifications you may have acquired through employment, study, or other experiences. Include membership to any organizations and any professional associations.

_____

_____

_____

_____

Agreement

I certify that the answers given herein are true and complete to the best of my knowledge and belief, and that I have made them in good faith.

   I authorize investigation of all matters contained in this application for employment as may be necessary in arriving at an employment decision, including a criminal record check with the relevant police authority, and a check of public available information, including Internet-based data.

   In the event of employment, I understand that any false or misleading information given in my application, its attachments, or interview(s) that I participate in (whether in person or via the telephone/on-line) may result in dismissal. I also understand that permanent appointment will be subject to an initial _____ month probationary period.

_____   _____

Signature of Applicant   Date

Sample Nondisclosure Agreement

This sample form is presented for illustrative purposes. It should not be construed as legal advice.

Agency Name

Agency Address

Declaration of Confidentiality

I, _____

(insert full name)

of _____

(insert address)

in the State [or Province] of [insert name of state /province], do solemnly and sincerely declare, that, except in the course of my official duties with [insert the name of the agency], I will not communicate or divulge, directly or indirectly, information relating to any matter that comes to my attention as a consequence of my employment, either now, or at any time in the future.

Signature: _____

Declared at: _____

(insert place)

this _____ day of _____ 20 _____

Before me: _____

Justice of the Peace

Summary of Selected Analog Audio Surveillance Devices

"The Soviets love bugs and place them everywhere. A Western traveler to Moscow must assume his hotel room is auditory."[1] Is it likely that this situation has changed under stewardship of the Russian Federation's President, the former-KGB counterintelligence officer, Vladimir Putin?

Here is a selected list of devices that illustrate how common electronic components, which are available from local electronic and science stores or online suppliers, can be used in audio surveillance. The devices and components are itemized with a brief description of their application. The list does not speak for all devices or electronic components that can be used in audio surveillance, but it represents what is available on the over-the-counter market and how an OPFOR can employed them in practice.

Microphones

Dynamic and Crystal

Microphones collect sound energy and two commonly used types are dynamic and crystal, and these are used for general purpose audio work. No electric current is required to use these. They are available in two directional patterns: omni- and cardio-.

Condenser

A third type of microphone is a condenser. These are battery powered and are usually more sensitive than dynamic and crystal microphones but are usually available only in an omni-directional pattern.

Tube Microphones

Tube microphones have a special function. Their main feature is a hollow tube (miniature) fixed over a microphone element. They are designed to be inserted through walls, floors, and so on.

Stethoscope Microphones

A stethoscope microphone is another specialized microphone with its chief purpose being listening through solid objects (e.g., floors, ceilings, and walls).

Contact Microphones

Contact microphones have the same function as stethoscope microphones.

Spike Microphones

Spike microphones have the same purpose as contact and stethoscope microphones; however, this device is distinguished by a spike-shaped electronic "pickup." The pickup works in the same fashion as a phonograph needle.

Shotgun Microphones

Shotgun microphones (sometimes termed *rifle mics*) are yet another special function microphone that utilizes a cluster of varying length tubes to achieve a directional pattern for listening. These are designed for overhearing conversations across large, open areas.

Parabolic Reflectors

Parabolic reflectors are a "dish-type" arrangement around a microphone to give directionality. They are similar in purpose to the shotgun microphone; however, the tubes of the shotgun are replaced with a parabolic collecting reflector.

Induction Coils

These are not microphones at all, but an electronic device that is used in place of a microphone to intercept targeted audio signals via electrical induction; so, they act like microphones. They are chiefly used in telephone surveillance. In general, they are able to be only detected by physical search.

Ancillary Devices
High-Gain Amplifiers

These are used to boost audio signals received from a microphone. They can be employed with contact and spike microphones and induction coils.

Frequency Equalizers

Equalizers are used to eliminate background noise and other sounds that interfere with the target conversation, for example, in electronic intercepts.

Remote Control Devices

These are typically a transmitter/receiver combination like those used by model hobbyists. They are used to switch surveillance equipment on and off from a distance.

Voice-Operated Relay

A voice-operated relay (VOX) is used to start and stop, say, a digital audio recorder. Its primary advantage is to conserve digital memory as it only records active conversations, not periods of silence.

Drop-Out-Relay

This device has the same purpose as a VOX; however, it is used to turn a recorder on or off when it is connected to a telephone landline. That is, when the handset is removed from the hook, the relay is "tripped," starting the recorder. When the handset is replaced, it turns the recorder off.

Wireless Microphones

Varieties

There are numerous varieties of what are termed *miniature transmitters,* and these range from the most sophisticated down to the very basic homemade, or store-shelf-purchased, devices.

Range

The transmission range of these electronic devices depends on the sophistication of the unit's circuitry, the placement of the transmitter (i.e., interference may be caused by buildings, nearby steel structures, etc. that shorten range), and to some extent the sensitivity of the communications receiver.

Power Supply

Some miniature transmitting devices use their own energy supplied via batteries. Others utilize the power of, say, telephone lines or even the AC power in the building in which it is secreted.

Frequency

Commercially purchased and homemade transmitters are reported to operate in the VHF and UHF parts of the radio spectrum—that is, between

25 MHz to around 512 MHz. This part of the spectrum includes the commercial FM broadcast band that lies between 88 MHz and 108 MHz.

Transmitter Repeaters

A repeater is used in conjunction with a miniature transmitter that is installed in the target premises. The low-power, miniature transmitter broadcasts its signal to the secreted repeater nearby. The repeater then boosts the signal strength and rebroadcasts the intercepted conversation on a different frequency so that a monitoring post can intercept and record the conversation for analysis.

Homing Transmitters

These devices are fastened to, or secreted in, the target motor vehicle. The purpose is to show the vehicle's location to the surveillant who is tailing at a safe distance. The older analog devices emitted either an audio tone or series of beeps. Tracking was accomplished via radio direction finding and signal strength devices. The target vehicle could be more easily located by the employment of two tracking units to triangulate the transmitter's position. Now, location data is send via a global positioning system (GPS) to a device with a map in the surveillant's car.

Laser Surveillance

The primary purpose of laser surveillance is to intercept audio communication. The device is sophisticated and operates by detecting minute vibrations produced on a room's window caused by people speaking inside the room. The device consists of a laser, which projects a beam onto the target window, and a telescope/decoder, which detects the vibrations and translates them into sound waves (audio).

Landline Telephones

Devices

Direct Tap: A direct tap is acknowledged as the easiest method to intercept a telephone conversation on a landline telephone as power is derived from the telephone line to operate the device. The actual tap is affected by the connection of a recorder (via, perhaps, a VOX), a transmitter, or headphones for live monitoring.

Near Direct Taps: These types of taps utilize induction coils. The installation can be configured to include headphones (live surveillance), a digital recorder (VOX), or a miniature transmitter and possible radio repeater provide greater distance to the listening post.

Note

1. Phillips, *The Night Watch*, 135.

Specimen Chain-of-Custody Record

This sample form is presented for illustrative purposes only and is not to be construed as legal advice.

Chain-of-Custody Record

I the undersigned state that I took possession of the documents listed below on the date and time specified. Transfer of these documents was made as indicated. Further, while in my possession the documents were secure and inaccessible to unauthorized persons.

DOCUMENTS_____

CLASSIFICATION_____

1) INITIAL POSSESSION BY: _____

Time: _____

Date: _____

Signature: _____

2) TRANSFERRED TO: _____

Time: _____

Date: _____

Signature: _____

3) TRANSFERRED TO: _____

Time: _____

Date: _____

Signature: _____

Index

About the Author

Henry (Hank) Prunckun, BS, MSocSc, MPhil, PhD, is a research criminologist at the Australian Graduate School of Policing and Security, Charles Sturt University, Sydney. He specializes in the study of transnational crime—espionage, terrorism, and drugs and arms trafficking, as well as cybercrime. He is the author of numerous reviews, articles, chapters, and books, including: *Terrorism and Counterterrorism: A Comprehensive Introduction to Actors and Actions* (Lynne Rienner Publishers, 2019); *Methods of Inquiry for Intelligence Analysis, Third Edition* (Rowman & Littlefield, 2019); *Cyber Weaponry: Issues and Implications of Digital Arms* (Springer, 2018); *How to Undertake Surveillance and Reconnaissance* (Pen & Sword Books, 2015); *Intelligence and Private Investigation* (Charles C Thomas, 2013); *Shadow of Death: An Analytic Bibliography on Political Violence, Terrorism, and Low-Intensity Conflict* (Scarecrow Press, 1995); *Special Access Required: A Practitioner's Guide to Law Enforcement Intelligence Literature* (Scarecrow Press, 1990); and *Information Security: A Practical Handbook on Business Counterintelligence* (Charles C Thomas, 1989). He is the winner of two literature awards and a professional service award from the International Association of Law Enforcement Intelligence Analysts. Dr. Prunckun has served in several strategic research and tactical intelligence capacities within the criminal justice system during his previous twenty-eight-year operational career, including almost five years as a senior counterterrorism policy analyst. In addition, he has held several operational postings in investigation and security.